# BLOOD BROTHERS

The Inside Story of the Cork Hurlers
1996–2008

# BLOOD
# BROTHERS

The Inside Story of the Cork Hurlers
1996–2008

## MICHAEL MOYNIHAN ∾

*Gill & Macmillan*

Gill & Macmillan Ltd
Hume Avenue, Park West, Dublin 12
with associated companies throughout the world
www.gillmacmillan.ie

978 07171 4432 7

Index compiled by Cover to Cover
Typography design by Make Communication
Print origination by TypeIT, Dublin
Printed by ColourBooks Ltd, Dublin

This book is typeset in 12.5 Minion on 16.

The paper used in this book comes from the wood pulp
of managed forests. For every tree felled, at least one
tree is planted, thereby renewing natural resources.

A CIP catalogue record for this book is available from
the British Library.

5 4 3 2 1

*For my parents Donal (1942–2007) and Mary —true rebels.*

# CONTENTS

# ACKNOWLEDGMENTS

I'd like to thank the following for their help with this book: Fergal Tobin, for his support all through, and everybody else at Gill & Macmillan; Tony Leen and everyone on the sports desk in the *Irish Examiner*; Declan Ryan in the *Irish Examiner* library; all my family, particularly my mother Mary, Katie, Helen and Abby, Daniel and Cillian, Sarah and Clare, Cliodhna, Liam and Eva, and Bobby and Breda in Waterford.

Diarmaid Falvey's advice and direction were superb, as always. Without him the book wouldn't have happened: end of, as he'd say himself.

The players couldn't have been more courteous and helpful, from the first day I got lost trying to find Timmy McCarthy's farm in Castlelyons to the last day of ringing Donal Óg Cusack to double-check some facts. They were as classy to deal with off the pitch as they were stylish to watch in action. Ditto Jimmy Barry-Murphy, John Allen and Donal O'Grady.

I wouldn't have finished the book without the help of my wife Marjorie. The frequent absences and lengthy phone calls were probably doubly hard on her as a diehard Waterford fan, but she still backed me all the way and made many practical suggestions that were hugely helpful. Her fellow Deise man Raymond Chandler said once that all he had ever written was done for his wife to warm her hands at.

When you borrow, you borrow from the best.

# INTRODUCTION

In 1995 the Clare hurling team ended their decades in the wilderness with an All-Ireland title. Depending on your familiarity with the Good Book, either Anthony Daly or Ger Loughnane played the part of Moses leading the lost tribe to the promised land, but there was no second-guessing the joy of the Banner followers. That was truly biblical.

For anyone not there in person, television did justice to the historic day, particularly Daly's stirring victory speech in the Hogan Stand. His words set the saffron and blue flags dancing all around him, but the future is visible over his shoulder, one small red and white banner waving even as the Clare captain speaks.

Cork won the curtain-raiser that day in 1995, the All-Ireland minor hurling final, having lost the previous year's decider, and the players harvested from that minor side would power the county's revival as a hurling power.

In itself that's not unusual. Using good minors as the foundation of a new dynasty at adult level is a tried and tested method of regeneration across the GAA, and two of those players debuted the following season when Cork plunged to a record defeat in the Munster championship at home to Limerick.

From that low point Cork's progress was slow: between 1995 and 1998 one Munster championship game was won. Then came 1999.

If they'd never achieved anything else, that season was a Hollywood script unto itself. The manager was on the brink of walking away before the championship started, but he remained and chose six debutants for the Munster championship opener; they faced the reigning champions in the All-Ireland semi-final but outgunned them; and in the final itself they were four points down with less than ten minutes left.

Most significant of all, perhaps, they threw down Clare in the Munster final, the team with whom they'd been locked in an Oedipal struggle for years. Cork had returned to the summit. Young and fearless, they looked set to dominate for years: the average age of the team was 23. If they had held down the decade that followed, the story wouldn't be half as interesting. Unmitigated success lacks drama; that grand wing back Montherlant was right when he said happiness writes white on the page.

They lost their way. A lethal combination of over-confidence and inexperience helped to sink them the following year against Offaly, and then there were successive first-round exits before a humiliating loss in the 2002 qualifiers against Galway.

The Connacht side had contested the 2001 All-Ireland final and had a nice line in promising youngsters coming through. Cork supporters streaming dejectedly from Thurles that day wouldn't have been surprised to hear they'd just seen a side that would contest the next four All-Ireland senior hurling finals. Those supporters would have laughed at suggestions that that would be the team in red rather than maroon, but after bottoming out in 2002, Cork reinvented themselves by doing something which no other GAA team had ever done. They went on strike.

What this book tries to do is show how a bunch of promising youngsters became driven men. As a storyline it's as universal as sport itself—and no less interesting because of that universality—but this Cork team became something different again. The 2002 strike is crucial to understanding that.

Nowadays the Cork hurlers are identified closely with the Gaelic Players Association (GPA), and some of the Leesiders have occupied prominent positions in that organisation. But back then player power was associated with Johan Cruyff and other easily offended Dutch footballers. The Cork players' strike had more to do with the team's journey than a player representative group. One player puts the case logically, instancing the day he and his team mates were pulled into a Tipperary hotel room before the 2002 league final and asked to take pride in the Cork jersey. He felt that pride in the jersey was driving their protest: 'It's because we respect the jersey that we do what we do, or not do, as the case may be.'

That combination of fierce devotion and logical decision-making characterised the team then and still does now. In 2002 they faced down the Cork County Board to improve their conditions, and they won, but in doing so they'd made a rod for their own backs. Cork had been winning All-Irelands in hurling for over a hundred years before the players went on strike, and they weren't short of people pointing out that they'd talked the talk in withdrawing their services. In 2003 they'd have to walk the walk.

The players reached that year's final. They reached the following three finals as well.

There were reversals and calamities, the bad hands that life can deal out to anyone. The team's star player had retired at 28. One of the cornerstones of the side destroyed his leg in a car crash the week of a championship game and was warned he might struggle to walk again. The most promising young attacker of his generation confirmed his potential by winning the Young Hurler of the Year award, and then left for another sport on the other side of the world. The manager who brought in the innovations walked away after winning the All-Ireland. A star forward was diagnosed with cancer at 29.

They faced down those reversals. The star player came out of retirement to win two All-Ireland medals. The man whose kneecap was driven halfway up his thigh in that car accident rebuilt his career to such an extent that he headed national fitness campaigns and became a cultural phenomenon. The man who replaced the departed manager took the team ethos to another level. The stricken forward shook off cancer as if it were just another sluggish corner back. The young man who went to Australia went with the blessing of his team mates, and he succeeded there against all the odds.

There were other milestones: disciplinary issues and media stand-offs, unforgettable speeches and famous visitors, casual innovations that were assimilated quietly into GAA culture. People forget there was a time when Cork's carefully placed cones and structured warm-up before games had spectators pointing in disbelief, for instance. Nowadays no serious inter-county team prepares for a game without a similar routine.

Almost as an afterthought, they reinvented the game. For decades in Cork there had been a belief in direct hurling based on touch and speed: players won the ball and delivered it quickly up the field to forwards who'd score independently. No man could run faster than a well-directed sliotar, where 'well-directed' operated as a synonym for goalwards.

Down the decades Cork had helped smother tactical innovation elsewhere. Galway had introduced the third midfielder as complementary to their running game in the late eighties, but it perished twice in All-Ireland finals against Cork's inexorable touch game, where the tactics consisted of delivering the ball as quickly as possible to lethal full forwards who then gorged on goals.

The twenty-first century Cork team didn't have predators to bother the green flag, so they adapted. They soon became known for a running and support game which was structured and purposeful: there was a plan and the players followed it, but to follow it they needed to trust each other more than anything else.

A group of players who'd trusted each other to go on strike didn't lack purpose. They believed in their approach and joined together, and in September 2006 they came within three points—one score— of three titles in a row when Kilkenny beat them in that year's final. As one of the Cork players says, it was the one time their opponents had the discipline to follow a plan they'd devised through to the end. They had to; it was a given that Cork would stick with their approach.

And that is the key to understanding the team and what makes them unique—their faith in each other. Their off-field attitude—taking on administrators, whether within the county in 2002 and 2007–8, or outside as happened after the Semple Stadium incident of 2007, facing down RTÉ in 2005, rallying around team mates under pressure—was paralleled by their faith in the on-field plan and belief in each other's commitment to it. A lazy description of their attitude—forthright, unyielding, articulate—might see parallels with that of the newly confident populace of Celtic Tiger Ireland, but it's deeper than that. This book tries to show how that bond developed between them.

'I feel those players are my friends,' says one of them. 'My best friends. I've travelled the road with them and we've had times when we've been down, when stuff has happened off the field—to all of us—and it's a fierce comfort to have those men around you.

'You go back training and you know someone like Seán Óg is going to drive on. And if he's going to drive on, and Sully is going to drive on, then I'm going to drive on with them. And if there's a million fellas outside the gate waiting for us, then we'll have a go off them as well if we have to.'

Every team says they're together. Few of them can prove it.

# EXITING WITH RESPECTABILITY

Sometimes a prophet *is* recognised in his own land.

Jimmy Barry-Murphy became manager of the Cork senior hurling team in late 1995, and it looked like a marriage made in heaven. When Tom Cashman and Tony O'Sullivan joined his selection committee, the 'Dream Team' headlines were as inevitable as night following day.

That was understandable. A generation of boys had grown up in the county chanting the three double-syllables of Barry-Murphy's name as they re-enacted one of his goals, and they had plenty of those to choose from. In 1973 he had scored the decisive goal in the All-Ireland senior football final against Galway—at 19—and he had repeated the dose in the hurling final five years later, seeing off Kilkenny. He had been elegant and skilful on the field of play, and modest off it, resigning from television punditry rather than run the risk of hanging a damaging nickname on a player.

To say his name alone worked a magic spell was no exaggeration: he retired in 1986 and Tipperary rallied the following season, but on the brink of their breakthrough at the Munster final replay in

Killarney, the followers from Knocknagow wavered. A mischievous rumour put it about that Barry-Murphy had been seen bringing his gear to the Cork dressing room. It wasn't true, but that was the power the triple name could wield.

With Cashman, O'Leary and Crowley by his side, Barry-Murphy wouldn't be long bringing Cork back to the promised land. That was the feeling within the county. After all, he'd served his apprenticeship with the county minors.

'I'd coached them for three years,' says Barry-Murphy. 'I'd seen the minors coming through. The third year we won the All-Ireland, and it struck me that if Cork were to get back to a decent level of hurling, then those players would have to come through and be the leaders in that.

'You never know with minors. It doesn't always follow that they come through—a lot of things must fall into place—but there were a few reasons why I thought they'd come through to senior level. I was hopeful in 1995. They were exceptional players and I saw no reason why they wouldn't come through to win All-Irelands for Cork. I'd have been shocked, really, if that didn't happen.'

But the landscape had changed somewhat since Barry-Murphy had been involved as a player, a mere decade earlier. On the inter-county scene Cork had been in the All-Ireland final as recently as 1992, losing to Kilkenny, and had brought Liam McCarthy south in 1990 as part of the double. But by 1996 those memories were receding quickly in the rear view mirror.

In 1995 Clare had needed Ollie Baker's late, late goal to slip Cork in Munster, and even then the game could have been rescued. When Cork mounted their last attack, it had taken a magnificent flick from Frank Lohan to deny Kevin Murray a match-winning goal. Accordingly, an accountant could interpret Cork's defeat as a loss to the eventual All-Ireland champions by a mere point and file a reasonably positive final return for 1995.

However, the victory empowered Clare. They had had to shrug off generations of defeat to create a winning mentality, and now that they had acquired that mindset, they weren't about to retire sated beyond the Shannon.

'They were the most feared team in Ireland,' says Mark Landers, who had a ringside seat for their watershed game against Cork. 'That was borne out off the field by their manager and on the field by their players. In 1995 I was on the Cork junior team and we played before the senior game, the Cork-Clare match. Barry Egan was lining up a sideline ball and Tom Cashman was behind him. Ger Loughnane strolled down and kicked the sliotar away, and Tom Cashman let him do it. He just put his hands up to the ref.

'After the game I said to him, as a Corkman, Tom, I couldn't believe you didn't take Ger Loughnane up on that occasion. You backed off him and you should have tackled him on it. He said, "That's not the way we do it in Cork." I said, that's fair enough. Clare were feared on and off the field until such time as teams would take Loughnane on along the sideline and take the players on out on the field. There were a number of years where I don't know if you could call it intimidation, but there was a lot of media hype about Clare.

'To be fair to them, they were a good, physical team. I found them fair and honest and they did what they had to do to win. I didn't have a problem with that. It was up to other teams to come up to the mark to match them.'

One team which fitted that description was the side Clare defeated in the 1995 Munster final, Limerick. At that point they were Clare's closest rivals in the province, a hardy, mature team who'd come very close themselves to an All-Ireland in 1994. Their agenda for 1996 had revenge against the Banner underlined in bold.

Cork, their first opponents in the championship that season, didn't rank quite as highly on Limerick's priorities.

Within the county, Cork hurling had also changed since Barry-Murphy and his selectors had come to prominence as players. That had been in the golden age of the seventies when the Cork club scene was dominated by the big three clubs, Glen Rovers, St Finbarrs and

Blackrock, who had divided the county titles of the decade between them.

Though revisionists would in time declare their grip on the county championship a bad thing, the county side had benefited from what was in effect a round robin tournament preparing them for action every summer. One much-decorated veteran of the Cork three-in-a-row team confessed as much in an off-the-record chat with this writer, pointing to Waterford's county championship in the same era for comparison.

'You had over twenty clubs in the senior championship in Waterford,' he recalled. 'Of course that diluted the talent. In Cork you had three very good teams, each with four or five inter-county players, playing high-pressure games in front of huge crowds. You couldn't get better preparation for big inter-county matches.'

The big breakthrough for the lesser lights in Cork had come in 1983, when Midleton had won the county championship. They didn't lack big names (John Fenton, Pat and John Hartnett, Ger Fitzgerald and Kevin Hennessy all featured with the county side) and were the only club in one of the biggest towns outside the city, but they showed that the big three weren't necessarily going to have it all their own way.

Decades later, it's easy to overlook Midleton's achievement, but because they were the first, they set the template. As late as 2006, Cloyne players, ahead of a senior county final appearance of their own, were still name-checking neighbours Midleton as the first club to show what could be done.

The lesson took a while to absorb. The big three drew on the underage strength they'd shown in the seventies to hold down the rest of the decade, but coming into the nineties other names began to appear on the roll of honour. Na Piarsaigh asserted themselves. Erin's Own came through. Divisional sides like Avondhu and Carbery had their day in the sun, while Imokilly got themselves organised.

The net effect was that Barry-Murphy and his selectors were

drawing from a different resource compared to the sides they'd featured on themselves. The power in Cork hurling had moved out from the city and was settling in the east of the county.

And in the north. For instance, the 1996 county title won by divisional side Avondhu was particularly interesting as the team was sprinkled with players from the county intermediate champions, a small club on the Limerick border which had spent decades yo-yoing from junior to intermediate and back down again. Now they were mining a golden seam of underage talent and using an unusual running and support game to bring results. In time, refined and tweaked, the Newtownshandrum style would reach a national audience, but Barry-Murphy's challenge was more immediate. And he knew it.

Quite apart from the clear on-field challenges, the manager had doubts about his own abilities.

'It was a huge change and in retrospect it was too soon for me really. Looking back, I wouldn't have done it, but again, when you're asked . . . We'd won the minor All-Ireland and in the euphoric state after winning that I said, we might as well drive on. This is an easy job.

'Nothing could have been further from the truth. I didn't realise how difficult it was going to be. I'd never handled senior players at any level, so that was new to me as well, and it was a huge learning process.

'For instance, what I found tricky was when it came to the harsh reality that some players' careers were coming to an end, but I think most of them realised that anyway. Tomas Mulcahy, for instance, was injured, and we brought him back for a couple of challenge games. It didn't work out, but he was very fair to me. He knew it himself, so we had no problem.

'There might be one or two players who'd be bitter about being left go, but you're always going to have one or two instances like that. But overall I didn't find it that hard because it was all new to me anyway.'

It was new to some of the other participants as well. Joe Deane had starred for the minor side in 1995, and he was the first from that generation brought up to the big show.

'It was a surprise to be invited in, but with Jimmy being involved we'd have been thinking we'd get a shot,' says Deane. 'I didn't expect to be called in that quickly. That time there were league games before Christmas, so I came on against Kerry in the league before the end of 1995. It was something different—Jim Cashman, Denis Walsh, Teddy McCarthy, Ger Cunningham, John O'Driscoll, Barry Egan— they were all there. I'd watched them all so it was a bit intimidating, but they made me very welcome.'

Deane had been earmarked for the top flight at an early age down in Killeagh, where they had high hopes for him long before he first came to prominence with the Midleton cbs side which won the All-Ireland Colleges title in 1995.

He wasn't one of the biggest, or fastest, but Deane was accurate and brave and he wasn't fazed by the big occasion. He had been an exceptional minor with one of the county's finest underage sides, a key player who was never daunted. But he still found the air thin at senior level.

'The speed, the physicality, everything really, was a big step up,' says Deane. 'We won league games that were played before Christmas but those were Mickey Mouse games. After Christmas we played three games and were trounced. We played Clare, who were All-Ireland champions at the time, down the Pairc and we clapped them onto the field.'

The challenge of facing up to the game's top dogs was brought home to the new man. By half-time he was sitting on the bench.

'I was taken off at the break, and the speed, the touch, the physicality—I remember thinking, we're miles behind here. It could take years to break into this.'

Barry-Murphy agrees. Clare were the standard and Cork weren't at the same level. 'They pushed up the physical stakes, the way they imposed themselves on teams.

'I didn't realise what was required, and basically we were going through a bad patch. Probably the players weren't good enough and we were exposed in several games regarding how far back we'd fallen.

'Cork had come close to Clare the previous year, but to be perfectly honest we'd fallen way behind the general standard.'

Another newcomer beginning his senior career was the 1995 minor full back, another youngster promoted to the senior panel. Given Seán Óg Ó hAilpín's status nowadays as one of Ireland's most famous sportsmen, it's hard to recall a time when he was an obscure teenager known more for his exotic background than his sporting ability. In time he would join the short list of Irish people instantly recognisable by their first name, or at least first name plus Irish diminutive; in early 1996 his elevation to the Cork senior panel was low key.

'I've a funny feeling that the management felt pressurised into bringing in players,' says Ó hAilpín.

'The core group of lads, the fellas I'd looked up to through the eighties and nineties, were still there: Teddy, Seánie McCarthy, Jim Cashman. They were in the dressing room when I walked in and with the greatest respect for them, the writing was on the wall for them. Jimmy brought in myself and Joe, but the selectors probably didn't see 1996 happening the way it did.

'It was like a boxer on the ropes—he still thinks he's got a chance and he'll hang in there. The selectors probably thought they might get another year, maybe two, out of those lads, so that they'd give myself and Joe and the other younger lads a bit of leadership. Unfortunately that didn't happen, and Jimmy was forced to use myself and Joe in 1996. And we weren't equipped for it.'

Ger Cunningham, then goalkeeper and the team's longest-serving player, sees the manager's perspective. 'You could see huge talent there, but when is the right time to throw young players in? They'd have played a few league games, but when is the right time? A good run in the league might have helped there, but as it was, facing into the Limerick game, there was uncertainty about some major positions on the team. And we had a good record in the Pairc; we had a good record against Limerick.'

For their opener in the Munster championship of 1996 Barry-Murphy and his selectors tried the proverbial mix of youth and experience. In Cunningham Cork had a goalkeeper who'd played in an All-Ireland final fourteen years earlier, while Jim Cashman and Teddy McCarthy had starred in the All-Ireland final a full decade previously. Deane would make his debut at corner forward; Ó hAilpín was in the subs.

Looking back now, Cunningham can see the problems clearly. For one thing, the first fifteen was anyone's guess.

'The team was unsettled going into the match. Wherever there was a problem Brian Corcoran was moved there, for instance. Tomas [Mulcahy] was back for a while; Teddy [McCarthy] came back. Jimmy would have been loyal to those guys and was maybe trying to get a balance, when a clear-out might have been what was needed.'

Deane, meanwhile, had the optimism and innocence of youth. 'Going into the Limerick championship game, we'd been beaten in our league games, we'd been beaten in our challenge games, and when you look back you'd say we were going desperate.

'But at the time I was thinking, this is the Cork senior team; we traditionally don't do well in the league; of course we're going to win against Limerick. I couldn't believe that we were beaten by that much, but based on how things were going in training and matches, it's no surprise.

'But that was the way it was going to league games in the late eighties and nineties. You'd see Cork players out of shape and the team getting well beaten, but they'd turn it around and become automatic contenders for the All-Ireland. I was convinced we were going to win that game.'

'It being Cork, people were saying all the time, Cork are Cork, that it'd turn around,' says Ó hAilpín. 'We didn't see the danger signs because you're new to the set-up and training with lads you looked up to, lads you saw do it for Cork in All-Ireland finals plenty of times.'

They weren't alone. The man at the top was of like mind.

'I thought that myself,' says Barry-Murphy. 'That was typical of Cork. We'd do it in the championship. I got it wrong.'

There's not much suspense in the story. Cork were beaten by sixteen points.

'They were all over us,' says Deane, even though, incredibly, they led at half-time by a point, 1–5 to 0–7. The final scoreline of 3–18 to 1–8 is a fairer reflection of the proceedings.

The other newcomer found it overwhelming.

'When you live in the moment, you don't realise the size of the task,' says Ó hAilpín. 'Looking back now you can see that bringing in a couple of nineteen-year olds, bringing them into a man's game . . . I don't care how good a nineteen-year old is, how good he was as a minor. Senior is a whole new ball game.'

With the ship holed below the waterline, Ó hAilpín was sent on. The removal of his club mate and captain, Mark Mullins, meant that technically he was captain; in practical terms he found the new ball game had a few unfamiliar rules.

'I was brought on in the second half. I came in at wing back. I was on Frankie Carroll, and I remember going in, looking downfield at a ball in innocence—you know, at minor level everyone would be just following the ball. Then I got a crack in the ribs. It's a frightening experience when you're not expecting it, and when I turned around there was a big smile on Frankie's face.

'You wouldn't want to wish that on anyone, that their first experience is getting hammered by sixteen points. The media, the public, everyone was down on Jimmy straightaway. In a funny way, though, I don't know if I'd have gone on and done as much if I hadn't gone through those times.

'And they were hard times. That invincibility about Cork had evaporated. I was a student going up and down to Dublin, to DCU, and you'd be a small bit ashamed that you were a Cork hurler after that match. I missed a lot of the fall-out. I was ticking over up there and I'd only see it at the weekend.

'We know what harsh times are. The lads who came in for 2003 lost an All-Ireland final, but at least they got to an All-Ireland final that year. In 1996 you were gone after one game. It was a cruel start, and while I don't know about Joe, I think it benefited me.'

Dazed by the crushing defeat, Barry-Murphy was grateful for any support he could get. The administration in Cork backed his rebuilding project.

'The county board stood by me and encouraged me, and we decided bringing in young players was going to be the road to recovery. But I didn't realise how hard it was going to be. I didn't realise how different senior inter-county had become compared to when I'd played myself. The Limerick game was an eye-opener as to how far back we'd gone.

'It was a hard time for me and the selectors because basically you're associated with failure. It was a diabolical performance against Limerick, and the Cork crowd responded. It was as if they knew how far we were gone, and it was amazing that a couple of years later you couldn't get tickets for Cork games in Thurles.

'One regret I'd have is that I brought in Joe Deane and Seán Óg, and it was probably unfair to them. I regret playing them that year. Coming into a team that was flying would have been one thing, but bringing them into a struggling side was a mistake. It was too soon, though I didn't realise how much the team would struggle. They probably needed another year or two, but they never blamed me for it and it worked out fine in the end. But it was a mistake.'

Barry-Murphy shouldered much of the blame for the defeat. In time it would be seen as the county bottoming out in hurling terms—Cork hadn't lost at home in the championship in seventy-three years—but forgiveness was in short supply in the summer of 1996, and the manager was a handy target.

'I felt harshly treated by the local media. I was hung out to dry by a number of articles that didn't portray me in a good light, but in hindsight I probably took it personally, which was maybe over the top from me. I was looking at it in terms of the co-operation I'd given the press since 1971 when I was a minor. Looking back I probably over-reacted, but I felt it was probably unnecessarily personalised and hurtful.

'We made up since, and I'd be the first to admit that we didn't realise what was needed to win at senior inter-county level, that I misread the situation in 1996. Our performance in Pairc Uí Chaoimh was shameful.'

For the youngsters, there wasn't even underage success to fall back on. They picked up an U-21 provincial medal but lost the All-Ireland semi-final to Galway on a wet, miserable day in Ennis.

'The U-21s were a great boost—up to a point,' says Ó hAilpín. 'I got cleaned out in the semi-final and Galway beat us well. So I'd had a bad senior start with Cork and a bad All-Ireland semi against Galway at U-21. The confidence wasn't great, given that I'd had a good run at minor level.'

Those who were close to the scene knew the size of the task facing Barry-Murphy. Mark Landers was on the fringes of the senior set-up and could see what was ahead of the manager.

'Jim came in with Tom Cashman and Tony O'Sullivan, and on the outside it looked fantastic, the dream team, but things were at an all-time low. To me the likes of Donal O'Grady, John Allen and Gerald McCarthy had a ready-made team, whereas after 1996 Jimmy had to build the team from scratch.'

That would take time. Barry-Murphy knew how the journey of a thousand miles would begin.

'Respectability. That was the first step,' he says. 'I wasn't thinking of winning All-Irelands after the first year; I was thinking more in terms of maybe exiting the job within a year or two with a bit of respectability for myself and the players. That's how far down my expectations had fallen and there's no point in saying otherwise.'

# WE COULD HAVE PUSHED ON

Diarmuid O'Sullivan got the phone call over Christmas.

'I was sitting at home and my father said, "There's a call for you." I said hello. The voice said "Jimmy Barry-Murphy here." I said, ah lads, which one of ye is winding me up? and put the phone down.'

Fortunately for the youngster, Barry-Murphy hit the redial button.

A year younger than the minor class of 1995, O'Sullivan hadn't been a guaranteed starter on the Midleton CBS Harty Cup side which had brought players like Donal Óg Cusack and Joe Deane to the attention of the hurling cognoscenti.

'That was the first big one, the Harty in 1995. I was a fifth year playing half forward and I didn't know how my hurling career was going to go. I suppose I would have liked to have been a forward, but I knew I wasn't good enough for that.'

O'Sullivan was big and strong, quick and skilful. In 1996 his father Jerry had been involved with senior divisional side Imokilly. One summer's evening he knew Imokilly would be short, and he brought Diarmuid along to make up the numbers.

'You're young. What would be better on a Tuesday or a Wednesday evening than playing a match?'

O'Sullivan junior says. 'I was put in centre back, and [Imokilly manager] Seánie O'Leary came over before the game and said, "You're young. Have a go. No one's putting pressure on you. Play away the way you want." That was the start of it for me. There was no pressure.'

O'Sullivan found senior hurling to his taste. He had an aura of confidence that carried through into that year's county championship and was noticed by Barry-Murphy. The Cork manager wouldn't have had far to look in any case: in 1996 O'Sullivan was carrying the hurleys for the Cork junior team because his father was a selector. The hurley-carrier would progress to left corner back on the senior team within twelve months.

Before that debut, though, came the apprenticeship. Though the O'Sullivan that all of Ireland would come to know later was expansive, if not ebullient, unafraid to take challenges head on, the eighteen-year-old who went down to Pairc Uí Chaoimh to meet his new team mates was a lot shyer.

'I'll never forget the first night I went training with Cork,' he says. 'I slipped into the dressing room and threw my bag into the corner. You had Ger Cunningham in the dressing room, Barry Egan, John O'Driscoll, Ger Manley . . . I kept going out to the toilet.

'When I came back out of the toilet I saw my gearbag being passed back out through the door and thought, Christ, what's going on here? Ger Cunningham said, "Lad, when you're old enough to come into this dressing room, you can come in." I went into the other dressing room and didn't open my mouth.'

There were other new faces to join O'Sullivan in the second dressing room.

'There was a big shake-up after 1996,' says Pat Mulcahy. 'The likes of Teddy Mac and those were gone, and the mainstays of the team were supposed to be the u-21s. But there were no fellas of 26 and 27 that would advise those lads. Almost everyone was new to the panel, and that probably hindered our performance at that point.'

Mulcahy had impressed with Avondhu in their county championship win of 1996. He was a clever defender whose intelligent support play was central to the rise of his club, Newtownshandrum, but by his own admission he was treading water in 1997 with Cork.

'I hadn't played minor for Cork,' says Mulcahy. 'I'd played a year at U-21, and suddenly after things going well in 1996 I was on the senior panel and, to be honest, I was in awe. There were eleven from Imokilly on it, a big UCC representation, and only three from all of Avondhu—myself, Fergal McCormack and Brian O'Driscoll.

'It was like there were two clubs and then the north Cork boys. It was difficult enough to get to know fellas because I hadn't grown up with that golden era of Donal Óg, Wayne and so on. To be honest, I don't think I improved that much in those two years, 1997 and 1998.'

Both newcomers warmed to their new manager, however.

'Well, if you couldn't get on with Jimmy . . .' says O'Sullivan. 'He was the most relaxed guy around. He and [trainer] Teddy Owens were a good pair, because Jimmy was laid back and there was a bit of cut and thrust about Teddy.

'For instance, I hate long-distance running, and I blame Jimmy for that. When I went in the first couple of nights they were still doing the long run up around the Marina, but Jimmy said, "You don't have to do that at all. Just follow Cunningham." We'd stay by the bushes and rejoin the lads coming down—well, we did until Ted cottoned onto us. But that was Jimmy's attitude. If you were good enough to hurl, he'd trust you.'

'Jimmy was excellent,' says Mulcahy. 'I was out in CIT at the time, and he was living a couple of houses away, and I'd go down to training with him. He was top class.

'Training was good too. They'd brought in Ted Owens and it was a lot harder. We did a lot of running around Pairc Uí Chaoimh, serious gym work for the first time . . . I suppose I was just happy to be involved, which was probably the wrong attitude. To say I was on the Cork senior hurling panel was a big thing for me.'

The introduction of Ted Owens as a physical trainer was a watershed. Owens worked the players hard and that helped to raise the bar. As Mark Landers puts it, Cork had traditionally been slow to absorb the new physical demands of nineties hurling.

'There was an attitude at that time that Cork weren't training as hard physically as other teams. Whether that led to under-performance nobody knows, but certainly when Teddy Owens came in, there was a huge emphasis put on physical fitness.

'What brought it home for me was a national hurling league game against Wexford, and the footballers were playing Dublin before us. We were sharing the one dressing room, and the difference in physique was dramatic. They were showering as we were going out and you could see that none of them was carrying any weight, while a few of the hurlers would always carry a couple of pounds.'

Ironically, one man who'd become synonymous later with fitness wasn't around for much of the hard grind that year.

'I missed a lot of the physical training in 1996 and 1997,' says Ó hAilpín. 'I was studying in Dublin and Jimmy and his management team brought in Ted Owens, and that was a good move. All I knew about Ted was that he was down in Castletownbere, and he brought something different to it. We were getting closer and closer to what you needed.

'Stories were coming out of Clare that they were running up the hill in Crusheen and all this stuff, early morning stuff, where we'd been doing two sessions a week down the Pairc. That changed and we were doing that much more.'

Still, it took a while for the benefits to show. Off-Broadway games in the second tier of the league weren't the best way to get ready for Clare.

'While it was great winning all the games, it wasn't ideal preparation to be playing Meath or Westmeath ahead of a championship game against Clare,' says Ó hAilpín. 'They'd been playing the likes of Kilkenny and Offaly in Division 1, good teams.'

That's the polite version. Asked now about the 1997 league, Joe Deane rolls his eyes.

'I was never as depressed. We struggled to beat Meath; we had to get a last-minute goal to beat them. Dublin beat us. There was a general sense of, where are we going?'

Seánie McGrath was a foot-soldier in the trenches alongside Deane. He had helped Glen Rovers to reach the semi-final of the county championship in 1996 and had had a decent campaign with the county U-21s. Pace and a superb first touch were always going to attract Barry-Murphy's interest, and McGrath's first senior game was against Dublin in the league late in 1996 in Pairc Uí Rinn. It was an inauspicious outing.

'I was shocking. It was dry but very heavy. My uncle Neville was at it and when I met him he said, "You were bad last week." I thought I'd blown my chance.'

Dr Paddy Crowley was involved in the UCC hurling club, and he offered a lifeline. McGrath was a student in the college but uninterested in playing Fitzgibbon Cup. Then Crowley persuaded McGrath to reconsider, and like so many players before and since, a successful Fitzgibbon campaign was the making of the Glen player.

'I made the panel for the league—Division 2—and we played Dublin in Parnell Park, Westmeath and London in Pairc Uí Rinn, Meath in Trim and Waterford in Pairc Uí Rinn. That was my best day.'

McGrath got 2–4 against Waterford, but describes his performance against Dublin, for instance, as 'crap', and he goes along with Deane in general terms. It was hard to see light at the end of the tunnel. In the narrow win over Meath, McGrath had a chance late on which went horribly wrong.

'I was one on one with the keeper and I kicked it. I nearly hit the corner flag. We laughed about it later, but at the time it was terrible. It certainly wasn't glamour stuff.

'Our aim was to make an impression, to get into the championship team. We played a load of challenge games that year, for instance, because we were in Division 2. The set-up wasn't like it is now. It was casual. Training was laps of the tunnel or else running around the Marina, and lads would duck in and duck out. It was more like club training. A bit of craic, I suppose.'

Clare were the championship opponents, then at their fearsome peak. They'd lost to Limerick, and Ciaran Carey's point from the ends of the earth the previous season, and they were anxious to make amends.

'Fellas looked up to them,' says O'Sullivan. 'There were stories about what they were doing, and whether those stories were true or not, they were repeated.'

'The Cork fellas were almost in awe of the Clare players,' says Mulcahy. 'Because you only had one game a year, that didn't help either. You were gone in May and you were waiting for Cork to play again twelve months later.'

O'Sullivan knew he was in the mix for a place in defence; he eventually learned of his selection in an unusual way.

'If you look at the overall scheme of things, we didn't even have the team. Brendan Larkin [of the *Irish Examiner*] came over to me as I came off the field for training and he congratulated me—he knew before I did!

'It was between me and Peter Smith of Midleton for the spot, and I'll never forget his attitude when the team was named. He came straight over and said, "I'm delighted for you. If there's anything you need, come and talk to me." We've had a lot of battles since in club games, but he didn't have to do that. It was a great gesture and it really made me feel part of the thing.'

McGrath, another debutant, was confident ahead of the Clare game. Self-belief powered his game, and he was on a high coming up to the championship.

'You've one huge advantage as an unknown quantity. I was

slighter than Joe. I was only ten stone. You could hear fellas saying, he hasn't a chance, but I was full of confidence. I'd had a good Fitzgibbon, a good U-21 and club campaign the previous year. I was buzzing.

'And of course you had a manager who gave nothing but praise. I might try a knack on the field and if it didn't work, I never felt he'd give out. I didn't feel the step-up because I was unknown. My pace was good and I could get away from fellas.'

In the dressing room before the Clare encounter, Pat Mulcahy recalls Barry-Murphy turning on the magic.

'Jimmy just had this presence. He was a brilliant orator; that was probably his great strength, and when he spoke there was no fella looking up at the ceiling. I don't think players spoke very much at all then, which would be different to now.'

'I was going out with a girl from Clare for two weeks that time,' says McGrath. 'Even that gave it a bit of spice. I was buzzing before it. I had no fears. Just one thought came into my head at the anthem: Jesus, this is it; here we go.

'I was on Frank Lohan, and I knew him from college. When you know someone it's different; it takes a bit of the pressure off. Though I remember [Anthony] Daly shouting in to Lohan, "Look after him, the small fella." And I remember shouting back out to Daly that if he came into the corner I'd look after him. That was me shouting back out to Anthony Daly!

'The first touch went well, and I knew I was on my game. At half-time Jimmy came over to me and said, "You're buzzing," and I said, I am. He told me to keep taking them on.'

At the break the score was 0–9 to 0–8. Cork had done well: O'Sullivan survived, Ó hAilpín thrived and McGrath carried on after the break where he'd left off, running, scoring, talking.

'In the second half I was alternating between the wing and the corner,' McGrath says. 'Daly was talking to me and I was talking back—not malicious. I have great time for him; he's a fierce character. Then they got the goal.'

Stephen McNamara's goal with five minutes left put Clare ahead decisively. It was the crucial score, and McGrath knew it.

'I said Jesus! or whatever out loud, and Daly leaned in and said, "You'll have loads of days. I was delighted to play against you. I hope I don't come up against you again."

'I had a chance of a goal late on, but Davy saved it. Coming off the field I was nearly in tears, I felt so sorry for Jimmy. He was a father figure. I was nearly saying sorry to him because we lost.

'We were playing for Cork, but there was more of a feeling you were playing for Jimmy. I idolised him. My mother is west Cork and years ago we were down there when Jimmy opened a pub, and I remember as a small child shaking his hand. It was like meeting God.'

For O'Sullivan, a decade afterwards, a final scoreline of 1–19 to 0–18 still seems like an opportunity lost.

'The funny thing was we were only two points down with time running out. We could have beaten them if we'd had the breaks. We could have done it. We could have pushed on.'

Ó hAilpín read some positive auguries in the game: 'We were beaten by the All-Ireland champions, but we had them on the rack for a long time, until Stephen McNamara got the vital goal with about five minutes left. That was a huge moral victory for us.

'In 1996 if we'd lost by five points, it would have been like a victory, given where we were coming from. As we learned later on, there's no such thing as moral victories, but there were good signs there in 1997. Progress.'

Even then there were knockers. McGrath had been a good discovery, but there were plenty of people to suggest he wasn't big enough to survive against defences as hard as Clare's.

'Yeah, I'd have heard a lot of that. It's part of the game. You're going to have knockers in every sport; it'd be strange if every fella was supportive.

'It was a huge motivation for me. If anyone said something to me I'd leave it go, but I felt like saying, show me someone with a touch like mine, or pace like mine, or a bit of cockiness like me. I had huge confidence in my own ability. I didn't give a damn.

'I felt that I contributed—I got a few scores or made some scores or won frees. Up to the time I finished in the championship my scoring average was just under three points a game, and I'd say to fellas, show me someone big or small who'll get that.'

His manager also asked the opinionated—of whom there were many at that time in Cork—to back up their theories.

'Several times I asked people who they'd pick instead, and nobody could say, "Well, this guy is getting a raw deal,"' says Barry-Murphy. 'We scoured the county and in the end we agreed that a youth policy was the only road for the future of Cork.

'Whether it would happen while I was part of the set-up or not I didn't know, but I said at one stage in 1997 that if you were to coach Cork for four or five years with Brian Corcoran playing and you didn't win an All-Ireland, you'd be very unlucky. It was hard to envisage him not winning an All-Ireland, but at that stage of his career it looked like that might happen.'

Barry-Murphy stresses Corcoran's importance to the team. Not only was the Erin's Own man the star player, he was the unofficial leader of the team.

'Brian was a fantastic figure for us. He was unbelievable for us. He was the spiritual leader, a huge help to me in that he had a way of getting involved with new lads. We were often coming back from league games up the country and he'd spend time with the new lads, without being asked, making them feel part of the set-up.

'Everyone looked to him for his performance in that he was man of the match for us on so many occasions that it was worrying to think of what would happen if he didn't play well.'

Deane also saw some silver lining in the early championship defeat, slim rations though they were. Not having senior inter-county commitments gave many of the players a chance to pick up silverware with the county at another grade.

'The lack of success at senior level gave us time with the u-21s. With no back door you had the whole summer with the u-21s and

Bertie Óg Murphy. Nowadays you see the preparation time the U-21 team has, and it's very broken. In our time we trained three nights a week as U-21s. That brought us on and was a big reason behind our progress later on.

'We were all playing together. We won two All-Irelands comfortably enough.'

For Barry-Murphy, one championship game a year wasn't telling him much about his players.

'If we'd had the system we have now, we'd have learned a lot more because you always learn more from your defeats. Take 2004, when Cork lost the Munster final and then drove on to win the All-Ireland, for instance.

'The minor team kept on, though, with Bertie Óg as U-21s, so it wasn't as if they weren't winning stuff. That was vital.'

With a minor success and an U-21 success, a senior title was the next step on the ladder. For his part, Ger Cunningham saw 1997 as the real beginning of the climb back up.

'There was more reality at that point, and that was probably the start of the rebuilding. Rebuilding takes more than twelve months. The older fellas were going, but you have to leave the younger lads time to settle in. At that stage I was 36, and I was looking over my shoulder.'

Cunningham had plenty of reason to be looking behind him. He had seen off two generations of understudies and had rarely been seriously challenged for his spot. (One of those understudies challenged this writer on one occasion to name any soft goal Cunningham had conceded—ever. Nothing came readily to mind.) But a youngster from Cloyne was bearing down on him. Donal Óg Cusack had a minor and U-21 All-Ireland medal at the end of 1997, and Cunningham acknowledged him as the heir apparent.

'I was impressed by his attitude compared to other fellas'. When we'd go training there was no comparison when it came to his attitude. The questions he'd ask at sessions were always sharp and to the point, while his talent was obvious.'

The two had a hidden history. The 1995 Cork minor hurling

selectors had asked Cunningham to test the contenders for the goalkeeping slot, and within minutes he had named Cusack as their No. 1 option. Now the youngster wanted the senior jersey. It wasn't a secret.

'Everything I was doing at that time was geared towards taking over from Ger,' says Cusack. 'Nowadays he's a very good friend of mine, and at the start I knew what my position was. It was, he's Ger Cunningham. I've to respect that. I wanted to learn as much as I could from him.

'Now, he'll tell you I was a competitive guy as well—we'd have competitions against each other in training, and he was who he was, but I loved the idea that I was taking him on.'

Cusack would have to wait to become the Cork senior goalkeeper, but not that long.

# THE YOUNGER LADS WERE STILL CHILDREN

Barry-Murphy's team was coming together. It was a slow process, but the pieces were sliding into position. He still had to fend off criticism, however. Some Cork supporters wanted more from their hurlers, more physique, to be precise.

'I remember being out several nights,' says Barry-Murphy, 'or in conversation with people at work, and fellas would be saying, we need a Tim Crowley, and I thought it was the most ridiculous comment of all time.

'If they'd been out there we'd have picked them. People were saying Clare and Kilkenny and Tipp were all huge men, and I was saying, I accept that, but are we supposed to pick big, useless hurlers?'

That was the vogue at the time. Clare, Limerick and Wexford had won All-Irelands and provincial championships with a muscular brand of hurling, and it was assumed that other counties would fight fire with fire—apart from Cork, whose team seemed to be getting smaller. Still, there was comfort early in the year, when the team won a competition, picking up the league title.

'We beat Clare well in the league semi-final,' says Seán Óg Ó hAilpín. 'Then we got a good win over Waterford in the final, a cracking game. One of the hottest days that year, big crowd in Thurles . . . it was a great step forward.'

It's a common theme. Diarmuid O'Sullivan remembers the fantastic buzz in Thurles on the day of the league final: 'It was as good as an All-Ireland medal to us at the time.'

'Even though a league mightn't be seen in Cork as huge,' says Ger Cunningham, 'it was a big medal at that stage to win, and they've not won many league medals since. So that was a big boost.'

And it had been a reasonable facsimile of a championship match, setting Cork up well for their championship opener against Limerick.

Much of the media focus was on Seánie McGrath after his debut against Clare the previous year. Some players don't cope well with attention—not McGrath.

'Ah, I loved it. As a young fella you'd read player interviews in the paper and say, I'd love to do that. When it happened it was brilliant.

'The profile of the team wasn't great, maybe, but at the time I was six feet tall and chest way out. I felt I was one of the key forwards and the team depended on me for scores. I thrived on that.

'Now maybe it put pressure on me, but after 1997 my confidence was high. I got a goal against Clare in the league semi-final and three points in the league final against Waterford.'

He surfed that confidence into the championship. Against Limerick some late switches by the Shannonside management played into McGrath's hands: 'Mark Foley was supposed to mark me but ended up at centre forward, so Jack Foley marked me instead.'

Without Mark Foley's company, McGrath plundered five points from play and established the platform for Cork's win. Two late goals made it 3–20 to 2–11, but Limerick couldn't reel Cork in. Barry-Murphy hugged all his players as they came back into the dressing room. He'd been vindicated.

'Seánie McGrath would have been the classic example of that size thing—people looking for bigger players,' says Barry-Murphy. 'He and Joe Deane were the corner forwards against Limerick and Seánie put the pride back in Cork hurling that day. To me that was what Cork hurling was all about.

'You didn't have to be big and strong. There was a place for everyone if they were good enough. The skill levels he showed that day lifted my heart, and he epitomised where we were going. He brought back the cockiness.

'There was no other road we could take. The rubbish I was listening to about big strong men—you couldn't just go out and pluck a Timmy Crowley or a Johnny Crowley out of thin air. They just weren't there.'

Ahead of the Clare game there was confidence, and evidence to support that self-belief. Cork had beaten Clare well in the league semi-final, after all, but it didn't take long for that achievement to be undermined afterwards. There were whispers that Clare had trained that morning, and though the Banner denied it, the fact that the story was given credence in the first instance shows the shadow they cast.

A decade later, Seánie McGrath still has no problem believing it.

'They were the team to beat. They probably trained the morning of the league semi-final all right. The championship was the focus for them.

'We beat them by eleven points in the league and probably got carried away a bit. We'd beaten Waterford in a good league final and then taken Limerick in our first championship win in six years. And Clare were in the long grass.'

On a bright sunny day in Thurles, Cork came out of their dressing room first against Clare. What happened next entered the folklore. Anthony Daly led Clare out, but instead of going around the rope cordoning off the entrance to the tunnel, they went over it.

'Anthony Daly tells the story that I said then, Jim, we're in trouble here,' says Dr Con Murphy. 'They were leaping out of their skins, and they were awesome at the time, in fairness.'

Awesome just about covers it. Seán Óg Ó hAilpín recalls the game as being a battle from the start.

'We had the wind in the first half and we were struggling. What went against us was they were more mature, more developed, more seasoned. They were hitting hard—fair and square—whenever they needed to.'

Still, Cork survived. It was nine points each at the break. But, as Diarmuid O'Sullivan puts it, Clare had a different gear.

'In the last ten minutes they hit us with a flurry of points and they were gone,' says Seánie McGrath. 'The public probably thought, Christ, they're gone back.

'But Clare were established; they knew about setting a team up. I always thought we were unlucky in 1998. We brought it back to two points with sixteen, seventeen minutes left, but Jamesie, Gilligan, Markham, they all came into it. They got on a roll and we were five or six down, then eight or nine. We were a bit unlucky, I thought.'

O'Sullivan was encouraged as well: 'They had been the bullies; they'd taken the physical approach. We were well beaten, but we'd put down a marker—this is going to stop; we're coming. We had a bit of cockiness about us because of the league semi-final, but they had a different gear.'

Barry-Murphy also saw some brightness on the horizon.

'Beating Limerick in Limerick was a great result, and we went to Thurles full of hope that we could take Clare. But they blew us away physically that day in the end.

'On the Monday or Tuesday after that, however, I watched the video of the game—not something I'd always do—and I saw that we'd missed a load of chances at the start of the game and yet with nine minutes into the game there was nothing in it.

'I think it was a lack of maturity or experience that found us out that day, but watching the video I remember it was the first time I thought, we're close to breaking through here. Even though we were well beaten in the end on the scoreboard, that wasn't a fair reflection of the overall game in my view. I said to myself we'll give it one more year; we're nearly there. Next year we'll have a great chance.'

Taking an overall view of 1998, Mark Landers sees it as part of a learning curve.

'We were riding the crest of a wave. We'd come from a scenario where we hadn't won a championship match since 1992. So the Clare and Waterford league games were good from a Cork point of view, and we'd beaten Limerick. But it was all within six weeks.

'Euphoria probably set in, along with a bit of fatigue. I don't know if fellas thought, we've a league medal, and maybe that was thought of as success.'

Recalibrating attitudes for championship success was one challenge. Other lessons absorbed against Clare were filed away, not all of them on the field of play.

'We went down to the Anner Hotel on the day we played Clare and we were mingling with the supporters,' says Landers. 'We probably weren't focused enough. That's nobody's fault. We'd just come more or less out of nowhere and suddenly it was, we were back.

'The sting in the tail was that Clare were in the long grass while we were immature, frankly. Ger Cunningham was in goal, but apart from that I was 26 and I was one of the oldest. We were also very light physically—some of the lads were under 21 still—and we probably didn't see the juggernaut coming. The younger lads were still children; that's how I saw it.

'You can't give a 21-year-old or a 20-year old the experience of a 25-year old, be that in life or physical experience. You get the odd exception, but when you bring along five or six lads that age at the same time, you can't expect them to stand up to lads five or six years older. That was the case in 1998, and we saw clips of Seánie McGrath and other lads getting roughed up by older Clare lads. And you were looking around to see who'd take them on.

'But in those twelve months the Cork team grew up. We'd learned about the physical side of things, and we took that into 1999. That was down to management and to older players—the likes of Fergal

Ryan, Alan Browne, Brian Corcoran—standing up when it came to the Munster final of 1999.'

The slow accumulation of experience was helping; so was the success at U-21 level. The team was gelling and lessons learned in the hard days would be carried forward, says Seán Óg Ó hAilpín, to the present day.

'Take new fellas coming into the dressing room. I'd put it down to an Irish thing. When you'd go into the dressing room you'd be in awe of fellas. That's why I'd never forget Brian Corcoran coming over to me and welcoming me. It made a huge difference.

'I know the way it works. You have to earn your stripes before fellas talk to you. You might be gone the following week and the other lads, the established lads, don't know if you'll be around. But it's also an Irish thing. We're probably not people who'd be the most open like that.

'When Setanta went over to Carlton he was introduced to the group and they all shook his hand, but that's not something we'd do, maybe. Nowadays when I'd see young lads coming in, I'd go over to them and introduce myself and ask what they made of the session afterwards to try to involve them.'

The fitness regime had also become more intense in 1998, says Ó hAilpín.

'What caught my eye that year was Ger Cunningham, and the fact he was training so hard—I think he was on the Nutron diet, he was looking lean—but the training was generally ramped up. Bleep tests, body fat tests, they were all part of the set-up.'

Ó hAilpín had issues to address which weren't related to his fitness. Living in Dublin spared him physically, but it wasn't doing a lot for his touch.

'When I look back on videotapes of some of the games, 1996 through to 1999, games I'd have thought I did well in, I'd be thinking, that's awful. I could barely hit the ball thirty yards. That was one of my biggest faults, my striking.

'The years in Dublin probably didn't help in that regard. I was playing hurling for DCU, but the problem was I didn't get enough regular ballwork. Physically I was fine. That was the least of my worries. And I tried to compensate for my hurling with my fitness; that was meant to compensate for my hurling.

'As the years went on I realised I had to address that, but in another way it probably saved me. I was involved with the Cork footballers, who did serious training under Larry [Tompkins], and given Teddy's training, I'd have been doing the two. Being in Dublin spared me that. Hurling-wise I suffered—DCU were a Division 2 side, and that had an effect—but I'd have been a dead duck if I'd stayed in Cork. I'd have been going here, there and everywhere. In the long run it helped me.'

Above it all Barry-Murphy's support for his players was a constant. It drove them on, says Seánie McGrath.

'If you're going to break in at inter-county level you need ability, but Jimmy gave me great confidence. After 1997 I got some publicity, but then the league didn't go that well for me. I got player of the tournament in the Fitzgibbon in 1998, but when I was poor in the league game after that, Jimmy would ring me and say, "Don't worry about that. We know what you can do."

'And then, for instance, when the Clare game went against me, I looked on the positives—I got two points in the second half to bring us back into it. People said I didn't have a great game, but I was positive.'

The outlook wasn't as upbeat for one of the other players. Ger Cunningham had put down sixteen years in goal for Cork and had saved the county on innumerable occasions. However, for the first time there had been whispers. He'd conceded two late goals against Limerick which had made the closing stages unnecessarily worrying for Cork. He knew the end was approaching.

'The Limerick game was the big one that year,' he says. 'Other than the fact that we'd won a championship match, which was the first win for most of the players, in terms of experience gained, that was a huge boost. The Clare game was a huge disappointment because we had expectations going into it.

'It was my last game, and it was probably my most pressurised match—a couple of scribes had put the pressure on after the Limerick game. It had been part of my life for twenty years, and knowing as well that things were going to turn, it was a huge change. But I knew it was nigh.

'The end of the Limerick game brought it even closer, and though the Clare game went okay for me personally, it brought the decision time near.'

The manager had a decision to make. Cunningham had been a legend of the game, a hero to all of Cork and one of the finest goalkeepers ever to pull on a jersey in any era, but there were other practicalities that had to be addressed. Barry-Murphy knew that the succession had to be managed carefully, but he also had to give Cunningham's successor game time. He met the incumbent late in 1998 for a chat.

'Ger had been great for us in 1998,' says Barry-Murphy. 'When we sat down to pick a panel for 1999, I felt Donal Óg had been sub keeper for long enough and deserved a fair chance. I met Ger and he asked me if we'd discussed the goalkeeping situation, and I told him there'd be no guarantees during the league, that we had to give Donal Óg a chance.

'Ger announced his retirement a couple of days later. It made it easy for us, but it was only fair to Donal Óg to give him a chance.'

With the master gone, the apprentice's day had come. Donal Óg Cusack had a clear run at the Cork jersey, but he knew the size of the shoes he was filling. He recalls Cunningham's last day in a Cork jersey for a championship game.

'What sticks with me was that Ger came over to me before the Clare match and told me he'd forgotten his contact lenses,' says Cusack. 'Now, that time we were so competitive with each other that I wouldn't even have told him that I wore contacts. I'd have thought for some reason that that was some kind of weakness. I'd have put them on before coming to training and that. But in the conversation we had the day of the game he asked if he could wear mine.'

The older man's focus was a lesson to Cusack: 'What struck me was that it didn't rattle him one bit that he'd forgotten his lenses. And then he put in mine, and wearing someone else's contacts isn't even like wearing someone's helmet. It's not ideal at all.

'During the game I watched him. I was thinking, this is bound to rattle him a small bit. But not at all. He made one of the greatest saves of all time against Niall Gilligan during the game. That was Ger Cunningham.'

## 1999 (1) ∿

# IF WE WERE GOING TO GO DOWN, WE'D GO DOWN WITH HURLERS

For all Barry-Murphy's optimism after the performance against Clare in 1998, the omens weren't that good early the next year. A swift mythology grew up about the lead-in to their first championship outing, for instance, centring specifically on a couple of notorious challenge games which Cork lost to Tipperary.

'Awful,' says Deane.

'Diabolical,' says McGrath.

'Shocking,' says Landers.

'The famous Tipp challenge games,' laughs Barry-Murphy. 'We were knocked back because we thought we were going well. We didn't go all out for the league in 1999 because we were going to give the championship a good whip, but the Tipp game knocked us out of our stride totally.

'Coming back in the car that night with Teddy Owens and Tom Cashman, they said they felt I needed to take a more hands-on role with the hurling training, to show more passion. I thought I'd been doing that, but we upped the hurling training. The Tipp games were probably a blessing in disguise in one way.'

Mark Landers agrees.

'Those games were the watershed for the year. It's hard to believe we won the All-Ireland in 1999 because Ronan Dwane and I used to travel to training together and we were saying early that year, this is the last year we'll be coming up here.

'It was going shocking. I spoke to Seánie McGrath before the first Tipp challenge; we were sitting up in the stand together. I told him how bad it was going and he didn't believe me. But that game was blown up early.'

Desperate measures were needed. The story that the manager resigned in despair after the second Tipperary challenge match grew legs quickly, but it wasn't that straightforward. There was no disputing the poverty of any likely Cork challenge in the championship, however. Dr Con Murphy, who had seen generations of Cork teams prepare for action, is unequivocal about the seriousness of the situation.

'Tipp humiliated us. We were in crisis at that stage, when Jimmy called some of the senior players in for a heart to heart. On the way home he called in to me and said he was considering resigning. He was wondering if it'd help, because it was going nowhere. It was the worst beating I'd seen Cork get ahead of a championship match ever. We were no-hopers.'

'I don't know if I was that close to resigning,' says Barry-Murphy now. 'But after the Tipp game I spoke to some of the senior players . . . I wasn't going to resign, but what I was thinking was, if I couldn't get the best out of the players, maybe there was another approach.'

His captain appreciated the honesty.

'Myself, Brian Corcoran and Fergal Ryan were called in by Jimmy,' says Landers. 'He said straightaway, "Lads, I think I'm the issue here. I can't get a response from the team." At the back of my mind for a fleeting moment I thought he might be right, but then immediately I thought, here's a guy who's open and honest, saying things are going bad. He's blaming himself and looking for a solution. That's a very honourable thing to do. He said he could have a manager in place within twenty-four hours.

'At that moment I said, no, Jim, you're not the problem. We're probably not as focused as we should be. The training should maybe be stepped up a little, but we're not going to let the ship sink at this stage. We can turn it around.'

'I threw myself totally into the hurling sessions from then on,' says Barry-Murphy. 'I tried to make everything into a match situation and it took off from there. But I was disillusioned. I said that if someone had something else to offer, that I was quite prepared to listen to it.'

Landers says the improvement was immediate.

'That meeting was a Tuesday and on the Thursday I was sitting next to Johnny Sheehan before we went out training, and he said, "Things are going bad." I said, Johnny, they are, but it's up to you and me to turn it around.'

They did. That Thursday night session was one of the best of the year, and as Landers says, the season took off from there.

For those with a mind to look, there had been some bright spots early on in 1999 as well.

'The Tipp game was bad but it was high scoring,' says Seánie McGrath. 'We played a challenge against Kilkenny that was a very high-scoring game as well, and I remember Eddie Keher writing somewhere afterwards that that was a fabulous game.

'We'd had a couple of decent league games in 1999: we'd beaten Wexford, Tipp and Waterford, for instance.'

Training also had a ferocious edge to it, giving the team a base of fitness that would stand to them later in the season.

'The training in the tunnels that time . . . I never went through torture like that before or since,' says Donal Óg Cusack. 'I wanted to be there. I was into training; but you'd wake up the following morning and say, Christ, it's only Tuesday. I've to go back down there. You'd nearly be nervous going back.

'What made it huge was the competition. Like, when Paul

Morrissey came on as a sub keeper, I'd be thinking, there's no way he's beating me in these runs. So we'd be competing with each other. When we were doing tests and myself and Paul were in the same group, Teddy Owens said to someone, "There'll be a fatality here, because neither of them will give in." We were in competition, which isn't good training. It couldn't be good training if you were trying for your personal best every single run.

'You'd come back into the gym after it and your head would be spinning. It was torture.'

There were one or two discoveries to bolster the team during the league as well. The alignment settled. Forwards were being uncovered.

'We couldn't be that confident after the way we'd been in the challenges against Tipp,' says Diarmuid O'Sullivan. 'But we'd gone to Gorey for a league game—we were still going in taxis at that stage—and Jimmy put me in full back. I was on Gary Laffan. It went well and we won by a point or two. Ben O'Connor came on and got a goal towards the end. That was the start of me at full back for the seniors.

'I'd played there for the U-21s. Bertie had asked me to play at full back and I'd given it a go. I felt if I could win All-Ireland U-21 medals, I'd be up to senior inter-county.'

Gorey was also the start of Ben O'Connor as a scoring forward with Cork. The quiet youngster from Newtownshandrum had been invited onto the panel in 1998, but had had too much going on with his club and declined. Early in 1999 he was still relatively non-committal, and the temptations of Highbury almost kept him off the team for another year.

'In March 1999 I got called in,' says O'Connor. 'I was supposed to be going to London with Jerry [O'Connor] and Jerry Ryan for an Arsenal game, but I got a call to the league game with Laois. I decided I wouldn't be asked again, and Arsenal were only playing Coventry . . . I was brought on for the last five minutes. The following week I came on against Wexford and I got a goal. But you take it as it comes. You don't sit down at the start of the year and decide to make the team.'

'I remember Ben O'Connor's first night with Cork,' says Landers. 'I introduced him and he sat beside me for the whole year. When you have good talents like him coming in, you need to make them feel welcome and take care of them. At that stage you might have had just Pat Mulcahy or Fergal McCormack from north Cork on the panel.

'When I came onto the Cork panel at 19, I felt intimidated among fellas who'd won All-Ireland medals and so on. It wasn't that I wasn't made welcome, but they were probably thinking, who's this whipper-snapper?'

O'Connor's goal beat Wexford and marked him as a coming man. On their way out of the ground in Gorey afterwards, a couple of Cork fans were asked by a knowledgeable Wexford supporter, 'Lads, whatever happened to Mickey O'Connell?' He wouldn't have to wait long for an answer.

Waterford were Cork's first test. They had reached an All-Ireland semi-final the year before, when they should have beaten Kilkenny, but more importantly they had been through the crucible in Munster. They had gone to war with Clare in the 1998 Munster final and replay, and were a hardened bunch compared to the Cork side Barry-Murphy picked.

There were six debutants: Donal Óg Cusack, Wayne Sherlock, Mickey O'Connell, Timmy McCarthy, Ben O'Connor and Neil Ronan. Understandably, Waterford were installed as favourites.

Dr Con Murphy points out that the team Barry-Murphy selected was true to his thinking on the game.

'If he was going to go down against Waterford, he'd go down with a young team, so he'd at least have blooded them for the future. That was his philosophy. In 1996 he felt we'd gone down badly with an old team, and he felt if he was going to go down in 1999 it would be with a young team and leave some kind of a legacy.

'He called for me on the morning of the game and he was physically ill, because it was the last throw of the dice.'

Barry-Murphy's time with the team all zeroed in on that one game.

'If we were beaten it was the trapdoor, but if we got through to the Munster final, and through the back door, we'd be playing in Croke Park,' Barry-Murphy says. 'I'll never forget the intensity of the players that morning in the Dundrum House Hotel. There was a fantastic focus. We picked a young team, a team that could hurl, because after the Tipp games we said that if we were going to go down, we'd go down with hurlers. We brought back Mickey O'Connell and he was inspired.'

O'Connell was superb. He and Landers dominated midfield, scoring eight and two points respectively. The captain's form hadn't been particularly good going into the Waterford game, so he was happy with the result.

'I'd won a senior county with Imokilly in 1998, won an intermediate with Killeagh and started a new job,' says Landers. 'I'd had a long season and was probably tired going into 1999, so I was under a bit of pressure. You were also dealing with the youngest panel of players going, though we built as the year went on. I think the players trusted me.'

'At half-time in that game Jimmy gave a very good team talk,' says Dr Con. 'He said he'd been with them since they were minors and that he was mad about them, but he said unfortunately they only had thirty-five minutes together unless they won. That had the desired effect.'

Despite a late Paul Flynn goal, Cork held out. Afterwards a famous photograph appeared in the newspapers of an exultant Barry-Murphy rushing out onto the field. The joy was evident, but not many people saw the significance of the manager's clothing at the time.

'I remember before the Waterford game we got Umbro boots and T-shirts from Fergus Burke,' says Seánie McGrath. 'We had no sponsored gear at the time and Jimmy wore the gear that day to thank him. Esat rowed in afterwards and gave us great sponsorship. But that's how different it was back then.

'Only when you look back you see the pressure. You'd say now that that was shit or bust, but at the time it was just another game.'

'When the final whistle went against Waterford, I felt some vindication for our approach,' says Barry-Murphy. 'At least we were back in Croke Park. That was probably being selfish, but at that stage it was like the promised land, given where we'd come from.'

Different players reacted differently. Debutant Wayne Sherlock remembers being drained for a fortnight afterwards. 'You wouldn't realise what a game like that takes out of you,' he says now, while Cusack, working in the city at that time as an apprentice electrician, remembers the after-effects.

'I remember going down to the shop for my breakfast and there were people handing out Esat flags in the traffic to drivers. No crests, just red and white with Esat on them. And then it struck me, how big it was.

'The Monday after we played Waterford I was on site, working away. The noise from the Waterford support that time was something I'd never heard before. And the next day on site there were big holes being drilled, and the noise from the Waterford support was in my head. Only a few hours earlier I'd heard that, and it kept flashing back into my head on site. It mixed in with the noise from the drills.'

The goal Waterford had scored was a scrappy one, but Cusack was a different character in 1999 to the confident goalkeeper of more recent years. Barry-Murphy had been careful to exonerate the new man from culpability in the Tipperary games in an effort to preserve his self-belief, and Cusack was finding his way: he had taken over from a legend and wasn't in a hurry to reinvent the wheel. Furthermore, there was a bad experience in the 1997 county final which coloured his approach in 1999 with Cork.

'I dropped a ball in the first few minutes that day and Sars got a goal. And I lost my nerve. It wasn't an enjoyable day because of that, and ever since one of my big things was to work on my head, to make sure I was in control of things. And that was my attitude in 1999: do your job. If there's 100,000 people there, ignore them. This is your team; just do your job.

'Being the senior keeper, I wouldn't say it was overpowering. It was something I was working towards, something I was trying to get my head around. I had great confidence in the lads around me. We'd all done well at u-21 together and I knew other lads from Imokilly. But having said that, I don't think I started expressing myself as a goalkeeper for a couple of years after that. Safety is a huge thing for a goalkeeper, and I'd have been geared towards that.'

Clare would be the opponents in the Munster final. The way Cusack remembers it, they were still the draw.

'We were training before the Clare game and I met a fella from Castlemartyr looking for tickets down the Pairc. And when I said I didn't have any, he said, "Well 'tis Clare I want to see, not Cork." And I remember thinking, well, it's Cork you'll want to see after Sunday. But that was the way people saw things that time. Not to mention the fact that it was a pretty thick thing to say to a young fella playing his first Munster final a few days later.'

Barry-Murphy was confident ahead of the game. Despite the fact that Clare had beaten Cork in every championship game the sides had played since 1994, the manager felt the tide had turned.

'I'd seen Clare play Tipp down the Pairc in the previous game and you have to be fair. Jamesie O'Connor, who was injured in that game, was a huge loss to Clare, no matter how you want to colour it. I felt if we couldn't beat Clare without him . . . he was a great player for them, but I felt this was our opportunity to put Clare away and start a new era for Cork. It would probably herald the end of the Loughnane era in Munster and start a new cycle for Cork hurling.'

Landers concurs on the loss of Jamesie O'Connor, but he was also trying to be proactive before the game.

'When I heard Jamesie had broken his arm, I felt it was a big help, but it wasn't something we thought about in the lead-up to the Munster final. I was looking for something from an inspirational point of view, and I showed the lads footage from the 1998 game.'

It had the required effect. When Landers brought the players into a room in the team hotel before the game, the clips electrified those present.

'Landers was dynamite before the Clare game,' says Seánie McGrath. 'Dynamite, boy. He showed us the clips of the 1998 game, fellas being targeted, and he said we needed to look after each other. Landers was a great character that way. He only made his debut in 1998, but he didn't care if lads were upset by what he said.'

Diarmuid O'Sullivan concurs on the video show: 'Before the Clare game, Landers brought us into a room and played a video of Anthony Daly walking past us, smirking. There was a real sense of, I'm still king here. Landers said, "If any of you still want to feel like that, the door's there." It got everyone going just before we got on the bus for Thurles.'

That focus remained intact during the pre-game parade.

'In the pre-match parade some of our lads were roaring at Daly,' says McGrath, 'They were telling him this was our day, that if he hit one of us he'd have to deal with all of us, that kind of thing. I was a good bit back in the parade and I remember thinking, we're up for this.'

'It wasn't a conscious thing,' recalls Wayne Sherlock. 'Landers had shown us the video. The hair's standing on my neck even talking about it now, so you can imagine what I was like at the time. I never saw fellas so possessed after that, because you could see the look in Daly's eye in the video. He knew he had us beaten.

'Out in the parade, because Daly was in fellas' minds, they started roaring over at him. That was the making of the team for the next few years.'

If Seánie McGrath had been closer to the front he might have seen more. Five years later Landers was on holiday in Lanzarote when a man offered to buy him a drink. He asked the player what had happened before the Munster final in 1999.

'When I asked him to be more specific, he mentioned what happened just before the parade,' says Landers. 'It won him £20,000. He said, "You eyeballed Daly for about thirty seconds before the parade and he looked away. When I saw that," he said, "I knew Cork were a driven team and put a wad of money on ye."'

The game was nip and tuck until a few minutes before half-time, when the ball came across the face of the Clare goal and Seánie McGrath, haring towards the end line, swung his hurley to keep it in play. It dropped in the Clare square and Joe Deane was on hand to sweep it home.

'I just remember the sheer joy,' says Deane. 'It was my first goal at senior inter-county championship level. It was a statement we'd arrived against Clare, the side who'd dominated for years. It was right in front of the Cork crowd on the Town End . . .'

For the man who flicked the ball back, it was indicative of the two players' approach.

'Fellas would say to me, you must be great pals with Joe Deane,' says McGrath. 'I wouldn't go drinking every Friday night with Joe— he was from Killeagh, I'm from the city—though we knew each other a bit in college. But I knew the kind of ball he liked, and vice versa. I knew he wasn't a guy who'd get upset during a game, that he'd score if he got one chance.

'I don't know if it was telepathic. To be honest, there was a bit of luck involved. I was just trying to keep the ball from going wide, trying to keep it in the danger zone. But the ideal fella to have there waiting for it was Joe, with the dainty flick. We never spoke about it; that was just our job.

'Looking back now, though, you'd say it showed something about our ability—and our cockiness. Lohan was giving some stick to Joe at one stage in the first half and his helmet flew off just as I was passing. I gave it a kick and drove it into the goal. Lohan came after me. He'd have blown me up onto the terrace and I just jogged around him saying, what's the problem? You could hear the crowd laughing up on the terrace.

'We got the goal and a point just before the break. It was 1–9 to 0–7 at the break. Half-time, Munster final, we were leading and we were buzzing.'

On the sideline, the man who'd scored so many vital goals himself felt the goal was a turning point.

'It was significant in that it epitomised what two of the lads on whom we depended, Seánie and Joe, were all about,' says Barry-Murphy. 'It was fantastic, and there was a great picture the following day of Joe running out, the blood running down from his eye. But it was also the goal which gave us the cushion to beat Clare.'

It wasn't over. Seán Óg Ó hAilpín saw the obstacles the team still had to overcome.

'It was huge psychologically. Before the game I'm not sure if fellas knew they could take them on. At times during the game we had them practically nailed into the coffin, but it still took a missed free from Davy Forde to win it. That'll tell you our mental state at the time.'

That Forde free, a surprising miss from the 21-metre line, was a huge let-off for Cork ('It must still haunt him,' says Diarmuid O'Sullivan), but a Munster senior hurling title doesn't come with caveats. The team's self-belief soared, particularly when Ben O'Connor scorched down the wing to nail what Barry-Murphy would describe as the trademark Ben point: boots scraping the whitewash off the sideline on the right wing, steepling the ball over the bar.

Ironically, O'Connor says now he doesn't remember a whole lot about his first couple of years apart from the length of the settling-in period.

'When you get into it first, you play away and you might do all right, but it takes you three or four years to settle into it. You've the odd fella like Shefflin who might get into it straightaway, but most fellas take a couple of years to get up to the pace of it.

'When I say the pace, it's everything—every inter-county hurler has pace. At club level your touch might get you out of trouble, but at inter-county level every player has that. And that's when it's level enough—you'll have stretches during a season when the ball is breaking everywhere that you're not. Inter-county level isn't as physical as club. Every fella is focused on playing the ball, and though you might get the odd belt, it's not as physical as club hurling.'

'There was a feeling after the Clare game that we were on the right track,' says Ó hAilpín. 'The team we'd found hard to beat, we'd finally got on top of them, and they were on the downward slope while we were on the way up. There were challenges ahead, but at that moment things couldn't have been better. Winning the Munster title was the be-all and end-all at that point.'

For Timmy McCarthy the contrasting outlooks of the older and younger players was vital.

'If you asked Corcoran or Fergal Ryan, they knew about losing to Clare, and though we were subs in 1998 and we saw them lose and we were disappointed, we'd never lost to Clare in our careers. It didn't affect us, while it might have affected the older lads.

'I think they really wanted to beat Clare in a big game and it was a combination of the two—they really wanted to win and we didn't know what we were getting into.'

The significance of a Munster final win over Clare wasn't lost on the manager either.

'I felt Cork were back as big players in the ballgame, which we hadn't been,' says Barry-Murphy. 'I had set Clare as the barometer at that time. They'd beaten us in 1997, bullied us in 1998 and we'd beaten them in 1999. I always felt it would herald their decline if we beat them in a Munster final, which it probably did. We went down the road of hurling, and we won playing real Cork hurling. That was important to me.'

Landers had twisted his ankle and had to come off, but he'd limped around the pitch encouraging his team mates. Beyond the passion he saw the lessons Barry-Murphy and the management had absorbed.

'When the final whistle blew . . . it was just fantastic,' he says. 'The supporters make it. It was the fourth of July, Independence Day. We weren't given a chance that day, but credit to Jimmy and his selectors, they'd learned from 1998 and going to the Anner, for instance. They solved that by bringing us to Dundrum House to keep us away from mingling with the supporters and to keep us focused.'

The mingling went on afterwards, as Diarmuid O'Sullivan recalls.

'Jimmy put his neck on the block that day and if we'd lost, Cork hurling would have taken a fierce blow. We walked down from Semple Stadium with Jimmy and everyone in the square was chanting for him and congratulating us, and for the first time you felt you were part of something.'

For Wayne Sherlock there was a particular vindication: 'I'd given a big interview the week before the game, and you'd be hoping you'd play well after giving an interview. In fairness, any fella who says he hates doing them is lying. It's nice to be recognised too; everyone likes that, though it's fair to say that some fellas are more confident doing interviews than others.'

Sherlock didn't have to worry. He was an integral part of the defensive effort against Clare. Now he and his team mates had to handle what Diarmuid O'Sullivan called the buzz.

'Wherever you went, fellas had polo shirts and jerseys on,' says O'Sullivan. 'You'd be young enough and immature enough that fellas would be chatting to you about what they were doing; nowadays you might snap at someone if they started talking to you about the match, which is probably too far the other way. But you'd be distracted by the whole thing, definitely. You didn't know what to expect.'

What they could expect was their first championship outing in Croke Park, and a part in one of the games of the decade.

# | CATCH US IF YOU CAN

Cork's reward for their Munster final win was a date with All-Ireland champions Offaly. Barry-Murphy freely admits that he'd had so much to concentrate on in surviving the Munster championship that activity to the east hadn't appeared on his radar.

'We were looking forward to the Offaly game. The pressure was off the team and everything else was a bonus. I'd lost touch with Leinster hurling in all honesty because I was so focused on Cork and the Munster championship.'

For his captain there was a simple imperative: to keep winning.

'We put the Munster final away,' says Landers. 'Some teams who win Munster championships see that as a pinnacle, but our attitude was, we're Cork, we're capable of winning an All-Ireland. We'd beaten the team feared in every county, but we wanted more.

'The big thing about the semi-final was going to Croke Park, and at that stage Brian Corcoran had been the only fella who'd played senior championship hurling there, so that was a factor.'

Wayne Sherlock, for instance, had never even been in Croke Park for a concert, let alone a match.

'Jimmy and the lads organised a session for us on the Saturday night before the game,' says Sherlock. 'We went to Croke Park, walked the pitch and pucked the ball around. And that was brilliant because it took the nerves away. It meant that your first experience of Croke Park wouldn't be running out onto the field to play the game itself.'

The nerves were further calmed by Fergal Ryan's imitation of Ger Loughnane on the sideline, but the players were ready. They knew it.

'We'd done the physical stuff, but here Jimmy came into his own,' says Landers. 'The hurling training was superb from the Munster final through to the All-Ireland final. I've often said to people that we were like two different teams in the improvement in speed and striking between the first round and the final.

'If you keep hurling into October-November every year, it shortens the time you're without the hurley in your hand. It makes sense. If you puck a thousand balls and another lad pucks a hundred, then you're going to be better.'

Seánie McGrath, meanwhile, was on the same level as his coach when it came to the opposition.

'Offaly were an unknown quantity, to be honest. We knew who the big players were, but as a team and as a style of play we didn't know what to expect. Jimmy spoke to me on the train and he said, "Croke Park is a massive stadium. I played there loads of times and it's made for you. Enjoy it." I slept well after that. I knew there was a good game coming, though my form had been up and down a bit.'

There was indeed a good game coming. The All-Ireland semi-final was the match of the year, a see-saw battle of superb scores and beautiful skills. Many observers didn't see the portents, but Cork's outstanding performance in winning by two points on a rainy, miserable day would turn out to be a good pointer for the final.

It wasn't all beautiful skills, of course.

'Having been taken off in the Munster final, I wasn't going to be too adventurous,' says Landers. 'It was a tremendous game. Brian Whelehan pucked an amount of ball, which was no disrespect to his man, because he was the best hurler in the country at the time. The Offaly players' stickwork was exceptional. They just never made a mistake.'

Offaly had cast all of Limerick into gloom in 1994 when they'd stolen an All-Ireland at the death with two late goals. Landers had that in mind late in the semi-final when one of those goalscorers started ghosting into position.

'There were two points in it and they attacked. The ball was down by the Nally Stand. I saw Johnny Dooley take off, and I remembered what he did to Limerick in 1994, so I ran after him, threw my two arms around him and dragged him down on the ground.

'I knew nobody was watching—the focus was all on the ball—so I kept him down and said, Johnny, you're going no further, my son. He was trying to get away and when we got up he gave me an unmerciful flake across the back. I remember thinking, that was worth taking. The ball was cleared upfield and they never got a chance of a goal after that.'

They didn't, but Cork added the points, scorching past their opponents in what was becoming a trademark racing finish.

'The game was a roller-coaster,' says McGrath. 'The focus straight after the Munster final game was, we'd enjoy it, and after Offaly the feeling was that no one would beat us. We'd developed a burst for the last ten minutes, something the team became known for.'

'That was the nature of every win,' says Seán Óg Ó hAilpín. 'In the last ten minutes we'd come hard. Ted Owens had been stressing the importance of fitness—allied to skill—and because of that we felt if we got a bad start, we wouldn't panic. If we could bring it back, then we'd back ourselves to win coming down the stretch.

'But the Offaly game was one of the hardest, definitely. It was the masters showing the students for long periods; they lived off half the possession we had, but there were hand passes and flicks, great scores. What helped them was that label of being piss-artists, that they'd be falling around drunk half the time. You'd try not to believe it, but it would seep in a bit, as we found out the next year. They gave us a lesson in 1999 as well, but our determination and youth got us through.

'Jimmy always said Offaly were funny. The times you don't expect them to play well, they come up trumps, and when you least expect them to do well, they can catch you. He was very cautious about the game.'

'I thought we'd win,' says Barry-Murphy, 'but I didn't realise how good Offaly were. That day—and 2000, when they beat us—brought home to me how fantastic they were as hurlers. That semi-final was an unbelievable game, and Ben got another point, just like in the Munster final—a trademark Ben point—to win the game. Winning games like that . . . such classy, serious games.'

'We were lucky enough, looking back,' says Sherlock. 'Whelehan and Corcoran were incredible that day; they were something else. You'd pay money to see the two of them. It was the best game of the year.

'The fact that it was in the rain, too, that was important, because you'd always hear this thing that Cork couldn't play in the rain.'

In goal, Donal Óg Cusack had a different set of challenges. Untested for most of the game, Offaly's late surge forced him to work on his concentration.

'That's one of the hardest things in goalkeeping and it's an interesting thing for a keeper. You warm up before the start for twenty minutes. But then you don't get a ball for twenty minutes in the game or whatever. And what can happen then is that you're dead, cold, in the last five minutes because you've had nothing to do for thirty, forty minutes. As a result I've worked on techniques to keep myself tuned in.

'The best example of that would be the Offaly game, which was very quiet until the last ten minutes, when a few dangerous balls came in. Now I'd have been thinking about that anyway, and I'd have chatted to my father about it.

'Of course by that time I thought I had loads of experience after playing minor and U-21, but the important thing was Jimmy gave me loads of confidence. The famous night against Tipperary when we got hammered, Jimmy said I was the only fella who'd played well. Maybe he had it in mind, I'll give them stick but I don't want to bring the keeper down.'

Timmy McCarthy is blunt in his assessment of the 1999 semi-final: 'We were just trying to get over the line. We didn't realise how good a game it was. Offaly were one of the teams of the nineties, and basically we didn't realise what we were doing.'

Kilkenny were the final opponents. They'd lost the previous year's decider to Offaly and were regarded as more experienced—and more motivated after 1998.

'Going into the final the impression we had was that they were confident and that Cork weren't rated,' says Barry-Murphy. 'Not by the Kilkenny team, but by others. The selectors and I focused in on this as our main chance, because you never know what's coming. I went to Croke Park as a young lad in 1973 and thought I'd be winning All-Ireland football medals for the next seven or eight years, but a lot of that football team never saw Croke Park again.

'And I think we got it across to the team that it's easier to win your first one. I hate that rubbish that you've to lose one to win one. In 1973 Cork hadn't won a football final since 1945, but I went into that game without a care in the world, and it's the only way to approach a final. It gets harder as you get older, as I found out to my cost in 1982 and 1983. The pressure comes on and you don't always deliver.

'We focused in on that. We were going to win; we had a great chance, and if it fell our way we'd take it.'

'That's the beauty of being young,' says Ó hAilpín. 'I find it harder to cope with All-Irelands now compared to then. When you're more mature, when you've played more, your fear of losing overshadows your will to win.

'In 1999 losing never came into the equation. I was young, in good health, confident in my ability and the team's, and Jimmy was always saying to us that the time to win your All-Ireland was your first time out.

'Whether it was arrogance or cockiness, I knew we'd win in 1999. But I couldn't say the same about 2004 or 2005. Even when we were beating Kilkenny well towards the end in 2004, I still couldn't relax. In 1999 there was a lot of media attention because I was in line for the double and all that. I didn't work that summer. I'd just finished my finals and I lived up in Na Piarsaigh or Pairc Uí Chaoimh. It was a great summer, a great time.'

Barry-Murphy's approach was the right one, agrees McGrath.

'Kilkenny were raging hot favourites, but Jimmy never made much of that. He never spoke about them. He focused on us. His training was superb—he was like a good managing director, with the right guys in the right places. Teddy would do the unpopular stuff, for instance, while Jimmy stayed popular!

'All the selectors were laid back because that was Jimmy's style, while the craic he had with Dr Con rubbed off on the rest of us. One night before the All-Ireland final Jimmy asked Dr Con if he could take us for twenty minutes and the whole place cracked up. There was a great mood. We slagged Con because Jimmy had "given out" to him.'

The practicalities of Barry-Murphy's approach—focusing on his own players—are borne out by Diarmuid O'Sullivan.

'Focusing on a particular opposing player, that wasn't the done thing. Jimmy's way was if you were corner back, you were corner back and you minded that. John Browne probably marked DJ for about fifty-five minutes of the game, and he was incredible the same day. I was on Shefflin and Charlie Carter was in the corner. Carey-Shefflin-Carter—not a bad full forward line.'

The captain, meanwhile, was a huge doubt in the lead-up to the final. Landers tore his knee cartilage in Kilworth playing a club game for Killeagh.

'I often told [selector] Fred Sheedy since, he should have been out filling in the rabbit holes,' he says. 'If it wasn't for Dr Con, I'd never have played in the All-Ireland final. I rang him, and though he was on holiday in Kerry, he told me to come down and see him. I went down and he said, "The cartilage is torn. You'll be a doubt." In fairness to him he made a few calls and he got me done the following morning.

'The help [physio] Liam O'Reilly gave me was fantastic. I trained with him in Bandon for three weeks, swimming, cycling and using weights, and Seánie O'Leary and Ted Owens came to see me eight days into the recovery programme. I couldn't train with the team— which, looking back, I can't believe the selectors accepted—and I lost seven pounds in six days. Johnny Crowley said, "You're gone away to a skeleton. We're concerned you're losing your strength." Liam had got me to a level I'd never been at before, and in the first twenty-five minutes of the All-Ireland final my performance reflected the work he did with me.'

One memorable night Landers arrived at Pairc Uí Chaoimh with a parachute.

'We hadn't seen Landers for about three weeks when we had the open day for supporters,' says Diarmuid O'Sullivan. 'The stands were filling up with people when, next thing, who comes out of the tunnel but Landers, who produces a parachute. Jimmy turned around, saw him and said, "Look at that . . ." There was Landers running up and down the line in front of the stand with the parachute flapping away behind him.'

Landers pays tribute to his midfield partner for pitching in.

'In fairness to Mickey, he did the parachute work with me. The other lads got a kick out of it; it had been serious until I started running around Pairc Uí Chaoimh with a parachute. They were probably thinking, what's the world coming to!

'I was lucky from a work point of view as well. I was left off for a month by the TSB. Dermot O'Brien, Tomas Mulcahy and Denis O'Sullivan put in the word for me and there was no pressure put on. That was a huge help.'

When the team was named, Landers was elated by his reward for all the hard work.

'Knowing I'd start . . . I couldn't put it in words. The team was announced, the press were there and I'd say suddenly ninety per cent of the reporters were in front of me. I'd been removed from the whole thing down in Bandon. But physically and mentally I was spot on. I was never in better shape in my life.'

The captain wasn't the only doubt ahead of the game. True to his nature, Timmy McCarthy doesn't make a big issue out of his race to get fit.

'Three weeks before the final I got injured playing for Castlelyons against UCC and I didn't train for those three weeks,' says McCarthy. 'I was only back two or three days beforehand; there was a fair chance I mightn't make it. I hurt my knee and I was getting physio two or three times a day, and I didn't know for definite I'd play until two, three days beforehand.'

McCarthy's secret vice—cigarettes—didn't help in the run-up to the big day.

'I'd enjoy them. I'm not proud of it, of course. I gave them up the last couple of seasons, but I'd have fifteen or twenty a day.

'When I was getting physiotherapy I was put on a treadmill a week before the final and I was put on the heart monitor. I'd had a fag before going in and my heart rate was 92. The physio said, "Seriously, you shouldn't be playing anything." This was a week before the All-Ireland!'

The day of the game sticks in Seán Óg Ó hAilpín's mind because of the downpour.

'Raindrops as big as sliotars. It was dry for the minor game, then it started pelting down and there was all the "Cork are sunshine hurlers" stuff.

'I never experienced anything like the silence in the Burlington at the meal before the game. We'd have had a few jokers on the panel, but there was complete silence, the calm before the storm. We went to UCD for a few pucks and then to Croke Park.'

Donal Óg Cusack isolates his attitude: 'It's like you have to do this thing; don't indulge yourself because that would be selfish. I was thinking, if only we could win this All-Ireland; if I could play well, then that would be everything I want.'

For Timmy McCarthy there was time for a quick fag. 'I had about six before the All-Ireland final in 1999, that morning; I was just bored.'

But the occasion did hit home for some of the others. For the captain, for instance, it was an emotional day. Mark Landers's father passed away when he was six, and as the bus rolled into the car park that loss came to mind.

'I cried going into Croke Park,' says Landers. 'I was thinking of my father. It would have been great to have had my entire family there. You'd hear fellas saying how important your family is, and it is. I didn't see home for two weeks trying to get myself ready.'

For all that, the Cork dressing room was serene, says McGrath. The atmosphere was calm ahead of the biggest game they'd ever played.

'Jimmy said, "I'm going to give out your jerseys,"' says McGrath. 'Teddy read them out, Number one, Donal Óg Cusack. I mean, it was like Christy Ring handing you your jersey. You were thinking, this guy is one of the all-time greats, and he's handing me my jersey. There's an onus on me to perform today. I owe it to him.

'He gave each of us a hug and a slap on the back. He'd shown huge faith in loads of fellas, and we wanted to pay him back.'

Landers's recollection of his greatest day is crystal sharp.

'I remember it all. The only blur from the final was that I knew where my mother was sitting in the Hogan. The stool we sat on for photos was over there and I looked into the crowd and couldn't pick out a face I knew, for the first time ever.'

The captain's self-assurance stood to him before the game began.

'When I went up for the toss, Denis Byrne [of Kilkenny] was as pale as a ghost and [referee] Pat O'Connor was worse. I was thinking, am I too relaxed? But it wasn't confidence; we were ready.

Pat's hand was shaking as he tossed the coin, and I said, Pat, you've refereed many a game, and this is just the All-Ireland final; don't worry about it.

'We won the toss and Jimmy had said to play against the wind if we did. The wind seemed to swirl and when Pat asked what way we wanted to play, I said, I want to play against the wind but I can't tell which way it's blowing.'

The game wasn't a classic. Both sides slithered around in the rain, trying to get to grips with the conditions, and it was eight minutes before the scoreboard operators earned their keep.

Cork won one crucial early battle, however, with Barry-Murphy describing the first ball Brian Corcoran caught over John Power as a huge bonus. Then it was first blood to Cork.

'There'd been ten or twelve chances before a ball broke to me and I slapped it over,' says Landers. 'It felt great—hitting the point that nobody could get—because I'd contributed. Of course I got another chance five minutes later and put it wide, and Jimmy started roaring at me to leave the ball into the forwards. So you couldn't have it both ways.'

It was diamond on diamond. Wayne Sherlock had his hands full early on.

'I was on Brian McEvoy and he had four wides in the first quarter of an hour. I was thinking, oh my God, because if one or two of them had gone over, I could have ended up with a totally different career. I was lucky enough.'

McGrath didn't get off to a flyer either, but the spirit was still good. Barry-Murphy's years of encouragement had armour-plated him.

'I went into the game buzzing with confidence. I'd done well against Offaly and I got four points for the club in the championship, so my touch was in. A couple of early shots went against me, but at the break Jimmy said, "You're creating chances, keep having a go." '

Further outfield, although Landers had prepared diligently, his withdrawal was inevitable.

'I'd have stayed on. Without being told, the selectors probably thought I only had half an hour, but while I was short of match practice, I was fit. Some of the subs said that three or four minutes after the break, the selectors turned to Frank Murphy to write the slip to bring on Kevin Murray, but five or six of the subs started shouting at them to leave me on.

'But I chased Denis Byrne at one stage and couldn't get to him, and he got a point, and they probably thought my race was run at that stage. But I don't have an issue with that. Winning the All-Ireland was more important than Mark Landers staying on the field. I wouldn't give up an All-Ireland medal for my own pride.'

Charlie Carter had a famous chance entering the closing stages, a glimpse of goal, but he put it over the bar. ('Every time he sees Donal Óg, he looks the other way,' says Diarmuid O'Sullivan.) The game was still there to be won entering the final quarter. Seánie McGrath had changed his hurley at half-time but, though he still hadn't made the scoresheet, the confidence was intact. Kilkenny were ahead, but they weren't out of sight.

'With twenty minutes left, I hadn't scored,' says McGrath, 'but Jimmy was still going up and down the sideline saying, "Keep having a go." I remember thinking, fair enough. I went out for the ball thinking, just get it into your hand.

'That was the most pressurised part of the game, those few seconds. I put huge pressure on myself to get the ball up into my hand, and once I did, I had a go for a point and whoosh—I felt all the weight just lift off my shoulders.

'For the last quarter of an hour I just wanted the ball. But it was the same for every player. Ben came into it; so did Timmy. The scores we got took pressure off other fellas, and it was a case of catch us if you can.'

'It wasn't a classic,' says Barry-Murphy. 'Conditions were horrendous, but what was great was that we were almost unstoppable in the last ten minutes. Seánie got great scores, Ben got a point, then Joe pointed a free . . .'

It was 12-11 to Cork when Kilkenny put the ball wide. McCormack and Cusack consulted on puck-outs before games as a matter of course. Now that work was about to bear fruit.

'For all the talk since then about puck-outs, that's one of my favourites,' says Cusack. 'It was a wet enough ball but Fergal came short for it and I took the risk. I hit it to him, he caught it, turned and got fouled.'

The free was fifty yards from goal. Deane strolled out from the full forward line to take it. He scored it—just about, he says—and edged Cork two ahead.

Kilkenny managed one more point. The removal of Power with ten minutes left was a huge boost for Cork, as Barry-Murphy freely admits.

'I had great respect for John Power. He'd won great battles for them, and when he went off I said to Tom Cashman, we have them now. That was a huge lift to us, him going off—an extraordinary decision—and Brian Corcoran thundered into it again for the last ten minutes.'

The clock hadn't quite wound down when Pat O'Connor took the whistle.

'He blew early,' says Landers. 'There was a scramble and he blew and the television cameras show the Cork panel thirty yards out into the field, and Pat O'Connor took the ball.'

'Jimmy was next to me when the whistle went and I was speechless,' says Sherlock. 'If you see the video, I'm just standing there. I was in shock.'

'At the end I remember saying to Sully, turn around, there's no way it's over,' says Cusack. 'I'd been asking the umpires about the time and the ref blew early. It was only when I saw the trucks coming on the field that I believed it was over.'

The goalkeeper heard a quiet word of congratulation afterwards for his daring puck-out for the winner. 'McCormack said it to me afterwards. "No one will ever remember that, but I'll never forget that puck-out you gave me."'

Barry-Murphy had reached the pinnacle, says Dr Con Murphy: 'Out on the pitch after the game he turned to me and said, "It doesn't get any better than this."'

There was work still to be done. As the players milled around, the manager went hunting for the captain. Landers was in the dugout, a little down after being taken off.

'Jimmy came over to me and said, "This is a moment in history. You're the captain of Cork; you're going to represent us in front of the world. Do us proud." That brought it home. Being captain means performing. I hadn't much prepared. I had the bit of Irish in the back of my mind.'

He did them proud. Landers let fly with a classic opener: 'Welcome back Liam McCarthy; we missed you a lot.' The Cork support went wild.

'People slag me over the first line of the speech, but that was all I had ready,' he says. 'To this day, though, I regret not mentioning Seán O'Leary. It still rankles because he was fantastic, one of the main reasons Imokilly won the county and gave me the chance to captain Cork. I couldn't remember if I'd said Johnny Crowley or Seán O'Leary, and I'm still disgusted with myself over it. He didn't hear his name.

'It was great to meet up among ourselves out on the field. During the lap of honour a lot of the Cork supporters stayed there, out in the rain, and I think that helped to form a great bond between the team and the support.'

After the final whistle Timmy McCarthy says he was lost in the moment. 'We didn't realise what we'd done. We were new kids on the block and this winning streak kept following us. When we saw the older lads, who saw first-round losses which meant six months' training gone . . . we didn't appreciate it. It wasn't until 2003, 2004 that we appreciated it, because by then we'd seen the downside.'

McCarthy appreciated something else at the end of the game. Diarmuid O'Sullivan saw the wing forward sitting on the grass, lost in thought, and asked if he was okay.

'I was just looking at that crane,' said McCarthy. 'I wonder how they got it up there behind the stadium.'

'At the final whistle I'd say my dad was the only fella who broke onto the pitch,' says McGrath. 'It was emotional—your mam's there, your family. It's all about being hard and tough, but then when the pressure's off the emotion comes out.'

After the game, trainer Ted Owens delivered the knockout blow.

'Ted is a great man for the drama, of course,' says Barry-Murphy. 'He pulled out the *Examiner* picture of myself, Tom Cashman and Tony O'Sullivan in 1996 looking down in the dumps, and it was symbolic of the journey we'd taken, I suppose. But it was touching.'

'Look, it was a cat final, but that didn't matter to us,' says Ó hAilpín. 'Corcoran had said, if we keep them goalless, we'll win, and he was right. We weren't conceding goals, though we weren't getting many either.

'Every now and again I look at it on video and I cringe. In the game itself I did all right. I didn't feel I played as well as I could have. But then again, in the football final two weeks afterwards I probably had my best game of the year, and we lost.

'Winning the All-Ireland was great, but it meant going on a list of winners, basically. Back then I never appreciated our wins anyway; it was all about the next session, the next match. That's all I was interested in. In 1999 I wasn't thinking of the winter and the team holiday. I wanted to get back training for the football All-Ireland.'

Going back meant returning to a county which had been nine years without an All-Ireland title, however. And Cork showed its appreciation.

'It was the greatest moment of my life, the thrill it gave to Cork people all over the world,' says Barry-Murphy. 'My desk in work is still full of the letters and cards I got from Cork people. I never realised what it meant to people.

'I told the young fellas coming down on the train that they didn't know what was coming. But neither did I. I wasn't expecting the outpouring of joy, the buses from all over west Cork . . . I even get emotional talking about it now. It was like the culmination of my involvement with Cork from 1973 to 1999.'

'I didn't think the welcome would be as big, but it was that big and more,' says McGrath. 'Your phone went off all day and all night; everyone wanted a piece of you. You had the Liam McCarthy up in the house. It got taken for granted.'

'It was the top,' says Sherlock. 'Everything was great: the meal, the Burlington, the train, but coming around Paddy Barry's Corner then on the bus . . . we were shocked with the crowd. We didn't expect that at all. You don't realise what hurling means to Cork people. After that you'd be wondering if people think about anything else.'

'We didn't realise the impact that final had on people,' says Cusack. 'Corcoran said we couldn't realise what we'd done, and he was right. But my mindset that time was, I need to go back training and to get ready. I got an All-Star that year I didn't deserve. Davy Fitzgerald should have got it. Now, the way things turned out since, I didn't get All-Stars that I maybe should have got.

'Jimmy was conscious of keeping our feet on the ground. And Teddy Owens was good like that too. Now we fell out during the strike, but in fairness to him he was one of the first guys to try and bring professionalism into the set-up.

'And in 1999, before the GOAL match, Teddy thanked the lads in the dressing room who were there and who wouldn't be with us in 2000. He said the way some fellas would live their lives in the next couple of months would mean they wouldn't be around the following season. And I thought to myself, that's not going to be me.'

Diarmuid O'Sullivan remembers the GOAL charity match. The Limerick hurlers came down and stayed on, and they had a great night. Not all the hurlers were there, of course.

Seán Óg Ó hAilpín had very little football under his belt because of his hurling duties and was back with Larry Tompkins and the footballers in Pairc Uí Chaoimh on the Tuesday night after the hurling final. He could hear Micheal Ó Muircheartaigh doing the commentary on the GOAL game above him in Pairc Uí Rinn; the RTÉ man's Kerry accent was clearly audible over the PA, drifting down on the wind to Pairc Uí Chaoimh, where the footballers were spilling their sweat ahead of their own big day two weeks in the future.

'But I loved it,' Ó hAilpín says. 'I was back training. I was happy out.'

# | LIKE VIETNAM

Facing into 2000 the future looked rosy on Leeside (no pun intended). Cork had won an All-Ireland with an astonishingly young team whose average age was 23. Excitable fans discussed a three-in-a-row, forgivable in the euphoria of victory, and they weren't alone. John Allen remembers how the season after the All-Ireland success began.

'I remember a county board official said out in Thailand on the team holiday that year, that the team could win three in a row because they were so young and so on. I remember thinking at the time that it was the wrong time and place to be saying something like that.

'Players can end up thinking, maybe we are this good, and that can work for or against you—when you don't make the extra effort. To be honest, I can't say I saw that in the dressing room in 2000, but the team that a lot was expected from in 1999 went downhill, if you like.'

Allen would play a larger role in the team's development down the line, but his involvement had begun on a small scale.

'In 1997 Denis Burns asked me if I'd fall in as a masseur with the Cork minors. I'd done a course in sports massage in Dublin and said okay, thinking it wouldn't be a big time commitment, and I enjoyed the year. During that season once or twice I'd have met the likes of Mark Landers, who'd have come down to us because I don't think the seniors had a regular masseur apart from match days.

'In 1998 the minors won the All-Ireland. I stayed on for the next year, but they were knocked out in the first round. Very soon after that the seniors were going to play and things were going very badly for them. I was out and John Crowley rang me and asked me to come down. I came down just before the first round of the championship. They'd done very badly and I think they were grasping at straws, really.

'They'd won the two U-21 All-Irelands. The core of that team was there, so a lot of them were young but had played together for a long time.'

An accident of geography helped Allen to bond with the players.

'I was in the same zone, the second dressing room, if you like. The two dressing rooms would be used in Pairc Uí Chaoimh for training, and I would have been in the second room a lot of the time, and there was great banter there—the likes of Sully, Alan Browne, Fergal McCormack and Wayne.

'There would have been a lot of slagging in there, and Jimmy and the other selectors wouldn't have been in there that often. Things rolled on in that year. We won the first game and came out of nowhere. I didn't see a defeat once I joined them, so it was a feel-good thing from that time on.'

At least one other member of the backroom team was ready to leave it behind, however. Jimmy Barry-Murphy had been involved with Cork teams from 1993, when he'd managed the minors for the first time. Facing into the new millennium, he was wondering if it was time to go.

'After 1999 I felt it was time for a change. I'd been there for four years. But the county board had stuck with me through thick and thin, and the lads had done me proud. I wondered deep down if I'd be able to make the hard calls. I'd have found it hard to take off lads like Brian Corcoran and Joe Deane, so I thought about dropping out but decided to give it another year.'

Some new players were introduced. A teenager called Ronan Curran remembers his first visit to the big show.

'Four of us were taken on to the training panel in 2000, and I played an Oireachtas Cup game. I remember sitting in the dressing room and taking in the characters. You'd be nervous, particularly when they're All-Ireland champions, but there was plenty of banter. It got more serious after that.'

With Brian Corcoran *in situ* there wasn't any need for Curran. In time the St Finbarr's man would set the template for modern play in the No. 6 jersey, but he was cut adrift as the 2000 season sharpened ahead of the championship.

The league campaign stuttered and stumbled. Pat Mulcahy remembers a couple of players coming back two stone overweight; understandable given the famine that came before the feast. But there were other changes, changes Diarmuid O'Sullivan picked up on immediately.

'We were All-Ireland champions and the spotlight was on us as a team and individuals. There was a difference. You knew you'd be judged differently.'

Seánie McGrath agrees.

'It's different once you've won an All-Ireland. An inter-county player is there to be knocked anyway, but when a county team goes from challenger to champion, everyone wants a piece of you.'

Cork were to see the change in attitude in their first championship game.

Limerick still had a fair sprinkling of their 1994 and 1996 All-Ireland sides for the Munster semi-final, and their promising U-21s leavened the senior side. Cork were generally expected to have too much class, and a nine-point winning margin would seem a fair endorsement of the difference between the sides, 2–17 to 1–11, but that's not how Seán Óg Ó hAilpín remembers it.

'We were lucky. Joe's overhead pull was the turning point. We expected a cakewalk and they gave us enough of it for long stretches. Then you had the Sully incident with Brian Begley.'

In the first, half O'Sullivan got involved with Limerick full forward Begley and lashed out, catching Begley across the back. In the weeks after the game some commentators returned to the incident time and again.

'It was an entanglement,' says O'Sullivan, 'but certain people— and I've refused to speak to them since—brought it up and brought it up for five weeks in a row. It started to get hurtful towards the end.'

'Diarmuid was Hercules in 1999,' says McGrath, 'knocking fellas off the ball; he was a legend. But when he did the same thing in 2000 he was a knacker. There was no consistency; it made no sense. He took it and gave it out.

'That was his way. In 2000 we played Ulster in the Railway Cup and we stayed in Dublin the night before. He was into wrestling and he was wrestling me around the place, and he did a jump off the top ropes—the hotel bed actually—and landed on me.

'My back was killing me and I told Teddy Owens I didn't want to play. He said no problem, but asked what had happened to my back. Ah, I was wrestling with Sully and he did a jump off the top ropes and landed on me. "Feck that," said Teddy, "you're playing." It was as if, it's only Sully, but he nearly broke my back. He was pinpointed a bit in 2000, but the team in general was there to be knocked.'

'In 1999 we felt not only that Cork were on our side, but the whole country was with us,' says Ó hAilpín. 'We were a young team and Cork hadn't been there in nine years. But as soon as you win it . . . you're there to be shot down. Diarmuid was part of that. Everyone wants to knock the champs.'

It wasn't all negative. Ó hAilpín delivered the long, dropping ball goalwards for Deane's crucial goal against Limerick, for instance, and that was a direct dividend from the All-Ireland success.

'My striking was starting to improve,' says Ó hAilpín. 'I think they were saying, we didn't think you could hit the ball that far, the time I dropped it in to Joe, because at that stage if I had the ball I'd either hand pass it away or kick it. If I went to strike the ball it might only go thirty yards.

'But that's the confidence that comes from winning. I noticed a big improvement in my hurling in 2000. I probably played some of my best games that year. I got All-Stars since then that I probably didn't merit in comparison with 2000.'

The win over Limerick set up a clash with the old enemy in the Munster final.

'There was huge hype,' says Ó hAilpín. 'It was the old firm again. Cork-Tipperary games had been out of the limelight for a while. It was in Thurles . . .'

At that stage Cork and Tipperary weren't the draw that Clare-Limerick had been for much of the nineties. But ancestral voices can't be denied. The manager in particular was exercised by the match-up.

'In the build-up, Jimmy said, "This is the game,"' says O'Sullivan. '"Cork-Tipp in a Munster final." That was Jimmy. He'd never lost to Tipp and this was his thing.'

After the Limerick game there was some attention being paid to O'Sullivan, and his likely opponent, Paul Shelly. Like O'Sullivan, Shelly was a cult hero to his county's fans. A powerful defender being asked to lead the Premier attack, Shelly wasn't a player likely to take a backward step. The Corkman was primed to begin well and put down a marker.

'That was really built up beforehand—myself and Shelley,' says O'Sullivan. 'The first ball that came down I caught it and cleared it, and I knew I was on a winner. He was a difficult character to handle, and it was tough moving him up from corner back to full forward.

'You'd have a bit of banter with him, but then you'd have a bit of banter with every fella.'

The banter stopped when Shelly won possession and bore down

on goal in the first half. He got inside O'Sullivan, who had to trust his keeper. Cusack jumped on the Tipp forward.

'Donal Óg got a tour of Semple on Shelley's back,' says O'Sullivan, laughing. 'I got a booking on the back of it for holding Shelley down, because I knew if he got up to Donal Óg . . . I sat down on top of him because I could see the look on Shelley's face inside in the goal, after carrying Cusack about ten yards in from the fourteen-metre line.

'I'm always amazed that no pub has a picture of him carrying Cusack around Semple Stadium. It was fantastic.'

'The Shelley thing?' says Cusack. 'Yeah, they still give it to me over that.'

Cork saved the penalty. The sides were level at the break, but after half-time the game loosened up. McGrath and Deane excelled, but while the Killeagh man is hazy about the day ('I know I got the man of the match award, but that's about all I remember'), McGrath had more reason than usual for wanting to do well.

'The TV show *Breaking Ball* used to have a feature where they'd follow a player around for a week. Well, it was supposed to be a week, but it was really only a day, and the cameras followed me around before that game. That night at training Jimmy asked who they were. I said it was *Breaking Ball* and I told him it'd be okay, but I could tell he wasn't too happy about it.'

Cork had eased out to a five-point cushion as the game wound down, but a Tommy Dunne goal and a Paul Kelly point cut Cork's lead to a single point. Cusack's puck-out found its way to the Glen Rovers man, and he had the chance to give Cork some breathing space.

'I missed it,' says McGrath. 'When I did, I was saying to myself, he'll blame the TV cameras for that, but the next puck-out was won by Timmy, and he kicked the ball on towards me and I put it over the bar. And to be honest, the celebrations were as much me saying, see, Jimmy, I was all right with the cameras, as anything else.'

As McGrath strolled off after the game he ran into Tipperary manager Nicky English.

'I knew Nicky a bit from the college scene. He shook hands with me and said, "Well done, Seánie—ya ballocks." We started laughing. For me he'd have been on a par with Jimmy.'

Cork had edged out Tipperary in an enthralling Munster final, but for Ó hAilpín there were worrying signs.

'I remember we were cruising when they got the goals to come back into it. We weren't putting them away, and you could say maybe that that was a sign, that it'd be part of our downfall later that year. But while you're winning games you're not too worried.'

His goalkeeper shared those concerns.

'We got by in 2000 because we had good players,' says Cusack. 'I was poor in that Munster final. I was within myself; I should have saved one of Tommy Dunne's goals anyway. But we were getting by.'

Self-belief wasn't in short supply elsewhere in the dressing room, however.

'Confidence? I'll tell you about confidence,' says Diarmuid O'Sullivan. 'Pat Ryan was very unlucky not to make the Cork team for that Munster final, and he was warming up during the game itself when we won a free. Jimmy said "Come on, Pat, you're going on." Pat says "About time too, Jimmy", jogged on and put the free over the bar—one of the most confident players you could meet.'

Cork drew Offaly in the All-Ireland semi-final, but Seán Óg Ó hAilpín puts the blame on a northern side for the Leesiders' shortcomings in that game.

'What killed us against Offaly was Derry. Derry had nearly beaten Offaly in their last game. The perception of Offaly was that they were older. They were drinking better than ever. And then they struggled against Derry.

'I was saying at home when the draws were being made, I hope we get Offaly, which was wrong, because when you're hoping for an easy one, that's when it can go wrong. Jimmy warned us, but the mindset was wrong long before that.'

Deane echoes the wing back: 'Offaly had been beaten well in the

Leinster final. They were ageing; there was no way we could see ourselves losing that game. There was overconfidence definitely. You could see it going up in the train. You could see it in the hotel the night before.'

The cockiness wasn't just a state of mind. Some players stayed up until 2.30 in the morning before the semi-final playing cards. It wasn't ideal, but early on the game was still going according to everyone's expectations.

'We should have wiped them out in the first twenty minutes,' says Barry-Murphy.

'We started like a whirlwind, but we didn't show that on the scoreboard,' says Ó hAilpín. 'We had tons of possession, while Offaly, typically, chipped away with a couple of points to stay in touch. Johnny Pilkington got four points off me, and two of them he didn't even look at the posts. I would have sworn that I had him under enough pressure to put him off for a couple of them, but fair play to him. And fair play to them.'

For all their possession (Cork had ten wides at the break compared to two for Offaly), the champions were just one point ahead at the break. Offaly scented blood.

'They realised in the second half that we were dead ducks,' says Ó hAilpín. 'Joe Deane was beating Kevin Kinahan up a stick with lovely ball being played in front of him, and then in the second half we were hitting the ball in high, into Kinahan's alley, and we made him look even better than he was with the ball we were delivering. That comes from pressure; we had time and space in the first half, then in the second half they got on a run.'

Offaly won by five points in the end. It was a stunning upset, and their players enjoyed the victory.

'The way they celebrated afterwards, you knew that was their All-Ireland,' says Ó hAilpín. 'Kilkenny beat them well afterwards in the final. But it took us a couple of years to recover from that Offaly game. We were like young American lads going to Vietnam and coming back shell-shocked.'

Offaly's unrestrained joy wouldn't be forgotten, but in the aftermath of the game Cork were desolate.

'The latter part of 2000 and 2002 were the real sickeners,' says Joe Deane. 'The 1996 defeat wasn't as much of a sickener. It was a new team, but winning the Munster final in 2000 reinforced that we were a good team, and it helped our confidence. Maybe it helped the confidence too much . . .

'During the game itself there was panic. We had enough chances in the last quarter of an hour to win, but we went for goals when there was no need. If it had happened three or four years later, I think we'd have won by three or four points. It was one that got away, a huge disappointment.'

There was one more heartbreak. In the shattered dressing room after the game, the manager had an announcement.

'I was very emotional in the dressing room afterwards when I told the lads I'd be dropping out,' says Barry-Murphy. 'I don't know how some of the players felt, but I certainly felt it.'

'Jimmy had wanted to go in 1999,' says Ó hAilpín. 'We knew that. We knew he was going.'

County board secretary Frank Murphy spoke in the hushed dressing room, saying it was imperative that Barry-Murphy stayed on, but the manager was shaking his head even as Murphy was speaking. The Barry-Murphy era was over.

It was a time of regrets. Seánie McGrath is unequivocal about the disappointment.

'For the group—and for me—it was a massive opportunity missed. I felt I hurled better that year than any other year. I'd scored consistently . . . my biggest regret, definitely.

'But against Offaly I missed a lot of scores, and after that I felt I was a target for criticism. I played in 2001, but my career started going downwards. That was the beginning of the end of me with Cork.'

And the end for Barry-Murphy. For the manager, however, it was the conclusion of a natural cycle.

'I didn't have the same hunger in 2000 that I'd had in 1999. There's no point in saying otherwise. I couldn't speak for the players, but I certainly didn't.

'I couldn't have gotten any more from the players, or out of myself. I get emotional even talking now about it. Having gone through what we did from 1996 . . . I remember at one stage my mother asking me why I'd taken the thing on, and there's no doubt your family's affected, but 1999–2000 was a culmination of a long period. Someone like Seánie McGrath would have been listening to me for eight years, between minor and senior.

'I missed it. You're talking to fellas every day about it, to selectors, Dr Con, players, press . . . I loved every minute of it, but I'm not sure if I'd have loved it if we hadn't won the All-Ireland in 1999.'

There were consolations. Barry-Murphy felt he was handing on a good side, one with appetite.

'We had quite a good year in 2000. People forget that. We beat Tipp in Thurles in a great Munster final. People thought we wouldn't have the hunger, but for the team's development it was huge. Normally there's a tapering-off of appetite after winning an All-Ireland, and given what Nicky English was doing with Tipp, I felt it would be a bigger achievement than winning the All-Ireland if we could go to Thurles and beat them in the Munster final. Cork love playing in Thurles, but it's still a hard place to go and win.

'That marked down for me that the lads would be around for years; that whatever else about that season, 2000, they'd have the appetite for more.'

# NOT MANY PEOPLE COME BACK FROM THIS

There was a new feel to 2001 for Cork. Tom Cashman took over from Jimmy Barry-Murphy. As a long-time selector he was well known and respected by the players. The championship draw was relatively kind—Limerick at home—and some new players were shaping up well for problem positions.

Fergal McCormack, for instance, had been inspirational for the county at centre forward, but a recurring ankle injury was limiting his appearances, so the emergence of Mike Morrissey, a powerful centre forward from Newtownshandrum, was opportune.

One of Morrissey's club mates was doing well at centre back too. By his own admission Pat Mulcahy hadn't been developing at inter-county level, so he took solace from the club scene in Cork.

'Bernie O'Connor taking over with Newtown was a huge turning point for me, for my confidence,' says Mulcahy. 'I felt I could say, I'm as good as any club hurler in Cork. Why shouldn't I be playing for the county? And things improved with Newtown as well. We got to the quarter-final of the senior championship in 1999 and won the county in 2000.'

And the rewards came. Mulcahy got his run with Cork, and in his favourite position.

'From the team's perspective, leaving myself to one side, training was going fine. I found Tom Cashman was a gentleman, and he gave me my chance, so I couldn't complain. I'd played full back for CIT and the club the odd time, but I'd been centre back mostly, and that was where I was most comfortable.

'At inter-county level, though, I probably didn't have the power for centre back. You don't need that power as much at club level, but the hits are serious for an inter-county centre back. You needed to be fourteen stone, fifteen stone to play a central position in inter-county hurling. That's changed a little, but at that point there were huge hits going in.

'To me those are the two big differences between club and county hurling. I don't think it's a skill thing. Some club hurlers have a better touch than inter-county players, but it's the combination of pace and power. Even if you're marking a guy at inter-county who looks like a small corner forward, he'll hit you hard, he'll be well made, quick and strong—and he's probably a centre forward at club level anyway. That's the difference, and it's probably the reason it took me so long to develop at that level.'

The training was intense that year, according to Seán Óg Ó hAilpín, himself no taker of short cuts in his preparation.

'Some of the training we did in 2000 was bordering on torture. I was back home and living in Cork, and running the tunnels in the Pairc . . . those were supposed to be warm-up laps, but they ended up as competitions. That was one thing that always stuck with me about that year, the pre-season stuff in January and February.'

Again, portents in the national league were mixed apart from one particular game against Wexford which would influence Cork's entire season. As Wayne Sherlock puts it: 'The game in the rain where they beat the shit out of us.'

'We were poor enough in the league,' says Ó hAilpín. 'Then up in Wexford, a wet, miserable day, we got flaked. Mike Morrissey broke his ankle and never really came back from it. Brian Corcoran broke his collar bone.'

'A filthy game' is how Dr Con Murphy remembers the match.

Morrissey, a vital central option in a lightish forward line, would never play for the county again. Corcoran was a major doubt for the championship outing against Limerick. The team were already without Fergal McCormack, so three of their biggest players were out of the running. When Murphy says Tom Cashman was very unlucky as a manager, it's not loose talk.

Still, there was optimism before the Limerick game. Training was fine, though in retrospect, 'fine' mightn't have been good enough.

'Going into the game I was confident,' says Deane. 'We maybe didn't think that time about how well training was going, whether it needed to be improved. Going into the Limerick game the preparation was okay.

'That changed later. In the last few years, coming to ten days or two weeks before a championship game, if a session was flat you'd say to the captain or whoever, look, training tonight was shit; we need to pick it up. In 2000 and 2001 you'd have just gone with the flow.

'I'd never have seen myself as a leader. I kept to myself and did my own thing without being vocal. At that stage Mark and Brian would have still been leading. They were still that bit older and would have been driving the thing.'

Then came the hammer blow. Seán Óg Ó hAilpín was involved in a car crash on the Thursday before the game.

'When I heard he was in a crash,' recalls Seánie McGrath, 'my first instinct was, is he still alive? When I heard he was okay it was a relief, and only then you think about the match. You're thinking, one of our best players is missing.'

For the player himself it was a harrowing time.

'It's forgotten because of the success I've had since,' says Ó hAilpín. 'The crash is like a bad dream now. I put it behind me a long time ago. Physically and hurling-wise I felt pretty good, but an act of stupidity on the road nearly cost me my sporting career. It happened on 24 May and we played Limerick on the 27th.'

Ó hAilpín had been on a promotional trip to Dublin and broke his journey in Tipperary to see a friend.

'Ironically, I was visiting someone in Templemore who'd been injured in a fall from a ladder, and I headed off through Loughmore to get to training in Cork, where I had the crash.'

He knew there was something badly wrong. When he got out of the car his leg buckled beneath him and he was rushed to Nenagh Hospital.

'I got onto Dr Con and he thought it was a prank call at first. I stayed overnight and the doctor there told me my kneecap was blown halfway up my thigh.

'Dr Con organised an ambulance to bring me to Cork Regional Hospital, and I was operated on. I was so naïve I thought I'd be okay for Sunday, for Limerick, with two days' rest. But the surgeon spelt it out for me. He said, "You won't be playing Sunday." I asked how I was fixed if we won, and he said, "You won't be playing for the next year."

'There was a silence inside me at that. It was pure fear. I didn't realise how serious it was until Dr Con said, "Not many people come back from this; we'll have to get you back walking." All I knew was playing the games, and maybe people thought I was boring, just training and matches, but I loved it.

'In fairness to Con, he spelt out what I had to do, and I have great admiration for him for that. He headed off out of my hospital room, and I bawled my eyes out.'

There was a knock-on effect for the team.

'We were just coming right, but the final nail was Seán Óg being in the accident,' says Mark Landers. 'I was thinking they'd slot Corcoran straight in, but what happened was that two or three fellas were moved around.'

'Pat Ryan came in and he was probably told late,' says McGrath, 'so his preparation wouldn't have been what he wanted. Then there were other positional changes that had to be made, which upset the team further.'

It got worse. The team were due to meet in Pairc Uí Rinn for the pre-match meal and then travel to Pairc Uí Chaoimh on a bus with Garda outriders. With the sun beating down, the players waited for the bus. And waited.

'It never showed,' says Dr Con. 'We were sitting in our cars waiting and waiting. We thought they'd show up, so in the end we were caught between heading off and staying for the escort. Eventually we headed down.'

The road down from Pairc Uí Rinn to Pairc Uí Chaoimh is habitually choked with supporters on a big championship day. That Sunday was no different.

'That was the start of it, up in Pairc Uí Rinn waiting for a bus that never came,' says Diarmuid O'Sullivan. 'Driving past the Venue bar, with fellas shouting abuse at you, hammering on the windows of the car. . .'

'When the team got to Pairc Uí Chaoimh they were in a distressed state,' says Murphy. 'And it, in my opinion, cost us the match. That was the last time Cork didn't take a bus to a big match.'

'At gone three o'clock you were getting into the dressing room,' says O'Sullivan. 'Then down to the gym and we all know what happened in there.'

The dressing rooms were full and the players couldn't get to the toilets. Towels were laid out in the gym and they urinated there.

'We were beaten before we went out,' says McGrath, 'though we put up a good score. The preparations weren't great that day. But having said that, you're still out on the field. I don't buy it one hundred per cent that we'd have won if the bus turned up. We were beaten by a more motivated team.'

Limerick had a better start and led by six points at the break; James Butler's arcing run and fine finish to the corner had jump-started them and they hadn't lost the initiative. Given Cork's off-field travails that wasn't surprising, but it wasn't a lost cause by any means.

Landers still holds that the resources Cork had weren't used to their utmost.

'We were probably gone a bit cocky, for instance, that we'd hold Corcoran, even though that wasn't said,' says Landers. 'We brought him on at half-time, whereas if we'd waited until the second half we'd have gotten a bigger impact from the crowd, and so on. We were six points down at the break and ten minutes into the second half we were level.'

Alan Browne's goal had brought Cork back into it. If they wanted a rallying point, their full back supplied it. Midway through the second half Diarmuid O'Sullivan howitzered the ball over the Limerick bar from deep in his own half, a point scored from halfway up the Marina.

'I got out in front and just got rid of it,' says O'Sullivan. 'There was no such thing as having a look that time. You got it and got it downfield, but it just kept going and going. Barry Foley's was a more important score, though. It was the winning of the game.'

As O'Sullivan says, Cork were in contention until the 69th minute, when Barry Foley cut a sideline ball over the bar—'from the corner flag', as Deane says.

'I put it out,' says Wayne Sherlock. 'I pucked the ball and got half-blocked and the ball went out over the line. I remember saying to the linesman, how can it be a Limerick sideline if their man blocked it? And then Barry Foley put it over.'

'They got a great score to win the game, but they wouldn't get it again,' says McGrath.

Even at that point the game might have been rescued. It was the first season in which additional time at the end of inter-county games was announced in stadia. Cork had a nasty shock in store.

'The first time ever in the history of the GAA that there was no injury time,' says Landers. 'I couldn't believe it when the announcer said that there'd be no added time.'

And suddenly it was over. Limerick had won.

'Everything went against us,' says Timmy McCarthy. 'Limerick won by a point, but they were the better team on the day. They deserved it. We nearly scraped home, but everything went against us. Even coming down from Pairc Uí Rinn, there was nothing organised for us . . .

'You have days you'd be looking one way and hit the ball over your shoulder for a point the other way, and there are other days when you try everything and it doesn't happen for you. That was one of those days.'

'We underestimated them,' says Sherlock. 'It was our first game at home in a few years; that probably added to the pressure.'

'On the Limerick side you had guys like James Butler,' says McGrath. 'He didn't have a long career with Limerick, but unfortunately for us he chose that game to have his best day. He got a great goal.

'It wasn't that Tom was a bad manager—he was quiet but was hugely respected—but various elements combined. Seán Óg's crash, the preparations, we were in limbo as to where to leave our gear in the gym and so on. A bad day.'

The sense that Cork could have done well in 2001 is shared by several players.

'Limerick had an outstanding year after that,' says Pat Mulcahy. 'But if we'd gone on then, everything might have changed—for me, for the team.'

'Pat's right,' says McGrath. 'If we'd won that, we'd have done well that year. We'd had a good league—beating Kilkenny, Laois and Waterford—and the year could have taken off for us.'

Landers is even more forthright: 'It was a fucking nightmare. I've no doubt we would have won the All-Ireland in 2001. We should have closed it out, but we didn't . . . that's where hunger comes into it, and Limerick were hungrier.'

The ramifications were various. Diarmuid O'Sullivan detected a slight decay in team spirit, for instance.

'After a game we'd always go out on the Monday night, but after the Limerick game you could tell something was wrong. Only three or four went out.'

The disastrous preamble to the Limerick game would be instanced the following year during the players' strike, but that was with the benefit of perspective. In the immediate aftermath the players accepted that accidents happen.

'The bus didn't turn up, but that could happen to a Premiership team,' says Sherlock. 'It happens.'

'The bus, that was administrative, a mix-up,' says Landers. 'The county board weren't at fault for that. The fact that we were peeing in another room, well, fellas do that because they're nervous. It wasn't a help arriving at ten past three, and if you've only seventy minutes to do your business, losing the first ten minutes because you're not focused isn't a help.'

Deane concurs.

'I don't think the fellas were thinking about it too much, certainly not going into the game. We were thinking more along the lines of, we were down three lads; we lost by a point after Barry Foley pointed a sideline from the corner flag. These things happen. It was a bad day at the office.'

A rumour wasn't long sweeping Cork that Tom Cashman had resigned on the sideline. In any event he didn't last long after the Limerick game, and Cork were in the market for a third manager in three years.

For Seán Óg Ó hAilpín there was plenty to ponder on the long road to recovery.

'I had a cast from hip to ankle; I was at home for three months with the leg up watching DVDs. What kept me going was Setanta playing with the Cork minors and Na Piarsaigh seniors.

'Being selfish, Cork probably had the worst year in a long time, being knocked out with no back door, but it was probably the best year to miss, though I was gutted for the lads. It would have killed me if they'd had a good run that year.'

When Ó hAilpín got the cast off, he had another shock in store.

'My leg was like a matchstick, all wasted away. I felt like asking the doctor to look in the cast for the rest of my leg. All you could see was bone. I couldn't even bend my knee at first, it had become so stiff.'

Ó hAilpín was friendly with Jim McEvoy, who'd done a bit of work with Ger Hartmann, the physio, and though Hartmann worked with athletes rather than GAA players, McEvoy's intervention got the hurler an audience.

'I met him [Hartmann] in August 2001 and he said, "There's a lot of work involved here," and I said I was willing to do anything to get back. I worked away on my own.

'It's amazing when you're so into the scene one day, then it's like you don't exist—no calls for training and so on. You're completely detached. Ger gave me a good programme and Jimmy oversaw it, and I went to Inchydoney and Schull and worked away on it.

'The leg got strong enough to jog on, and that was a huge relief in and of itself, but my fitness was gone. I went for a run one time in Muskerry RFC and I could barely manage two laps before I was out of wind.'

Going into 2002 Hartmann was holding Ó hAilpín back; only in March would he let the player get back onto the field.

'I played my first game back for Cork on 15 March 2002 against Derry—which is famous for other reasons, Niall McCarthy bleeding on the bus—and the knee held up. I was cagey enough, but it held up. It was a start.'

By that time Cork had a new manager, and new selectors. Bertie Óg Murphy, who had guided them to two All-Ireland U-21 successes, was in charge. It looked a marriage made in heaven: the new coach had handled many of the players at U-21 level, and promising minors were coming on stream.

Yet less than twelve months later the team had crashed out of the first round of the championship again, had created unwanted GAA history by going on strike, and Murphy had resigned.

# IT TOOK A WHILE TO BE COMFORTABLE IN WHAT WE WERE DOING

It was a year that would be remembered for different reasons, but not for Cork performances in Thurles or Croke Park. The team did participate in the 2002 Munster championship, though it was a short trip with an unhappy arrival. On a dank, wet evening in Semple Stadium they took on Waterford, a game few of the players care to remember. With his customary frankness, Donal Óg Cusack reduces proceedings to their constituent parts.

'I remember making a great save in the first half, and a mistake in the second half that cost us the game. The Waterford fans have never let me forget it, but what really made it worse was that I was in the middle of the whole thing.

'The goal was one of those balls—you don't know if it's the full back's or it's yours. I half-went for it, but it skidded in front of me. And we lost the game as a result.'

Cusack's recall isn't quite accurate. The goal Tony Browne scored from midfield helped Waterford, but it wasn't the decider. Ken McGrath was unable to start the game due to an arm injury, but the

Mt Sion star came on in the closing stages and struck over the winner for Waterford at the Killinan End.

'McGrath didn't start,' says Wayne Sherlock. 'But he finished us.'

The story of 2002 starts earlier than that, however, back with the league final, or back further with an innocuous get-together in the Na Piarsaigh dressing rooms.

Donal Óg Cusack was to become one of the best-known sportsmen in the country largely by default. Brian Corcoran's unexpected retirement in 2001 meant the goalkeeper was the only member of the Gaelic Players Association (GPA) on the Cork hurling panel.

'Corcoran and I were the only lads in the GPA,' says Cusack, 'and I took it on when Corcoran retired. One thing that did annoy me was the Player Advisory Group [PAG]. It was a bluff. Seánie [McGrath] was our representative and I knew he wouldn't do anything for it.

'He was a pal of mine, but I got pissed off when he described the GPA as "Farrell's gang". I was nothing in the GPA at that time, but I felt we had to go with the GPA.'

Seánie McGrath didn't feel being a member of the PAG would be a problem in the dressing room, though he turned down the chance to join the GPA.

'Maybe when you get tagged as a certain type of player—a bit of a joker—you're not seen as being political. I got away with it in those terms—"Seánie's a bit of a character."

'Frank Murphy asked me to go on the PAG after 1999 and I thought it was a huge honour. James Nallen and Dara Ó Cinneide were on it and Jarlath Burns was chairman. He was very good; he'll make a good president of the GAA in time.

'Donal Óg asked me to join the GPA, and I didn't know much about it at the time other than that it was a player organisation. I said I'd join. No problem Ogie, I'm in with ye. But when I got up the next day I thought I'd been asked to represent Cork with another group—they didn't do a whole lot but I had good time for them— and I felt it wouldn't be fair on that group. They were honest-to-goodness guys; some of them were club guys raising concerns about the club scene, and I felt if they picked up the paper and saw I'd gone to the GPA they'd be thinking, what an asshole.

'So I told Donal Óg that out of respect to the PAG, I'd stay with them, that I wasn't against the GPA, and he was grand with that. Part of it was the fact that I didn't know much about the GPA; part of it was that I was trying to get my place back on the team. For me that was hard to take; that was my focus in 2002–3.

'I had good time for the GPA; they did fantastic work, but you're selfish. You're just trying to get your own game right. In addition, I was working for the family business, and my father gave me great leeway, but I still had responsibilities there in sales and scheduling. That whole player thing wasn't high on my agenda. I wasn't in the frame of mind to go around fighting the county board.'

For John Gardiner it was the year he arrived. He was involved with twelve teams that season, but the most important was the Cork senior hurling team. The dominant minor hurler of his year, an imposing centre back with an immaculate clean striking style, he still found top flight hurling an unforgiving arena.

'It was a huge step up. Realistically you're only a young fella, and you're playing against men. In my first championship game I was on Ollie Moran, a huge man, so I really felt that day I wasn't up to it. But the training had been a culture shock. I'd been training hard with CIT, with the club, but it was nothing compared to training with Cork.'

Another culture shock came after a meeting in Gardiner's own club after Cork trained one evening.

'There was a players' meeting held at a Cork training session up in the club,' says Gardiner. 'Bertie Óg was outside the dressing room, and there was a report in the paper that he'd been locked out of the dressing room. That was never the case.

'I suppose I hadn't seen what had happened before. I thought those meetings were normal practice.'

Mark Landers fleshes it out.

'The GPA meeting in Na Piarsaigh . . . there weren't too many players involved in it, but when Teddy Owens tried to come into the dressing room, the door was closed and Bertie Óg took it as a sign that he was locked out, which couldn't have been further from the truth.

'We were told on Tuesday night that a bus was leaving on Friday for a league game in the North. That was unrealistic, asking your boss for a day off with that kind of notice. Nobody was blaming anyone, but in Jimmy's time we flew—and Jimmy never flew. He hates flying.

'Yet here we were, years later, taking a day off to go to the game on a bus. We went into a meeting then to talk about the GPA, and we didn't know until afterwards that Teddy had tried to get in. We went down to the Commons Bar for food and were told that Bertie Óg had gone home disgusted.

'Out of absolutely nothing there was a problem. We said to Teddy that we weren't happy with the arrangements for Friday, but we added that we hadn't locked anyone out of the dressing room. Three of us got into a car and rang Bertie and put him on speaker; we apologised to him, said there was no issue with him or his staff, but that we had a problem with the arrangements.'

It was never personal, says Landers.

'Bertie Óg was a great manager,' he says. 'I was really looking forward to working with him, but the way circumstances went, he got caught in the middle. He probably took the wrong stance at the wrong time, but I couldn't have foreseen how things would develop over the next twelve months. Nobody could.'

There were good and bad signs in the league. Cork did well enough to qualify for the final, against Kilkenny, but one game left poison in a wound that would eventually burst. When Cork played Derry, Niall McCarthy got a bad gash in the face and had to sit on the bus from Derry to Cork: one of the other player's strongest memories of that year is of McCarthy bleeding into a handkerchief, looking at the blood-soaked cloth and then pressing it back against the wound over and over again. When Cork got back home, McCarthy was brought to hospital to be stitched. His ordeal wouldn't be forgotten.

Cork faced Kilkenny in the league final. The GPA was casting around at the time for a way to make its presence felt, and Cork came to an agreement with their opponents.

'We'd decided we wouldn't stand in for the picture before the game,' says Cusack. 'But when we came back to Cork, Alan Browne suggested we leave out our jerseys and roll down our socks. I told Andy Comerford, but he told me things weren't going well above in Kilkenny. Then he rang me on the Saturday night and said, "No one else is doing it, but I'll do it." And I told him that we'd never forget it.'

The morning of the league final didn't go well. Cusack was in tears before the game as mentors pleaded with him not to go ahead with the protest.

'I felt we had to go ahead with it,' he says. 'Some fellas did; some fellas didn't.'

'We were pulled into a room in the Dundrum House Hotel and told about famous Cork hurlers who'd worn the jersey, the likes of Jamesy Kelleher and Christy Ring,' says Seán Óg Ó hAilpín. 'We were told we'd be doing them a dishonour by not treating the jersey properly.

'I don't know if you'd call it a threat, but some players were going to do it anyway. Alan Browne didn't feel strongly about the GPA and didn't feel like doing it. So be it. But I'd battled for years with the likes of Donal Óg and Diarmuid; if they were going to battle, I was going to row in with them. At first I was only going in for their benefit, but then I saw the bigger picture.'

Cork were slow to start, but wired into the game, though Kilkenny won with a late point. Dr Con Murphy remembers thinking that at that stage Cork had the potential to win the All-Ireland. For the players the disappointment of losing wasn't helped by the winners' attitude.

'It left a fierce sour taste in our mouths regarding Kilkenny,' says

Cusack. 'It did. What made it worse was Peter Barry being quoted in the papers saying it was all about the jersey and so on. That was like sticking a knife into us. Of course, what we've learned since is that journalists could manipulate that kind of thing.'

'The reason we feel bitter about that to this day is that it looked worse for us,' says Ó hAilpín. 'What we took from that was that they weren't looking at the bigger picture. They'd won a battle but they weren't looking at the war. What they did didn't help. It wasn't a war Cork were fighting; it was a war for player welfare.'

The players headed back to their usual watering hole after games, Mulligan's Bar in Parnell Place in the city. But even there the omens were bad.

'There were a couple of things said,' says Cusack. 'Fellas were praising the Brownes for not joining in the protest. And I knew we were doomed from then on.'

The unease was palpable. People were unaware of the lack of organisation behind the scenes, but the players were getting more and more annoyed by it, as evidenced by Timmy McCarthy's memories of the time.

'There were things you'd notice. You'd be asking management what time the bus was going to something and nobody would know, and you'd be thinking, well, if they don't know, who knows? That kind of thing. It was badly organised.'

Cusack felt that the organisational side of things had progressed under Jimmy Barry-Murphy's leadership, but that that forward motion had come to a stop.

'We liked Bertie Óg. He'd come up with us. But the thing wasn't organised. It wasn't what it was supposed to be.'

The tension between management and players wasn't supposed to be there. It dated back to the early-season meeting in Na Piarsaigh, which came to the surface when selector John Meyler told Mark Landers to take a good look around Pairc Uí Chaoimh, as he wouldn't be seeing much more of it.

John Allen wasn't working with the players that season, but he could see the dissatisfaction growing.

'The fact that the players weren't happy with the conditions they were playing under—things not being delivered on time, meals not being good enough, hassles about expenses—was probably a contributory factor to how they did. The structures weren't clear enough to address problems, so nobody was able to take responsibility and sort things out—x was blaming y, and so forth.

'Then you had strong people saying, we're not taking this any more. They got everyone together, which took a lot of organisation. From being in the dressing room I knew certain players were involved in the GPA; certain players weren't involved in the GPA; you had a player co-opted onto the GAA players' organisation. You had three different groups! Bringing all those players together was difficult, but it showed that the players were determined to change that.'

After Cork lost to Waterford in the championship, they were drawn against Limerick in the qualifiers.

'Fellas were tough enough to get on with it at the same time. We beat Limerick,' says Cusack. 'I remember Meyler hugging me after that game, but there was fierce distrust. But by the time of the Galway game . . . you had the selectors giving out T-shirts to fellas on the way up.'

There was an added complication. Diarmuid O'Sullivan's flirtation with football had become a full-blown affair by the time of the Galway game.

'I always felt I was a good footballer and we won the East Cork junior championship in football in 2001 with Cloyne,' says O'Sullivan. 'Eamon Ryan, the Cork senior football selector, approached me about challenge games and it was something I wanted to try. I was on the national league panel and made the team for the Munster final against Kerry at corner forward.

'I'd been full forward all along, but Colin Corkery came back and he was full forward. I was taken off at half-time and felt hard done by because any ball that was got outside the field was targeted at Colin. On at least three occasions in the first half when I was on my own in the 21, wrong options were taken. I felt aggrieved because of that.

'The replay was on in the Pairc and I was brought on with about ten minutes to go and got a point. As I was coming out, I saw Declan O'Keeffe on the ground and I gave him a nice kick up the arse. After the game Larry said, "That was a nice one you gave O'Keeffe, and if any fella deserved it, he did."'

It wasn't as light-hearted in 2002. The Munster football final would have the hurling qualifier between Cork and Galway as a curtain-raiser, and the fact that O'Sullivan was on the football panel didn't go down well with some of the hurlers.

'The U-21s were the golden boys, and to be fair to them they'd achieved a lot,' says Pat Mulcahy. 'They were the core of the team. But I remember when we played Galway, Ronan Curran was wearing number 30; I was number 28.

'Two weeks before the Galway game I asked the selectors if I could play in a challenge game, knowing that even with injuries I had no chance of playing. I was told I couldn't play, yet the day of the Galway game Diarmuid played football. I said to myself that day, what's the point? From that perspective I certainly felt like a second-class citizen.

'I sat next to Curran on the bus on the way home and I remember saying to him, shaking my head, that's it, I'm finished. And in fairness to him, he said, "You'll be playing next year", though I said, not a hope. I was packing it in. I couldn't take it any more.'

Mulcahy's dissatisfaction was shared by others.

'You could see lads were getting annoyed, so many different things were going wrong,' says Ronan Curran. 'I was a sub, obviously, and I don't think we were being treated properly at that time either. There's a big difference between now and then. Now everyone's treated the same, and there's as much work put into the subs as the first fifteen because every fella has to progress. Back then it was as if the subs were pushed to one side, if you like, and a lot of us were getting ticked off with it.

'It shouldn't have been like that. Because most subs are younger, they need to be progressed so that they can come into the team a few years later. That's changed now, but back then there were other issues as well, and you could see something needed to change.

'I found it very frustrating. I gave it up for a while in the middle of 2002 because I couldn't take sitting on the bench any longer. Maybe I was wrong, but I thought I was at least worth a go; it was worth taking a look at what I could do. I was there from 2000 to 2002, three seasons and I got one league game, against Derry. You'd be thinking, what do I have to do? I was doing well in club games and training.

'Jerry O'Connor would have been in the same situation, and look where he is now, All-Star and former Hurler of the Year. In 2002 when I gave up, I got a call to come back and I said no. In training one night that year I was put behind the goal to puck the ball back out to the lads who were on the team. You don't feel good after that; your confidence goes down and you don't feel part of the thing.'

It was an eerie day when the hurlers faced Galway. The team bus came through to Semple Stadium along deserted streets, as everyone was already inside the stadium for the football game.

'[Chairman] Jim Cronin came into the dressing room and could hardly talk to us,' says Cusack. 'We were thinking, Jesus, Cork have been beaten. Sully was a ball of sweat. And when he was allowed to play, that was the finish for me. I was either getting out of it or I was going to do something about it.

'As I said, you were hearing that this was a glorious thing, playing for Cork, but the fellas saying that weren't doing anything about it.'

Dr Con Murphy had had a close-up view of the Munster football final as a curtain-raiser, and the Tipperary footballers—powered by Declan Browne and Brendan Cummins—had Cork on the rack as time ticked away. Cork football boss Larry Tompkins threw every card on the table, which meant Diarmuid O'Sullivan was on the turf in Semple Stadium half an hour ahead of schedule.

'Diarmuid was put on for the footballers with twenty minutes to go,' says Murphy, 'and he was sprung with good reason: the footballers needed him. But that was the last act for the dual player in Cork. I remember it was a hot day and I was out on the pitch with Diarmuid before the hurling game pouring water over him. He was boiling up after the football game.'

Cork got a goal against the run of play against Galway, but it was a long, slow descent after that. With fifteen minutes to go, Cusack came outfield to speak to Fergal Ryan. 'He said to me, "We're in trouble; it's collapsing." At that stage we were just in damage limitation.'

'While I felt I did as well against Galway as I'd done in previous games, my hurling was beginning to suffer,' says O'Sullivan. 'I wasn't training as hard as I could. It was a strange day, but I don't regret doing it.'

The day was so strange that Cork had a player put off; as O'Sullivan says, it takes a real supporter to produce the name unprompted (Timmy McCarthy). Other players had days to forget.

'Against Galway it was the utmost humiliation,' says Seánie McGrath. 'I was put on and taken off. I was disgusted. For me 2002 was a disaster, and that's why I didn't get too involved in what happened afterwards.

'We all went our own way after that; we didn't leave as a group. I don't think anyone went to town after it. Nobody wanted to talk about it. It felt like a death in the family—that certain players might go, that the manager might go.

'It was obvious that it wasn't a happy camp, certainly not in comparison with 1998, 1999. A lot of us had been used to that, so we were dreading what was coming in 2003.'

'We couldn't understand how Sully could be allowed to play football and hurling the same day,' says Cusack. 'And we knew that nothing surer, Diarmuid would be playing football.'

The first rumblings of the strike came in a radio interview given by Donal Óg Cusack in August 2002. He was frustrated and felt someone had to act. He took the lead.

'We'd have felt our ambition was to play for Cork,' he says. 'You were led to believe it was something special, something you'd go for hammer and tongs. But then when you got involved, you realised there was a lot of bluffing going on, absolute bluffing. You had fellas saying, this is a great thing, but they weren't putting the effort in. They were disrespecting the honour it was supposed to be.

'I'm immune to it, but fellas saying we'd be disrespecting the jersey because of things we do. That's all wrong. It's because we respect the jersey that we'd do what we do, or not do, as the case may be.

'We had made progress with Jimmy, but that progress had stopped dead when he left. The momentum was lost.'

Pat Mulcahy was driving into the city in mid-August when he switched on the radio.

'I was unbelievably disillusioned with the whole thing, and then I heard Cusack on the radio, and I was delighted.'

'It was the right thing to do,' says Diarmuid O'Sullivan. 'That was how we felt as a group of players.'

The goalkeeper didn't hold back on the radio, outlining the difficulties the players had in preparing properly and the toxic atmosphere between players and management. It caused uproar.

The county board didn't read the signs, but then again, the likelihood of a strike wasn't on anyone's radar at that point. The players organised themselves, but meetings with the board through September and October didn't yield progress on key issues—having medics at games, proper gear being supplied on time, gym access— though those weren't necessarily top of every player's agenda.

'I felt the fellas who shouted the loudest on the panel got the most respect,' says Mulcahy, 'and the quiet fellas didn't. I didn't think everyone was treated equally, which was wrong. There were issues with the gear and so on, and I could see where people were coming from, but that wasn't the biggest issue I had.'

'My take was I regarded myself as a fallen star at that stage,' says

Seánie McGrath. 'I'd won an All-Ireland and a Munster medal the following year, and I was focused on getting back up the ladder. That's all I was focused on. I was selfish. Players are like that.

'I wasn't thinking about meals and buses and so on. I felt the new management team mightn't have much time for me, so I felt I had to impress them. But I couldn't eat after a game, so I didn't miss anything there. Going into the Limerick game, I didn't think we were right, and when I was taken off in that game, I just left. I went home, I was so cheesed off.'

Convinced that the board were stalling, expecting the players to run out of steam, the panel lost patience early in November. It was clear the board weren't about to make concessions; meetings between both sides took on an edge, but there was no movement. At the end of the month the players outflanked the board completely by announcing their strike at a press conference in the city centre.

It was a tense time for all concerned, but for some it was worse than for others. Diarmuid O'Sullivan's father Jerry was a member of the county board, for instance.

'I wasn't living at home at the time but it was hugely stressful,' says O'Sullivan Jr. 'To this day we've never spoken about it. We were in a no-win situation, both of us. I'd always confide in him, but I knew there'd be a press conference one Friday, and when he rang me I had to say no.

'It was very stressful, but it was probably worse for my mother having to choose between her husband or her son.'

The players had certain advantages. They were dictating the agenda with the media, for instance, and there was a natural sympathy with players rather than administrators among the public, which was strengthened by stories of Niall McCarthy's nightmare journey from Derry earlier in the year.

They also had a huge asset in Diarmaid Falvey, a solicitor and club mate of Cusack and O'Sullivan. He gave himself over totally to the cause, and his advice and coaching of players before negotiations with the board was a key element to their eventual success. One

senior player puts it baldly: 'We would have gotten nowhere without
him.'

In the battle for public sympathy, nothing was left to chance.

'A few of us made points to the paper,' says Mulcahy. 'My point
was simply that things that worked thirty years ago wouldn't work
now. I remember at Newtown, training for that year's county final,
one of the lads said, "That's you finished; you'll never again play for
Cork."

'Landers asked me to get involved, to sit at the top table as maybe
a north Cork representative, and I was slow enough. I didn't feel I'd
made enough of an impact on Cork hurling—that I'd played one
match and not done well, and I could have been seen as a begrudger.

'I'd made my point when asked, and if a new selection committee
had never picked me again for Cork, I wouldn't have had a problem
with it, because I felt I'd had to make my point. It didn't bother me
doing what the lads asked, apart from sitting at the top table. I felt
that was for senior players who'd contributed more to Cork.'

Not all the players agonised.

'I supported them all the way, but if I'd been threatened with not
playing with Cork again, it wouldn't have bothered me,' says Timmy
McCarthy. 'I'd have headed off to Australia or something. GAA has
never been the be-all and end-all for me. I don't know what would
have happened if they'd thrown us out, but I don't think that was
ever going to happen.

'But then, I was away from it all, I wouldn't be meeting people. I
can only imagine Seán Óg, for instance, walking down the South
Mall that time. He'd have been annihilated.'

It was unknown territory for every player. John Gardiner was the
newest member of the panel and can recall the debates within the
panel.

'Now you can look back and say it was the right thing to do, but
at the time I remember saying all I wanted to do was to play hurling
for Cork. Fellas were telling me what had happened, and it was the
right thing to do, but we were apprehensive about it, particularly as

I'd only played a few games for Cork at that stage. I was probably the most disposable guy on the panel.'

Gardiner wasn't the only player worrying. Joe Deane was a poster boy for Cork GAA as a whole.

'It took a while to be comfortable in what we were doing,' says Deane. 'Cork hurling had been in a good state for a hundred years, and who were we to say things were shit—was that a cop-out for not putting in the effort ourselves? We had to be comfortable in criticising the management and the county board, and it took me a while to become comfortable in what we were doing.

'We felt we could proceed only if every fella on the panel bought into what we were doing, that it was the right thing. During the strike I realised that when it finished there'd be added pressure on us. Fellas took it on themselves that winter to look after themselves, that we'd have to train hard because it would be thrown back at us if we didn't do well. People would be quick to say, ye got everything ye wanted, so the players took it on themselves, without saying so publicly, to mind themselves.'

'The strike was a culmination and a combination of a lot of things,' says Seán Óg Ó hAilpín. 'It wasn't just 2002, but probably thirty years. Players had accepted things for years, but what brought it to a head was when we were badly beaten by Galway that year it was, the players don't give a damn, which really annoyed fellas.

'How can you perform when you're not on the same level playing field as others? People thought the Cork hurlers got the best of everything, which was bull. I wouldn't say we won the strike. We just wanted fair play. The conditions we wanted, that was just a no-brainer. When you start off you just want to wear the jersey, but as you get older, you hit 25, 26, and you realise the system is wrong.

'One reason we got involved was not just to benefit us, but to benefit future generations of Cork players. Mark Landers was prominent in the strike and he's well gone; he was coming towards the end even then. He had nothing to gain from the strike. The strike was coming, but we didn't drop a bomb; we went through the process with the board first. We gave them a chance.'

Eventually the board took that chance. In the middle of December the player demands were met, but for some of the participants it was an end, not a beginning. Bertie Óg Murphy and his selectors had walked away.

'I liked Bertie Óg,' says Cusack. 'I still do, even though our relationship was fatally wounded that time.'

'I feel sorry for Bertie Óg,' says Timmy McCarthy. 'He'd done a lot for us. I think he made the team of today and he doesn't get the credit for it.

'What he did for us at U-21 was unbelievable. He guided us along, he didn't pressurise us, he looked after us game-wise, we were all playing loads of games and he really looked after us that way—didn't kill us with training. He'd give you a night off if you were playing too many games. Other fellas might demand that you be at training every night anyway. It was unfortunate he came in just as things were going wrong in the camp.'

'Bertie was the unluckiest coach involved with Cork,' says Dr Con Murphy. 'He was just in the wrong place at the wrong time. All the players would still tell you they had great time for him.'

The team medic also took some hits in the crossfire between players and administrators.

'I always felt I was a player's person,' he says. 'I was unwittingly dragged into it, but I felt it was friendly fire.

'It's significant the way society has gone, that people have higher standards. Times have changed. What was accepted when I started with Cork has changed totally. It was an accident waiting to happen.'

The players regretted that friendly fire, as Dr Con puts it, as deeply as anything else.

'We offended Dr Con, who was a great friend to the players,' says Mark Landers. 'He was one fella who there was no gripe with. The fact that he got caught in the crossfire is something we'd always regret. I certainly would, because there was no hurt intended towards him; he'd always have been seen as a friend to the players.

'My own career was coming to an end, and whether I liked it or not I was being forced out. The other side of that was, I was coming to a realisation that I didn't need Cork hurling either, that I'd achieved what I set out to achieve. I wanted to forge a career, and in some respects I wouldn't have been as dedicated as I needed to be to play at that level, but it wasn't made any easier. Players aren't stupid; they can sense that.'

Facing into 2003, then, the team was without a manager and hadn't won a first-round game in Munster for two years. Coming out of Semple Stadium after the qualifier defeat to Galway, Cork fans had been understandably despondent.

The Tribesmen had a rich vein of underage talent coming through and had contested the 2001 All-Ireland final. Asked if it was reasonable at that time to expect Cork rather than Galway to contest the next four All-Ireland senior hurling finals, Diarmuid O'Sullivan is frank: 'No. Not a hope.'

# | I DON'T DO POINTS

Donal O'Grady could guess what county board officer Jim Forbes wanted to see him about in the Shandon Court Hotel late in 2002. Forbes had been charged with getting a successor to Bertie Óg Murphy and he soon came to the point in the conversation, asking if O'Grady was interested.

'I said I was but that I had certain conditions,' says O'Grady. 'And if those weren't met that I wasn't interested. I said I'd take a couple of days and I'd get back to him. I talked at home about it.

'I'd never thought about it, but when it came up I felt it would be interesting. It was there for the taking. I'd be going to matches and analysing them anyway rather than watching them as a spectator. That's the way I am. But I would never have been thinking, they should be doing this, they should be doing that. Every fella has his own way of doing things.'

It was in keeping with O'Grady's subsequent reputation as a manager that he laid down the ground rules and dictated the terms of his new post. Attention to detail and superb organisation would characterise the O'Grady regime; as one player said, anything he could control, he controlled.

O'Grady met Cusack and Deane for a chat. They didn't know each other at the time, but the new manager came away with the sense that the players wanted to give themselves the best chance they could to compete.

'The key thing with O'Grady was Seán McGrath as a trainer,' says Cusack. 'He'd have been part of the Teddy Owens thing and was respected absolutely. I didn't have much of a relationship that time with Donal O'Grady, but Seán Óg said, "Give this guy a chance. He'll be a good man." I was so close to Seán Óg that that was enough for me.

'But by the time he left, you'd have trusted O'Grady with your life.'

The new manager had won an All-Ireland medal in 1984 at full back and had been a Cork senior selector two years afterwards. Determined and a confident communicator, as befitted a long-time TV pundit and principal of an elite Gaelscoil, O'Grady was a strong character who'd worked briefly with some of the older members of the team as a backs coach in 1997. The players were soon reacquainted with his obsessive focus on the skill of the game. And with time management.

'When I heard O'Grady was appointed, I thought, nice one. I know Donal; he taught me in school,' says Seán Óg Ó hAilpín. 'He was principal when Setanta was in school; we'd be comfortable with him . . .

'Obviously I didn't know him as well as I thought. The first game was an A's versus B's match in the Old Mon Field. It was to start at 11 o'clock, and I strolled in around ten past. Donal gave me a look that I knew from school—he came over and basically read me my rights, being late as an established player didn't give an example and so on.

'And that showed me a new regime had come in; under previous managers I'd have gotten away with that, but O'Grady showed things had changed. And I should have known anyway. That was the last time I was ever late for O'Grady.'

Other players had similar experiences.

'O'Grady asked us all to fill a notebook with what we thought after training and so on,' says Ben O'Connor. 'Then every fella got a schedule, when buses were leaving and so on, and you weren't late because you knew exactly when things were happening.

'The year before O'Grady came in, myself, Jerry and Paul Morrissey were travelling up to training together from Newtown, and I'd say we were never on time. We just didn't leave in time to get to training—always late. But that was kind of accepted.

'With O'Grady, though, the big thing was time. He was always on your case over being on time. But the other side of that was if you had a few nice days during the summer and you'd trained Tuesday and Thursday, he might say to you, don't bother coming in on Friday, take it easy at home. As long as you played ball with him and you were there, the odd time he'd give you a night off. He'd know when fellas were under a bit of pressure at work or whatever, and you'd be taken out of a certain drill or exercise.'

'I think the county board underestimated O'Grady,' says Ó hAilpín. 'They saw him as a good coach, a good disciplinarian, a guy to crack the whip. But he turned out to be the best thing ever. Because of the spirit of the strike he was allowed to pick his own selectors and after that things started falling into place.

'For instance, we had good managers, but some people thought if you wore a red jersey you were the finished article. O'Grady took the opposite view. He'd do basic stuff, but that was stuff you'd never been taught. You'd be told what to do but your technique wouldn't be broken down. When Setanta and Aisake went to Carlton, they were told about holding the ball to kick it, that kind of detail. And that was O'Grady's approach too.'

O'Grady himself didn't see a need for formal aims to be stated for the players.

'I didn't sit down and say, these are the targets or anything: the target with Cork is always an All-Ireland. Every player on the panel would know that and we didn't need to have a big meeting to decide that.

'I did say to them that we'd base everything on our performance: that if we could get that right, everything else should be okay.'

As the team played challenge games and time went on, O'Grady felt the team would have a better balance with certain players in certain positions—and a definite approach to their playing style.

'Certainly the big thing was to get the players thinking,' he says, 'not to hit the ball aimlessly and so on, but to think about what they were doing with it, how they could serve the needs of the lads up the field, to work with each other.

'Donal Óg Cusack was obviously a deep thinker on the game, a fella who was trying to see how things would progress. There was no opposition to the plans we had, what I was laying out as the plan. The full forward line, for instance, would have realised that the plan involved getting good ball into them. It grew out of that.

'John Gardiner, for instance, would have had a habit of belting the ball across the field when he was in possession. I spoke to him about that and pointed out he was putting the other backs at a disadvantage when he did it. It took him a while to change that, but he did.'

O'Grady offered proof along with instruction, but the technology didn't always have a cutting edge. The laptop analysis for which the team became famous was preceded by a television-vcr combination which had to be lugged around. 'And you had to wait for the video to scroll back to what you wanted to pick out then,' as O'Grady says.

He found willing pupils on the team, though he was aware of the pressure they were under.

'Most fellas took it on board fairly quickly,' he says. 'They could see what we were trying to achieve. You were looking for the perfect performance, even though you were never going to get that, but what was more important was that the players were enjoying it. It wasn't a question of total hurling, but for the first time I think the players realised that every fella was depending on every other fella.

'There was huge pressure on the players early in the year. They'd made a big stand and become household names in the country because of the strike; before that they'd have been known to hurling fans, I suppose, but that made them even more well known. If they hadn't gone on strike the GPA would probably have been still-born, I'd say.'

The attention to detail didn't run to ecumenism. In previous decades players might have built dual careers in hurling and football. Not in the twenty-first century, however.

'It's impossible now,' says Tom Kenny. 'In 2001 I was on the training panel for the [Cork] footballers. In 2002 I said I'd give the hurling a go, but I was back with the footballers in 2003. I remember the night in Fermoy the hurling management named the team for the Tipp game in the NHL. The footballers were playing that weekend as well and I was thinking of going with them, but I was told I'd be wing back against Tipperary.

'I played in the first round of the Munster football championship against Limerick, but after that myself and Seán Óg sat down with Donal and Larry [Tompkins] and we said it wasn't feasible.'

Other players had similar experiences.

'We were training in Ballygarvan in early February,' says Ó hAilpín, 'and I arrived early—obviously, after my lesson in the Old Mon Field—and O'Grady called me into the car. He'd heard I'd been approached by the footballers.

'"*Cad mar gheall ar an peil?*" he asked me.

'"*Bhuel, tá fonn orm imirt peil,*" I said.

'He took out a chart with sessions made out for February and March, and it went on to September, and the All-Ireland final, sessions to prepare for Cork versus x. And he said, "This is the hurling schedule. How can I prepare the team properly if I don't know when I'm going to see you?"

'I thought he was mad. Here we were; we'd been beaten out the gate by Galway the previous year; we were thinking it'd be great to just get over Clare in the first round. But that showed his intent. He believed, and that rubbed off on the players.'

Another talented footballer also got the treatment.

'One night Donal called me over and said there were rumours I was interested in playing football for Cork,' says John Gardiner. 'I said, to be honest, Donal, I was thinking of giving it a go. And O'Grady said, well, he'd have no problem with that. Then he said, "You won't be considered here, of course, if you do. I'm not telling you not to play football; you just won't be considered for the hurlers."'

On a practical level, O'Grady had to rebuild the team—not from scratch, but major surgery was needed.

'In my two years we had to replace seven players on the team,' he says. 'Half the team, basically, but we got the balance fairly right overall.

'There was a debate about where to play Joe [Deane]: up front, full forward or corner forward. We played him full forward and even though people said he was too small, we felt that wasn't as important as the quality of the ball going into him. That was what the emphasis was on. If the ball going into him was good, that was what mattered.'

That was full forward. Other central positions needed to be filled, most crucially the centre forward and centre back roles.

'Well, Niall [McCarthy] hated right half forward anyway,' says O'Grady. 'He'd do okay at left half forward, but he preferred the centre, and it suited him. He was physically very strong, very fast, and even though his shooting wasn't always reliable, he'd give you everything he had.

'Ronan Curran didn't impress us early on, mind you.'

Curran had been doing exams in CIT, but in his first big game for Cork that spring, against Galway, he was off the pace. He had a reputation as the centre back-elect, and his manager was worried that he'd gone back.

'I said to him after that, are you okay?' says O'Grady. 'And he told me he'd been doing exams all the week and he was exhausted. I told him he should have told us; we'd have rested him. But once he settled, he was the centre back. No doubt about that.'

Other players motored into contention. In a game against Clare early in the year O'Grady unearthed another jewel.

'Tom Kenny was wing back that day, but he'd been drawn into the middle. The ball went over his head, out beyond Jamesie O'Connor, who had a ten-yard start on him. Tom took off and within three strides he'd caught up with Jamesie, dispossessed him and come away with the ball. He had huge athleticism, but because he'd been with the footballers we had to do a lot of work on his striking. But as a youngster with Farranferris he'd taken frees, so I knew his striking was basically good.

'We had him at half back all that year because I felt that pace in that line was a huge help. A lot of people wouldn't see that Tom is covering back to mark a player by his own square one minute and then he's up at the other end supporting the play the next. People watching wouldn't notice him shadowing opposition players, so even now a lot of the work he does at midfield isn't noticed.

'To be honest, we were lucky in the players that came along—the likes of Tom, who's become a major player on the team ever since. We were always looking at him as a right half back. It's the balance thing again: we wanted Gardiner at midfield with Mickey O'Connell, with John to stick around the middle and put any loose ball over the bar, and Mickey to travel.'

Significantly enough, given where he later settled, Gardiner didn't enjoy his 2003 posting.

'I didn't like playing midfield. Not at all. In 2002 I played all the league games in midfield, then I played wing back against Limerick in the championship and centre back against Galway. But I think O'Grady knew that I wouldn't be strong enough for centre back. He needed a new centre back.

'Myself and Mickey did okay at midfield. He travelled and I spent most games in front of the half back line, where I was told, and it worked. But I wanted to go back to the backs. When Tom came out, that freed up the wing back position.'

Then there was Setanta.

Seán Óg's little brother stretched after minor, and a forward who topped out at six foot six was always going to attract the interest of the senior selectors. He was studying in WIT, however, so O'Grady didn't see much of him until the youngster made a name for himself in a league encounter.

'First off, he was a great character,' says O'Grady. 'We played a league game down in Wexford, and he came on at right corner forward. You could see he was a fantastic talent. He got an awful battering at one stage, coming in along the 21-metre line, but the talent was there. You were saying, here's the man for the next ten or twelve years, particularly if he was as dedicated as Seán Óg.

'He brought something else to the dressing room as well. He was always last—always—onto the bus, and I went in one day after we played Offaly to put the run on him and he was still in the shower, singing *'Amhran na Mainistreach'*, the North Mon song.'

'I remember him singing a lot of R Kelly,' says Diarmuid O'Sullivan.

'Setanta used to call me sir,' says O'Grady. 'I'd point out to the other players that he was the only one showing me due respect . . .

'He brought a bit of irreverence to the whole thing. He'd always have a bit of a quip for you. If he disagreed with something, he'd say it in such a way that it'd be a laugh rather than taking someone on. Which isn't to say he wasn't focused before games—he was—but he had that youthful attitude. Bring it on, if you like.'

His older brother enjoyed the company.

'If I had my way I'd have the three of them playing with me,' says Seán Óg. 'Setanta had felt annoyed he wasn't looked at in 2002; he'd done well in trial games. He headed over to the States for the summer, then he came back to WIT.

'The game that did it for him was the league game against Kilkenny. He had a good game on Philly Larkin, who was a very good player, and that game marked him out. We'd been suffering without a target man for years and suddenly he was an option.'

Much like Diarmuid O'Sullivan before him, Setanta had been a familiar figure at Cork training sessions before being invited along officially. When his older brother first made the Cork team, he'd thumb in from Blarney for training. Often he had company.

'Setanta would come in with me and puck the ball out from behind the goal,' says Seán Óg. 'JBM would give him a ball then afterwards and he'd be delighted.

'But I knew back then that he was destined for good things. No kid thumbs it from Blarney to the Pairc just for a sliotar. He was delighted to meet Joe Deane and the lads. When he broke in, he was thrilled to play alongside Joe and Alan Browne and so on.'

From early on the legend gathered pace. The story quickly sprang up that the younger Ó hAilpín had dismissed directions to take his point, the immortal GAA advice, with the equally immortal retort: 'I don't do points.'

O'Grady laughs.

'I heard that story all right. It could have happened. In the Wexford game I mentioned, I remember he headed for goal, coming in between the 14 and the 21-metre lines, and he got a desperate belting off the backs, a few shoulders and so on.

'After the game I said to him, either lay it off or take your point. You wouldn't get such a hammering. Supposedly, he said, "Look, Sir, I don't do points." I don't remember it, but it could have happened. He certainly would have given me a look which said, points? That's not what it's all about.'

His closest friend on the panel fleshes out the yarn.

'Setanta's saying was always, I don't do points,' says John Gardiner. 'And you might laugh, but it was true. If he did get a point it was like, shit, I didn't get a goal. Anyone else would be delighted with a point in a championship game, but he'd be disgusted if he couldn't get a goal.'

Other relationships needed more work. As Donal Óg Cusack puts it, 'Sully and himself didn't see eye to eye.'

Diarmuid O'Sullivan played full back for the hurlers against Limerick in the first round of the league. Then he played for the footballers and when the hurling team was named for the second league game, he wasn't even in the subs.

'I thought, hang on a second . . .' says O'Sullivan. 'O'Grady said to me that I wasn't right. I asked how. He said, "You're not fit; get yourself right and come back to us."'

O'Sullivan continued with the footballers for a while, playing against Kerry under lights and heading north to Crossmaglen the following week: 'I came on at half-time up there. The first thing I tried was giving Kieran McGeeney a shot, but he gave me a slap first.'

Eventually reality set in and O'Sullivan had to choose. He rang football selector Eamon Ryan and said he'd be concentrating on hurling.

'I had great time for Larry [Tompkins, the manager]. I couldn't ring him and upset him.'

Team trainer Jerry Wallace came to O'Sullivan and offered to help him sort himself out. The full back did torturous sessions of extra training with Wallace in the mornings. It was slow work, but he was seeing the benefits, and when the team went to Waterford for a challenge, he was named in the corner and did well.

But the 1984 full back and the 2003 full back were never close.

'I felt he could be abrupt. He wasn't into the arm around the shoulder,' says O'Sullivan. 'In hindsight he was right; no one is bigger than the team, and we needed a kick in the arse. But I remember we trained one Sunday morning, and Setanta and I were having fierce belting matches in training. We played one Thursday night and we leathered each other, and Setanta was jumping around.

'The next ball, I gave him a right lash and said, you're not so happy now; wait til you're on Frank Lohan and you'll see skelping. So the next ball, the two of us pulled about so high over the ball, and with that O'Grady sent him over to the other side. But to be fair to Setanta, he loved it. The harder you hit, the more he'd hit back.'

The following Sunday, O'Sullivan was at full back in training and when he went to pick the ball, Brendan Lombard, who was on the panel, came in to challenge.

'He caught me with a shoulder up under the chin and knocked me back. When I recovered I saw the ball—and Lombard's leg—and I pulled as vicious as I ever did. The hurley broke and the ball went one way and the hurley went the other way. It flew off and hit Paul Tierney in the balls.

'It looked desperate. O'Grady said, "Get off the field now," to me, and I said, what's wrong with you? We had a roaring match out on the field, so I went in and got my bag and said, that's it, I'm finished.'

O'Sullivan headed for the dressing room, steam coming from his ears.

'Seánie O'Leary came out to me and I said, that's it. I'm not being treated like a child. Jim Forbes came over and only for him I'd have walked that night.

'Forbes said O'Grady wanted me to apologise in front of the whole team and I wouldn't because I wasn't in the wrong. Jerry Wallace, Jim, Seánie—they all came into the dressing room to get me to come out, but I wouldn't. I was heading down the tunnel, but Jim Forbes told me to calm down and to think about it. I said I wouldn't apologise.

'Eventually we agreed that I'd apologise to Lombard and Tierney. I went out and apologised to them. But I was on the way out, down the tunnel and away. That was the start of our relationship.'

O'Sullivan's late arrival onto the team meant he'd missed out on O'Grady's remodelling of the team's style.

'I'd been out of the scene and I remember the other backs were messing around in a league game,' says O'Sullivan. 'They were hand passing the ball backwards and forwards, and I was roaring at them to let the ball off. Seán Óg said, "Look, this is our game now", and I said, first I heard of it. I kept hitting the ball long, doing my own thing.

'And O'Grady came to me after that game and said, "When you get the ball, look around and see what's on."'

It was the first sighting of the running game.

Once synonymous with Newtownshandrum, it would soon be recognised as Cork's default approach. Pat Mulcahy was used to hurling neo-cons in Cork bemoaning the lack of direct play from Newtown. He soon heard the same lament about Cork's new approach.

'What people said about the style never bothered me,' says Mulcahy. 'Bernie O'Connor used to call it the running game with Newtown, and O'Grady called it the possession game. I don't think O'Grady ever admitted that it was copying Newtown's game, but I noticed that before, you were on your own. You won the ball on your own and you struck it on your own, and if you couldn't do that you were gone.

'When O'Grady came in in 2003, whether he picked it up from Newtown or not I don't know, but it was all about support play in defence from then on. With the club as a centre back I'd always make myself available when the full backs had the ball. With Cork, O'Grady encouraged players to support each other. You'd know there was another player to back you up if you were in trouble, and of course that would help your confidence.'

Clare provided the first test of the new game. They had contested the previous year's All-Ireland final, and if the edge had been blunted from their 1995–7 vintage, they still had plenty of power with which to take on a new Cork team in the Munster championship opener. O'Grady realised that.

'There was huge pressure on the Cork players to perform in Thurles that day, with 40,000 people watching them,' says O'Grady. 'If they hadn't won, people would have been saying, ye were very strong in November. There's always wags around. Maybe that applied in the All-Ireland final; there was still that pressure to deliver.'

'They felt under terrible pressure; that was clear,' says Dr Con Murphy. 'It was unthinkable in previous eras to do what they'd done. Credit to the county board, too—everyone moved on and it worked out well. A lot of people were hurt at the time, but it happened for the right reasons.'

On the morning of the Clare game Donal Óg Cusack noted a newspaper headline, 'Now it's time to walk the walk'.

'We were expecting that,' he says. 'The day the strike ended we were saying, we have to win.

'It was a huge battle to win. But pressure? There's always pressure when you play for Cork. Our advantages were the new players, who brought some freshness to the thing, and the fact that anyone who was with us, we felt they were one hundred per cent with us—the selectors, the backroom.'

'The lads who were there a while probably felt under pressure after everything,' says Ronan Curran. 'For the likes of me, Tom and Setanta it was different. We were just excited. We weren't thinking of the strike because we'd got our chance.

'I knew from the strike on that everyone was together, that there was something to prove. Lads backed each other up. You'd be a bit nervous, but I remember thinking, this is where you wanted to be after complaining constantly for the last few years; you'll have to do something or you're a right gom. There was a real buzz around that day. Everyone was expecting something different.'

'It was an adventure,' says Pat Mulcahy. 'Setanta, Ronan, Tom, they hadn't been heard of, then they were starring. It was probably the most enjoyable for me. Despite any criticism or whatever, as long as I had a coach who totally believed in me, that didn't bother me.

'I thought the crowd respected us because of the strike, and then you had the Setanta factor. From 2003 on, you had the core support still there, but a new group of supporters fell in behind the team, which was outstanding.'

The marker was laid down early. After a few minutes John Gardiner put in an emphatic blockdown: the Cork crowd rose, and a thought flashed through O'Grady's mind: we're back.

'I remember that block,' says Tom Kenny. 'For myself there was one ball after four-five minutes. Niall Gilligan got the sliotar about twenty yards out and went for a shot. I just stuck out the hurley and blocked it out for a 65. That gave me confidence because we'd spent weeks blocking and hooking. I wouldn't get easily flustered anyway, but that kind of thing gives you confidence.'

There were other signs, as Pat Mulcahy recalls: 'I remember when Timmy lifted Davy Fitz out over the line after a minute or two thinking, well, he's up for it anyway.'

Joe Deane scored a spectacular goal following a terrific Ben O'Connor run, and Cork never lost the initiative after that. Curran looked settled; so did Tom Kenny, while Setanta Ó hAilpín's schooling under Diarmuid O'Sullivan stood to him against Frank Lohan.

'He threw himself around,' says Seán Óg Ó hAilpín about his brother. 'He was ready for the Lohans and wasn't going to back down.

'The feeling among a lot of Cork supporters was that we'd be doing well to compete. They weren't expecting a whole lot, but the game was over at half-time.

'Ten minutes to go, the game's sewn up and it was like happy days again after 2002. For the likes of me, Donal Óg, Diarmuid, it was like a second coming. During the winter of 2002 we were assuming the worst, that if it didn't work out we might be looking for a new sport.'

'Just winning that day probably set the tone for years to come,' says Tom Kenny. 'Clare were favourites, it was Donal's first game, and even though we didn't maybe feel it, there was a lot of pressure on us. There was a lot of relief after that game.

'It's a funny sensation. You're focused on the game. My thing is when you head out and hear the announcer say, *anois, a chairde, foireann Chorcaigh*, and the roar. You're tuned in from that on; you're fully switched on. It's a phenomenal sensation. I'd gone to a lot of games in Thurles and then all of a sudden, after being injured in the league, I was in the middle of it.'

All the players remember one unforgettable moment. With the game in the bag, the Cork supporters started singing.

'Surreal,' remembers John Gardiner. 'Twenty minutes to go and they're singing "The Banks" up on the terrace. Never heard that before while the game was still on.'

Waterford lined up against Cork in the Munster final. They were reigning champions, but Cork had momentum. That didn't mean it was plain sailing. Many observers were surprised when Diarmuid O'Sullivan was taken off early in the game. Those close to the team were surprised he'd even started.

'I spent two weeks in bed with a virus before that,' says O'Sullivan. 'I shouldn't have played. I did a fitness test on that Friday night for Seánie McGrath, and it took everything I had to convince him I was fit.'

'Diarmuid shouldn't have been playing,' says O'Grady. 'We felt, though, that if we didn't start him, Waterford would have gotten a boost, so the idea was to start him and take him off. Waterford were playing Paul Flynn at full forward, and we felt Pat Mulcahy would be better suited to marking him, which he was, as it turned out.

'I think Diarmuid enjoyed playing corner back for a while because it gave him a break from full back, which is a ferociously responsible position: one slip there and you're gone, while if you make a mistake in the corner you may get away with it.

'But on top of all that, he'd been sick all the week of the Munster final, and he shouldn't have been played. The idea was to march him around, and after a few minutes to take him off. As it happened, I don't think he wanted to come off, but he had to, and Mark Prendergast did well when he came on, dispossessing one Waterford player in the second half and delivering the ball for Joe Deane's goal.'

Waterford started well, with John Mullane scorching past O'Sullivan for an early goal and point.

'We fell behind, but I wasn't worried,' says O'Grady. 'I felt when they were on top, right lads, we're in a game, let's see what we can do. I was confident.

'In the first half we were playing into a gale, and people probably didn't notice that we brought Timmy out as a third midfielder to block the ball coming through to Ken McGrath.'

McGrath, a wonderful centre forward before he became a superb centre back, occupied the minds of the Cork defence.

'At the time I didn't know how good or bad Waterford were,' says Ronan Curran. 'Going into that game I knew I was marking Ken McGrath and I was under pressure to hold him. I was just thinking of my own man. That day they had a lot of wides, but it was a good win, the start of a lot of great games against Waterford.'

Cork needed a spark against the wind. Setanta provided it.

'We were struggling, and then he got a half-chance,' says his older brother. 'Declan Prendergast was doing well on him, but when Stephen Brenner hesitated, bang! In the end we won well, but it was a see-saw for a long time. Any time we'd go ahead, Mullane would bang in another goal.

'But the one thing about Setanta was he always had huge confidence in his ability. That's something, when I look back at my own career, that I didn't have. Early on if things went against me, the head would go down, but not Setanta. If the first ball didn't go his way, that never bothered him.'

'That was his value,' says O'Grady. 'Six foot six, pace . . . he reminded me a bit of John Fitzgibbon in that goals were his thing. Having said all that about the game, though, Ken McGrath hit a lot of wides that day.'

Mullane ended the day with a hat-trick, but once again Deane's coolness under pressure yielded a crucial goal for Cork to give them a decisive lead.

'It was a title,' says Gardiner. 'Given where we'd been, it was a monkey off the back.'

Another problem landed into O'Grady's lap around the time of the Munster final, however.

'Ger Canning would come down for team news,' he says. 'But we'd always play as selected—this is us; change if ye want, was our attitude. He asked me before the Munster final what I thought of the new balls, and I just looked at him. I know nothing about that, and Cork weren't informed of it, I told him.'

A new set of sliotars had been introduced, and when O'Grady saw them in operation he wasn't happy.

'One thing about the 2003 ball was that if you hit it anyway wrong at all, it'd start to spin and then it'd head away wide. Early on against Waterford, Ben O'Connor got a free, and I thought it was an All-Star ball he had, but when he struck it, I could see it start to spin and it went wide.

'Look at the way those balls were introduced. Kilkenny were given a dozen of them in April or May and were asked to try them out. They came back and expressed their satisfaction, and the ball was introduced to the rest of the GAA world.

'If every county had been given the balls at the start of the year, it would have been different; but if we play with ball x and another county prefers ball y, then a compromise should be reached. But just giving it to Kilkenny and saying, well they're happy with it so everyone else has to use it? It was a joke.

'If we'd lost you'd be viewed as a right incompetent manager. You wouldn't have known what balls were being used. But that was the level of communication.'

The team was getting to know their manager along the way.

'He was a terror,' says Timmy McCarthy. 'I get blood infections working on the farm, cutting my hands on thorns and that, and I'd be on antibiotics so I couldn't train. O'Grady would be giving out to me. "Why aren't you wearing gloves? Teagasc are doing a survey to get farmers to wear gloves"—that kind of thing.

'Now if I thought Teagasc were doing surveys on gloves instead of the EBI of cows . . . O'Grady was a pantomime; he'd do anything. But a brilliant coach. Everything was practised, down to picking the ball with two hands on the hurley. He left nothing to chance. Anything he could control, he'd control it.'

'O'Grady knew your personality,' says Mulcahy. 'Once or twice I

'What Cork hurling was all about.' Jimmy Barry-Murphy on Joe Deane's goal against Clare in the 1999 Munster final. Seanie McGrath joins in. (*Irish Examiner*)

'If we were going to go down, we'd go down with hurlers.' Jimmy Barry-Murphy at the final whistle, Cork-Waterford, 1999. (*Irish Examiner*)

'He blew early.' Wayne Sherlock, Cork celebrate as referee Pat O'Connor blows the final whistle in the 1999 All-Ireland final. (*Irish Examiner*)

'It doesn't get any better than this.' Jimmy Barry-Murphy and Timmy McCarthy celebrate at the final whistle, 1999 All-Ireland final. (*Irish Examiner*)

'See, Jimmy, I was all right.' Seánie McGrath. The Corkman points against Tipperary in the 2000 Munster final. (*Irish Examiner*)

'Like young Americans coming back from Vietnam.' Seán Óg Ó hAilpín and Diarmuid O'Sullivan chase Offaly's Paudie Mulhare in the 2000 All-Ireland semi-final. (*Irish Examiner*)

'Six foot six, pace . . .' Donal O'Grady on Setanta Ó hAilpín, who gets a standing ovation on his substitution against Wexford during the All-Ireland semi-final replay, 2003. (*Irish Examiner*)

'I never hit as much ball as in that match.' John Gardiner on the Cork-Kilkenny All-Ireland final, 2003. He and Diarmuid O'Sullivan are dejected at the final whistle. (*Irish Examiner*)

'We couldn't get back into it.' Donal O'Grady on losing the Munster final to Waterford in 2004. Waterford's Declan Prendergast celebrates as Joe Deane looks on. (*Irish Examiner*)

'Feeding nuts to a monkey? I didn't mind it.' Diarmuid O'Sullivan clears past Wexford's Larry Murphy in the All-Ireland semi-final of 2004. (*Irish Examiner*)

'The important thing was to keep to the plan.' Donal O'Grady issues instructions to Donal Óg Cusack and Diarmuid O'Sullivan in the 2004 All-Ireland final. (*Sportsfile*)

'I didn't hear it much in the early days.' Joe Deane on Cork supporters chanting his name. Here he goes for the ball with Eamonn Corcoran of Tipperary in the 2005 Munster final. (*Irish Examiner*)

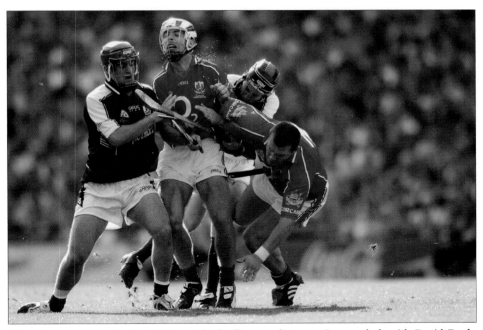

'There's an opportunity here.' Diarmuid O'Sullivan and Ronan Curran clash with David Forde and Niall Healy of Galway in the 2005 All-Ireland final. (*Irish Examiner*)

'As good as we ever played.' Donal Óg Cusack on the 2005 Munster final. Neil Ronan celebrates his point against Tipperary in the second half. (*Irish Examiner*)

'Is fada an turas.' Seán Óg Ó hAilpín lifts the Liam McCarthy Cup for 2005. (*Sportsfile*)

'What's keeping him?' John Allen was unaware that Diarmuid O'Sullivan had been grounded as he came upfield in the All-Ireland qualifier against Limerick, 2006. (*Sportsfile*)

'Frigging bees.' Ronan Curran on Kilkenny's tactics in the 2006 All-Ireland final. Here Kilkenny's Henry Shefflin reaches ahead of Diarmuid O'Sullivan. (*Irish Examiner*)

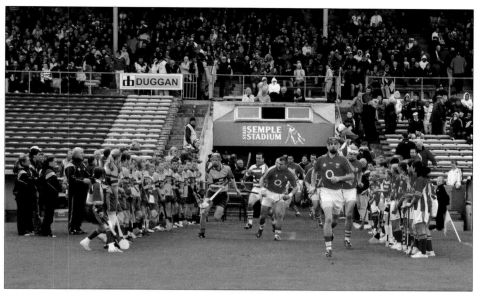

'Your instinctive reaction is to hit.' Donal Óg Cusack on what became known as Semplegate. Clare's Frank Lohan and Cork's Diarmuid O'Sullivan clash before the ball is thrown in for the start of Cork v Clare in the Munster championship, 2007. (*Irish Examiner*)

'2007 was the Dan the Man show.' Sean Óg Ó hAilpin on Dan Shanahan, seen here scoring a goal for Waterford in the All-Ireland quarter-final of the same year. (*Sportsfile*)

'The Thursday I knew was a huge day.' Donal Óg Cusack, seen here with footballer Graham Canty, arrives for arbitration talks at the Rochestown Park Hotel, 14 February 2008. (*Provision*)

went to training in 2003, and he watched me during the warm-up. He'd say, "You look tired. Go on in and tog on, have some food and head off home." He was very astute. He'd always be watching the quieter lads in particular.'

'Donal instilled a lot of confidence in me, Ronan, John and Setanta,' says Tom Kenny. 'In league games if I was wing back, he'd say to me, "Keep batting the ball away from your man." After the game you'd be thinking, out of five balls I only blocked one and cleared another, but Donal had a way about him that he'd tell you, "I asked you to bat the ball and you did."'

Seán Óg Ó hAilpín could see O'Grady improving players.

'In the Kilkenny league game Tom made a great solo run and then barely hit the ball. He reminded me of myself when I was playing football. O'Grady switched John Gardiner out to midfield then and moved Tom back to wing back: he had more of a reputation as a footballer at that time, and the Kilkenny game seemed to prove it. But then O'Grady's coaching kicked in: now Tom Kenny would put the ball over the bar from his own half.'

'He brought in discipline, tactics we'd never had before,' says McCarthy. 'He brought in Seán McGrath and Jerry Wallace. What we were looking for, he brought with him.'

McGrath and Wallace brought a cutting edge to the training sessions, and the players responded.

'The training was totally different,' says John Gardiner. 'It was all outdoor, and with Seánie McGrath as trainer it was very, very tough. It's not a coincidence that we were on top while he was training us.

'It was more scientific. Everything was timed. That was something new for us. Before that you'd do a hundred metres—out and back, out and back—but with Seánie he'd time you and say, your time was such-and-such the first run; why wasn't it that fast for your last one? He introduced hydration, checking your urine . . . This was a massive change.

'Seánie's character was such that when he was there, you had to be switched on. There was no messing, no chatting at training. He wouldn't tolerate it. You were there to work.'

'Seán was a huge help,' agrees Ó hAilpín. 'We trained very smart rather than very hard. He knew when to work us hard and when to ease off. He'd look at sprint times and if they were sluggish, he'd realise we were slightly overcooked, for instance, but he'd work us very hard when we needed to. So the fitness was good. The organisation was good. It was all going well.'

The cult hero of 2003, meanwhile, was making hay.

'It was an incredible summer,' says Seán Óg Ó hAilpín. 'As the months wore on, nobody in the family saw Setanta. He was here, there and everywhere.'

There was more to come from the young man with the goalscoring touch.

# | CAN THAT FEELING

Cork drew Wexford in the semi-final. They'd turned Waterford over in Nowlan Park in a thrilling qualifier game, but the consensus was that Cork had momentum and would prove too classy.

That's not how it turned out.

'It was a great game,' says O'Grady. 'For the spectators it was a fantastic occasion, a beautiful day, big crowd, a great contest . . .'

That's the overview. The game itself was a kaleidoscope of small details. For instance, Ronan Curran found his first senior outing in GAA headquarters trying enough, and not always because of the opposition.

'We went up the week before to get used to the new Croke Park, to try the new surface, and the difference was unbelievable. We knew we'd be under pressure because Wexford had played there a good few times. We were nervous—it was the first big game in Croke Park for a lot of fellas.

'I know I was trying to get my bearings and it was very hard the first day—you'd lose the ball in the stands—but it showed the second day that we were used to it.'

Curran also noted the differences underfoot.

'It was unbelievable. It wasn't too bad in Thurles because there was some give in the ground, but Croke Park was like a rock. Early on against Wexford, Damien Fitzhenry hit the ball out and it bounced around the half back line—which it should never do, of course—and Pat Mulcahy was coming onto it.

'Pat had his hurley up in the air, but it bounced clear over his hurley, nine feet or whatever into the air, so we were thinking, Christ, we'll have to be careful here, and not let the ball bounce, obviously.'

'I went out to a Wexford puck-out on our 45,' recalls Diarmuid O'Sullivan. 'The ball bounced over my head and wide. It was unreal.'

'You'd notice it in puck-outs,' says Tom Kenny. 'Donal Óg would be known more for finding his man rather than going long, though he's gone long as well. But you'd notice the new ball bounce on twenty, thirty yards at times, and it was negating the game of hurling. We've had a few issues with sliotars since, but that was noticeable.

'We were in Croke Park before the Wexford game and the surface was hugely different to Thurles. I had to change my boots to six-stud and you'd be a couple of games getting used to them. Your feet would be at you.'

O'Grady was keen to nullify one of Wexford's trump cards, even if his method wasn't widely appreciated.

'Beforehand I'd noticed that Rory McCarthy had had a great game against Waterford in the qualifiers down in Nowlan Park. He'd been exceptional at midfield, and I told Mickey O'Connell he was to keep him out of the game. Mickey was involved for maybe the first ten minutes of the match but not afterwards, because we were keeping the ball away from McCarthy—and Mickey—by using John Gardiner a lot.

'The thing was, I heard afterwards that Ger Loughnane had said on television that Mickey should have been taken off, but if so, Rory McCarthy should definitely have gone as well because neither of them was getting the ball. Rory got the goal late on, fair enough, but it shows what people don't pick up on.'

Wexford jumped out to a hefty lead and were pouring forward, but although O'Grady was tempted to start switching things around, he held tough.

'We were in trouble during the second half, but we decided not to change the team around because we weren't being overrun in any one place. Sometimes when you start making switches, it can unbalance the team. It was a bit of a finger-in-the-dyke situation at that point, so we said we'd leave things as they were a while.'

The new star was instrumental to the recovery. Cork won a free in the middle of the field and John Gardiner was approaching the ball.

'Diarmuid told me to go away,' he recalls. 'He hit it in long and Setanta got up and caught it, and clung to it.'

'In fairness to Setanta, he got a great goal to bring us back into it,' says O'Grady. 'He made a great catch, swivelled and kicked the ball with the outside of his boot into the corner. That got the crowd going and gave us self-belief.'

'Setanta caught it with his wrong hand, if you like,' says Seán Óg Ó hAilpín. 'He'd say himself if he'd kicked it properly Damien Fitzhenry would have saved it, but he miskicked it and it looped past Fitzhenry.'

The youngster's distinctive goal celebration—an apparent 'calm down' gesture with his hands—fired the Cork support, even if its provenance remains a mystery to this day. ('I don't know where that came from,' says Seán Óg. 'It didn't come from me, anyway.')

Alan Browne then put Cork three points up with a fine score from the sideline.

'The last ten minutes showed again what Seán McGrath and Donal O'Grady used to say,' says Ó hAilpín. 'Get into a two-horse race with ten minutes left and back yourself. A lot of the Wexford lads were a bit older, and we drove it on. But of course they still equalised . . .'

The game was more or less over when Wexford surged downfield one last time. It had been a breathless seventy minutes, but the closing seconds were even more dramatic.

'My philosophy would always have been, if a guy made a run, then you should keep inside your man at least, because even if the ball breaks, you're between him and the goal,' says O'Grady. 'But Rory McCarthy made a great blindside run—Sky Sports would have shown it from forty different angles.'

Tom Kenny was central to the endgame: 'In the first half we'd been comfortable enough, but it got a bit shaky in the second half. My overriding memory was their equaliser. I was going out for the ball and Wayne was behind me, but for some reason I flicked the ball away from him.'

Rory McCarthy snapped up the ball on the Cork 21. Though Diarmuid O'Sullivan was bearing down on him with unmistakable intent, the Wexford man lined up a shot from an acute angle.

'If you gave it to him ten times, he mightn't do it nine times out of ten,' says O'Sullivan. 'But it was a great goal.'

McCarthy's shot flew past Cusack for an equaliser that was beyond dramatic.

'I wouldn't mind, but I played well enough that day,' says Cusack. 'I felt I was solid enough. I handled a couple of bouncy balls that day and one that came out of the sun. Ger Cunningham was the only one who spotted how hard that one was, for instance. People don't understand when a keeper is looking into the sun because they're looking the opposite way.

'But Rory's goal . . . it was like someone handed you a million euro and then changed their mind and took it back. We were there and then it was gone.'

Although his side had lost a lead with the last puck of the ball, O'Grady was reasonably happy.

'I rarely felt much pressure on the sideline, for the simple reason that there's not much you can do, only see what's happening, but I remember that when Alan got the point I was thinking, that's grand—we won't get beaten anyway. They were hardly going to get four points, and even when they equalised we weren't going to throw ourselves on the ground either.

'I was happy enough. It was our first game in the new Croke Park on the new surface. A lot of the lads had blisters afterwards, and our first session after that was on a Wednesday, a light session, for the replay the following Saturday.

'As far as I remember, Wexford had a golf outing that week, so they were going to be out in the sun for a couple of hours, which wouldn't do you much good.'

It didn't. Before that, however, O'Grady had work to do with his charges.

'A high ball had come in against Wexford and Paul Codd got it and stuck it,' recalls Pat Mulcahy. 'O'Grady spent half an hour with me at training the following night showing me how to defend a high ball. This was before training actually started.

'Now I didn't agree with him, but he convinced me otherwise. He was that good.'

There was more good news in Diarmuid O'Sullivan's thundering return to form. It had evoked an unforgettable line from TV commentator Cyril Farrell in the drawn game.

'Against Wexford the first day, after twenty minutes O'Grady came down and told me to go in full back,' says O'Sullivan. 'I caught a couple of good balls that day. I had a right tussle with Larry Murphy.

'The "Feeding nuts to a monkey, Ger?" They should never have got rid of Cyril. He was great for live games. Did that bother me? Not at all. Cyril is genuine. There are other guys who'd be different, but I always had good time for Cyril.'

'The draw stood to us,' says John Gardiner. 'You got more used to Croke Park. As for the balls. . . when it was up in the air you'd lose it sometimes with the building going on, not to mention the fact you had the new ball. I got a bag of them again a few months ago and I still couldn't get the hang of them in the ball alley.'

There was some unexpected fallout when attention was drawn to certain players' hurleys during the draw. Seán Óg Ó hAilpín, Paul Codd and Damien Fitzhenry had had the Paddy Power logo on their sticks, and there were some suggestions of suspensions for stealth advertising.

'I've nearly forgotten that,' says Ó hAilpín. 'Paddy Power approached us to put the logo on the hurleys, but there were a good few players approached—from Kilkenny, Tipperary and Wexford, the other semi-finalists.

'When we heard there were a few guys we felt better about it. We never saw any controversy coming up. There was a few quid in it, but afterwards there was consternation; there were people saying we'd be thrown out of the championship.

'Donal didn't have a problem with it. If he'd come to me and said, this is an issue, I'd have said, no problem. Other managers would have pulled it, but in a way that showed us that O'Grady was on the side of the players.

'Setanta was supposed to play with a branded hurley, but he didn't. As a 20-year old we felt he was better off without the pressure. But the publicity Paddy Power got out of it, you couldn't buy that.'

The controversy fizzled out, memorable only for Codd's characterisation of those criticising the sponsorship as 'tinkers and rogues'.

The replay had its highlights, but an early Timmy McCarthy goal set Cork on their way to victory—an illegal goal, as McCarthy himself admits.

'Niall dropped the hurley for my goal; it should have been disallowed. Wexford were going well enough that year. Whatever else happened that year, we were never going to give up; we weren't going to die on our feet.

'We were super-fit, so it was a case of keeping going for the result. And fitness has really been a big part of this team's success. You'd always know with ten, fifteen minutes left that you'd be able to keep going flat out. You'd never think, I'll take it easy for ten minutes here to save myself for later. You could keep going flat out all the time; you knew you could keep going. Seán and Jerry were terrific that way, so professional.'

There were obvious drawbacks for Cork facing into the final. The two Wexford games didn't quite equal Kilkenny's familiarity with Jones's Road.

'That's a downside of not being in a final regularly,' says Ó hAilpín. 'Comparing 2003 to 2006, people were used to Cork being in the final by 2006. In 2003 it was new to a lot of lads, and it had been four or five years since we'd been there. For instance, I remember having a fry the morning of the 1999 final. In 2003 that was gone—porridge for breakfast, and so on.'

His manager agrees.

'Cork hadn't been there for a couple of years,' says O'Grady. 'Kilkenny, I always felt, had an advantage in playing in Croke Park so much. They knew the place, they knew all the officials; it has to be an advantage to play in the stadium that much.'

The pressure was real. Though Gardiner praises O'Grady for minding his players as much as he could—'He told us not to answer our phones, to run interviews through a selector and keep the younger players away from the media'—not everything could be covered. Cusack and his captain had an unnecessary disagreement the week of the final, for instance. 'Alan Browne said to me that week that I should be the proudest man in Croke Park the day of the final. The week before there was an article in one of the Sunday papers and Alan had said a few things.

'I genuinely liked him, and I'd always have had him on the Cork team, but I rang him and gave out to him. And he said sorry, but then he was upset, and I was upset that he was upset, and if I'd known he'd get that upset I'd have maybe left it.'

And on the day, one late malfunction cost Cork. O'Grady still regrets it.

'We were given a time to come out, 3.06 pm or 3.04 pm, I can't remember which. So the way we worked, we tailored everything back from the 3.30 throw-in. Having looked at other finals, we factored in the time to meet the President, the anthems and so on. That all took about eight minutes. So eight minutes before the game your preparation was finished—you couldn't tell the President you wouldn't meet her because you were off working on your sideline cuts.

'The last speech was given, we were ready to go, and as we were letting them out, the stewards held us back in the tunnel. There was an Irish Nationwide presentation being made to the brothers who'd played in All-Ireland finals or whatever, and they were lined up in front of the tunnel. Either you'd have had to go through them or around them to get to the field.'

O'Grady had a split-second decision to make. His reasoning was that a player might run into a person on the field, or get injured getting tangled up in tv cables.

'We had to hold them for a couple of minutes. That upset lads because emotionally they were ready to burst out onto the field. We were blocked, and once they got out they were a bit *trí na chéile*. We'd usually spend a bit of time hitting the ball over the bar or taking 65s before going into the actual warm-up, and maybe that came against us in the game, the fact that we didn't put in that time before the warm-up.

'It was the one thing, when you sat down at the end of the year, the one thing that went wrong for us. Every other thing had been planned for. It was the one thing that caught us. We were only out when Kilkenny came out. We were supposed to come on and get our photo taken, but when we got on the field, Kilkenny came out and got their picture taken, so we were put out a bit.'

It wasn't the only blow. O'Grady's full back had burst out onto the field a little too quickly.

'I pulled my hamstring going out on the field,' says Diarmuid O'Sullivan. 'We were mad for it, and I remember running out and then . . . it upset me, definitely.'

'We definitely played the occasion in 2003, particularly in the first half,' says Ó hAilpín. 'We'd prepared well, but we had a bad start. That showed the nerves.'

Kilkenny settled quickly, while Cork struggled. Tom Kenny, for instance, was on a hurler-of-the-year run of form until the final. His last game of the year would provide a slightly different challenge: marking Tommy Walsh, an acquaintance from UCC.

'At the time we'd have been friendly enough,' says Kenny. 'It didn't bother me that I'd be marking him, and knowing Tommy, it wouldn't have bothered him either.'

Walsh wired into the game with three quick points to set Kilkenny on their way.

'The first fifteen minutes were tough all right,' says Kenny. 'I remember the first ball. It broke out to midfield and I should have gone for it with Tommy. The second ball I got drawn into a challenge and he got the ball popped out to him and scored. The third point was a great score; I'd hold my hand up.

'After that I went to midfield, and I remember I got two chances and if I got them now I think I'd have scored. I passed one off and I got blocked. That's experience. You could put it down to that first fifteen minutes, even though I should have put it out of my head.'

Timmy McCarthy doesn't beat about the bush on the reason Cork lost.

'Eighteen wides, yeah. Things didn't go, frees didn't go over. But if we'd won that, we mightn't have won another one. We didn't take a goal chance or two; we only got a couple of points in the first half . . . it was brutal.

'There was a lot of pressure on; we'd been on strike; we were expected to win and we probably put too much pressure on ourselves and worked ourselves into a tizz about it.'

The manager tried to work them out of that tizz. Ó hAilpín remembers dreading the half-time break, as the Cork players headed for the dressing room six points adrift.

'Usually when we'd played well, O'Grady would feck us out of it at half-time. We were expecting a lambasting. But it was the opposite. "I'm going to say something strange," he said. "You're playing well, but unfortunately that's not showing on the scoreboard. Ye've had all the possession. Compose yourselves; that's what we've been telling ye all year."'

He calmed them. When Cork returned for the second half, they improved and started chipping away with points, while Kilkenny found it harder to get scores.

'Wayne Sherlock marked Eddie Brennan out of it; Pat Mul was doing very well on DJ and we had them on the back foot,' says Ó hAilpín. Then his younger brother picked a Kilkenny pocket and bore down on Hill 16: goal.

'Setanta's goal brought us right back,' says Ó hAilpín Sr. 'We were like one big engine moving, but after that we had a couple of chances that we missed. Setanta maintains one of his shots went over the bar but was waved wide; another thing was the Kilkenny selector who threw a hurley at Setanta from the Hill 16 end, and nothing was ever made of it.

'When you have Kilkenny on the rack, you have to take your chances. And we didn't.'

Niall McCarthy hit the post and Kilkenny broke upfield. They worked the ball to Martin Comerford—'it bounced over me,' says Ronan Curran—and he closed on goal, presenting the defence with a dilemma.

'I would have come out to Comerford, but Seán Óg was coming to him,' says Cusack. 'Now that's not Seán Óg's fault, because he was meant to come to him, but I stopped.'

'Comerford finished the game,' says Ó hAilpín. 'He got the ball and I got a half-block on it, and the ball just passed Donal Óg at the near post. If he'd hit it properly Donal Óg would have saved it, but the ricochet took it past him. He was moving the other way.'

His goalkeeper had been caught in no man's land.

'Comerford went to strike the ball across me,' says Cusack. 'I moved my weight to go that way, but Seán Óg got a bit of it, and I had to change my weight. It bounced, I went for it and didn't stop it.

'It looked a bit of a jammy goal, and it was, and I said it to them at the All-Stars [in 2007] that Eddie Brennan's goal against Limerick was the same, but Brian Cody said to me that night, "We practise those in Kilkenny."'

The county final in 1997 stood to Cusack at that stage; he settled himself, retrieved the sliotar and drove on, but the comeback had been deflated. The game had gone from Cork.

'I hadn't a great year in 2003,' says Cusack. 'I got a lot of criticism that was deserved. Now a lot of it was magnified by the strike, but a lot of it was justified. But honestly, I just picked the ball up and looked for the next target.'

For Cusack—for all of them—the disappointment was visceral.

'It's desperate. It's so bad that if I was trying to rest in the morning and the match comes into my head, I'd have to get up out of bed. It would torment you.'

Tom Kenny's college mate sought him out.

'Tommy came over to me afterwards, in fairness,' says Kenny. 'In 2004 I went over to him, because in fairness he'd done it for me. It's only right to go and talk to lads.'

'We'd lost games as a group before, but this was heartbreaking because we knew we had a chance,' says Ó hAilpín. 'If it had carried on like the first half we'd have had no complaints. We weren't good enough, but it was there for the taking.

'We got in a huddle in the middle of the field and Donal Óg said, "Can that feeling that you have today and I've no doubt we'll be back next year." And that was the start of 2004.'

O'Grady spent the winter dissecting the defeat.

'You could say this, that or the other, but we didn't play well in the first half. Maybe we lacked a bit of composure. If you look at how that game went, we were six points down at half-time. We'd missed some easy enough chances, but halfway through the first half we'd had a few chances that fellas maybe only half-went for.

'Setanta had had a good goal chance and could have stepped across his man, the way we practised in training, but he didn't. We were beaten in the end, but at least in the second half the crowd got their money's worth. We got to a winning position but couldn't press it home. We hit the post and when the ball came back we didn't have someone on the break . . . Afterwards the players knew it; they were thinking, we should have won that one.'

'The way I look back on it now is the two games on either side of our three-in-a-row bid,' says Ronan Curran, 'the finals in 2003 and 2006. In 2006 we weren't near them; they were too hungry and we didn't look like we had that extra gear.

'But in 2003 the bit of inexperience hurt us; there were one or two things that went against us. We hit the post, in defence we left them through for a goal, and while I'm not saying we should have won it, we had the chances. Kilkenny won on the day, but it's a regret that we didn't win that year.'

Pat Mulcahy agrees with his centre back: 'If we made any mistake we overestimated them. It was an adventure; pressure wasn't a huge factor, but we definitely overestimated them. It was a game we should have won, one that got away.

'We were all over them; we got within a point, and then maybe showed a little naïvete. They got a poxy goal and it was all over. It was O'Grady's first year too, and we definitely weren't the finished article. The following year, and 2005, we were playing as more of a team. We were more individualistic in 2003, maybe, in the forwards; we passed the ball around better the following two years.'

There was one more disappointment left in 2003. O'Grady hadn't made up his mind to stay on as manager, but early in October he got a phone call from team statistician Eddie O'Donnell asking if he'd decided.

'I said I hadn't, and Eddie said there might be some news that might influence the decision.'

Setanta rang O'Grady and met him in the Commons Bar. He had

been offered a professional Australian Rules contract with Carlton and was going to accept it.

'I just wished him good luck,' says O'Grady. 'I might have said to him to consider his options, but he wanted to go. One of the other teachers in the school told me subsequently that whenever Setanta had written Irish essays about what he'd like to do as an adult, he'd always mentioned Aussie Rules, or professional sport at any rate. He wouldn't have had any problem getting a job in Cork, but I wished him the best and said I hoped he'd get on well.

'But it was a blow. He was a player who could conjure up a goal. If he was one on one with the keeper, more often than not he'd get a goal, and you're always looking for a finisher like that.

'Alan Browne was gone as well, and he was another big loss. People didn't give him enough credit, but he was a great player. He contested everything and fellas didn't see the work he did. In 2003 Joe Deane had a great game against Clare in the first round, for instance, but Alan Browne stayed in on the edge of the square for that game and Brian Lohan was pulled and dragged everywhere. People didn't appreciate that. We'd had a good balance in the full forward line in 2003, so that was a blow facing into the next year.'

The news filtered through in different ways. John Gardiner and his Na Piarsaigh club mates had been training for a football league final that winter when the Ó hAilpíns came to training one evening with an Aussie Rules ball.

'We were saying, yes boy, we'll have a game of Aussie Rules here for a bit of a change. So we were thumping each other around the hall in Na Piarsaigh for a couple of weeks and then the lads go off to Australia. They were training with us!

'He was a huge loss. And he was my buddy as well. All of a sudden he was gone. He was a huge loss to Cork, not to mind Na Piarsaigh.'

'I saw Setanta one Friday. He was getting a lot of throat infections at the time and I said he needed his tonsils taken out the next week,' says Dr Con Murphy. 'The next thing he was in Melbourne! We all wished him luck but he was a huge loss. He was the most exciting thing to hit Cork since JBM. He had a huge future, and suddenly he's gone. I remember thinking, this is a disaster for us, but obviously I wished him well.'

Donal Óg Cusack had had his suspicions.

'I had an idea. Now I feel more sorry than I did in 2003, 2004. The odd time now I'd think, it's a pity he didn't stay, but I was happy he was doing it. I still am, though it would have been great to see how he'd have developed as a hurler. But I wrote him a letter wishing him all the best. We were all genuinely delighted for him.'

Setanta's older brother says now that it wasn't a clear-cut decision.

'It was tricky for him, deciding what to do. He'll tell people it was a great opportunity, but it was a toss of a coin whether he'd go to Australia or not. We'd discussed the pros and cons, and he didn't see his life out there at that stage. He'd had a good 2003 with Cork and saw that as a start, but he decided in the end, "I won't get the chance again so I'm giving it a go; if it doesn't work out I'll come back and take up where I left off. Otherwise I'll never know."

'That was the deciding factor. He met O'Grady for a chat because he felt he owed it to him. O'Grady said he didn't want him to go because he was a vital part of the squad, but he wished him well if that was his choice. And Setanta said he'd never forget O'Grady for that.

'He was a few days in Australia before it came out, but that was enough. If it had come out before that, they'd have bombed Cork Airport! I know some people still resent the fact that he left. Some people said, fair play, but others said he was leaving Cork down. But he hasn't regretted his choice at all.

'The reality is that we won two All-Irelands without him, and if people were hurt when he left, it was far more hurtful to him to see us win two All-Irelands without him while he was getting the shit kicked out of him in a new sport. He came back for the 2004 final and I knew he was questioning his decision, but he's living his dream now.'

His club mate put down a scratchy Christmas. Everywhere John Gardiner turned in Cork he felt a jab.

'I got more stick that winter than anyone else. Fellas say it jokingly, and you laugh along, but it's not funny. Every fella thinks he's the first to say it, but when you hear it over and over again . . .

'We were over Kilkenny that day and they were lucky to come out with a win. Obviously they played well, but we owned the ball in the first half, particularly me. I'd say I played more ball in that game than I ever did.

'Fellas say it to me about missing all the frees that day. I took three frees, but I missed four shots out of my hand. Everybody was the same, missing frees in front of goal, things you'd never do again. If we'd had those chances a year later we'd have won, stupid though that might be to say. Kilkenny were good, though, and they had the experience.

'I did more training that winter than any other year, though, I was so keen to get back into it. If you feel you've left something behind you, then you want to have another go at it.'

That winter O'Sullivan and Gardiner appeared on the *Final Words* TV programme, which looked back over the hurling season. One of the scenes replayed showed O'Sullivan bursting past Kilkenny attackers like skittles.

'At the time that was maybe a motivational thing,' says O'Sullivan. 'It was just part and parcel of the game. When we were contacted for *Final Words*, it was hard to do. The only thing was that that show made John Gardiner look desperate, and he'd played very well for us that year. Things didn't go right for him in the final, and I thought they were trying to knock a young fella's career.

'That motivated us in 2004, the interviews and scenes they showed in that. That drove us on.'

## 2004 (1) ∿

# YOU WON'T DROP ME AGAIN

O'Grady didn't see the team for a while. He didn't go on the team holiday, and speculation mounted that he mightn't come back as manager, but he did. There was unfinished business.

'I'd like to have had the time back before the 2003 final,' he says. 'I'd have left them out instead of holding them back. That was the only thing I'd have changed about the whole year. You'd learn a lot in the time you're manager, obviously.'

Some things hadn't changed, however.

'In 2004 the first hurling session we had was in Pairc Uí Rinn,' says Diarmuid O'Sullivan. 'Wet, miserable day, every fella's touch very poor that early in the year. And O'Grady called us in and said my touch was poor! I asked if my touch was worse than anyone else's . . .'

The two had another shouting match in front of the group. O'Grady put the drill back on, then called O'Sullivan over and issued the full back a frank appraisal of their working relation-ship.

'He said, "Look, this is my last year, like it or not, so we can try to get on with each other or we can carry on like this. You don't have to like me and I don't have to like you. We'll leave it like that." It was fine after that.

'There was no negotiating, no messing. I definitely matured as a player because of him. He brought a lot of us back down to earth.'

Early on in the year, O'Grady also addressed the All-Ireland final goal Donal Óg Cusack had conceded.

'He came up to me and said, "I've watched it about a hundred times and I can't fault you for it,"' says Cusack. 'He said that to me over by the red gate in Pairc Uí Rinn. I remember thinking, that's great, and then I thought, I'm going to pay this man back.'

On the basis that a rising tide lifts all boats. the signs were good early on. Newtownshandrum rattled through to an All-Ireland club final victory, and their county players enjoyed being spared the early-season drudgery of stamina training with Cork.

'I'd say 2004 was probably the best year,' says Ben O'Connor, 'not because we won two All-Irelands in one year, but because we had no pre-season. There was no hard slog in January, February and March for us, and while we were involved in the club campaign, O'Grady told us we didn't have to come in to county training. "We don't want to see ye any more now."

'After Patrick's Day he gave us another four weeks off after that. He knew we wouldn't lose a lot of fitness in that length of time, and that was the best way to deal with it.'

The manager had more pressing concerns on his mind. Replacing Setanta Ó hAilpín was the challenge early that year.

O'Grady had worked with Brian Corcoran when Jimmy Barry-Murphy had brought him in as a backs coach in 1997. He'd gotten to know the Erin's Own player and felt he got on well with him, and 2004 wasn't the first time he'd tried to talk Corcoran out of retirement.

'I wouldn't say we went after him, but I'd rung him in 2003,' says O'Grady. 'There were rumours that time he was coming back, but he'd said then he wasn't. Then he came back to Erin's Own, and when I rang him to see if he was available for Cork, he said he was but he didn't want to play in the backs.'

O'Grady wasn't interested in using Corcoran as a defender; he just wanted to see how close the player was to match fitness. Erin's Own were playing Killeagh in Pairc Uí Rinn, so the selectors went to see Corcoran. The backroom team saw enough to suggest he might have something to offer the team, even if the rust was obvious.

'Having lost Setanta, Corcoran coming back was huge,' says Dr Con Murphy. 'I'd regard him as the player who contributed most to Cork in my time since 1976. Setanta was great crack, he had sex appeal for the team . . . he'd put on his Fitzgibbon Cup jersey then throw on his Cork jersey—of course, he wouldn't fit in either of them now—but having Corcoran come back was a huge boost.'

The players agreed.

'We needed something big to replace Setanta,' says Ronan Curran. 'I'd say it's understated what Corcoran meant to us. He was our hero when we were growing up. Of course, you can only imagine what it would have been like with the two of them, Setanta and Corcoran.'

'We'd played and won All-Irelands with him,' says Diarmuid O'Sullivan, 'but it was huge for the likes of Tom, Niall Mc, lads who'd never played with him. What he brought to the dressing room was huge presence. He knew how to say the right thing at the right time.'

Corcoran was brought on against Waterford in the league and got a great reception. Then there was the challenge game against Clare. If the Tipperary challenge games were harbingers of doom in 1999, this was far better news.

'A lovely sunny Saturday in Ennis, and that marked the return of Corcoran for me,' says Seán Óg Ó hAilpín. 'He got 3–2 off Brian Lohan and I was thinking, he's back on song.'

'He was excellent that day,' says O'Grady. 'He did well coming on against Limerick in the championship, and he was on the team from then on.'

Apart from Corcoran's return, however, one miscalculation early in the year would have far-reaching consequences.

'During the first period of the league that year,' says O'Grady, 'we didn't want lads on the bench all year, so we gave panellists a chance in every match and we got into the second phase of the league, but we had no training done by April. We had to give the players back to the clubs.

'Against Limerick we just wanted to get through, but because we'd missed out on April our fitness was off against Waterford.'

A late score conceded against Limerick—shades of 1998—took the gloss off the scoreline, but for one player it was a special day. Brian Murphy made his debut alongside the men he'd worshipped.

'You'd think someone like Sully wouldn't get nervous before a game, that they all just walk out, but everyone gets nervous,' says Murphy. 'For me the big thing was Brian Corcoran; he was the be-all and end-all to me growing up, and I never thought I'd talk to the man, not to mind play with him.

'I remember Wayne was outstanding. He, Sully and Donal Óg got me through the game really. Times you'd need it, they'd be encouraging you constantly, keeping you on your toes and concentrating.'

Despite a full stadium, Murphy could hear Sherlock's encouragement across the pitch. The new man settled well; O'Grady wasn't too surprised.

'He has great speed, strong, but above all he has great balance. The man he'd be marking, no matter what he does, Murphy can set himself straightaway and not lose his stride. His balance is superb.'

He'd taken a while to settle into the group, by his own admission.

'I was playing corner back in the Fitzgibbon with CIT,' Murphy says, 'but Ronan Curran was centre back, and he was immense. I was looking at him and saying, he's miles ahead of me; I'm years away—if at all. Fitzgibbon was about as good as it got for me at that time.

'For me the pressure was in training three or four days a week. That was a huge change after training two or three days a week, and not training that hard at that. I used to take days off college and go to sleep for the day after it.

'I wasn't used to it. Obviously it's a big eye-opener, inter-county senior training. The big mistake I made was going flat out, say, in the very first sprint at training. You'd learn to pace yourself a little bit, but at the start you'd see Seán Óg ten yards ahead of you; you'd be starting to panic a little bit. You play against these guys in club games and you realise they're fit, but you only realise just how fit they are when you see the work they're putting in.

'The real killer was the way it caught up on you. After Tuesday you'd be fairly okay, sore, but then on Thursday you'd train as hard, then there was Friday or Saturday . . . Seán McGrath was a brilliant trainer, but at the time he was the hardest man in the world.'

Murphy would need all his reserves for the Munster final. Waterford were a different prospect to Limerick. More settled than they'd been in 2003, they'd survived a scorching day in Pairc Uí Chaoimh against Tipperary and were ready for Cork. The game would enter the pantheon of Munster finals.

Cork began well with a bobbling shot from debutant Garvan McCarthy creeping under Stephen Brenner's hurley, and it soon became a game for the ages.

'We started in a whirlwind,' says Seán Óg Ó hAilpín. 'We got a lucky goal but Tom was flying, the points were going over. But they got goals at vital times: Eoin Kelly got a goal; Dan Shanahan got a goal.'

His fellow wing back had his hands full.

'I was switched over to left half back on Dan Shanahan and they started raining ball down on him,' says John Gardiner. 'There were scores going over that day that were incredible; it was a hundred miles an hour.'

'We played superb hurling in the first half,' says O'Grady, 'but one crucial decision went against us. Corcoran had the ball and Ben O'Connor was inside him, and as Corcoran was just about to pass, the referee gave a free against him. I couldn't understand why, but if Ben had got that goal . . . Still, we were four points up, having played against a strong breeze.'

Soon after the resumption there was a brief row in front of the Cork goal, and John Mullane got a red card. Waterford looked there for the taking, until Paul Flynn steadied the ship. Standing over a free forty yards out, the Waterford star lined up his shot.

'I honestly thought he was going for a point,' says Ó hAilpín. 'It didn't seem a rocket of a shot—and Flynn can whack it when he wants—but we weren't expecting it.'

Flynn's dipping shot flew into the right-hand corner of the net and the crowd exulted.

'I didn't think he'd go for it either,' says Brian Murphy. 'I thought he was too far out, but he had the balls to try it. It was a fantastic shot; it had dip and swerve. It changed the game totally.

'And they played better in the second half. Whether it was the psychological thing of having a man down or what, the longer the game went on, we didn't play with cohesion. We were pucking the ball long and waiting on the breaks. I could see it slipping away from us.'

'The funny thing is this,' says Diarmuid O'Sullivan. 'The way he was lining it up, you half-knew he was going for it, where Shanahan stood . . . Flynn is incredible. He's not in the game and then in a minute he has 1–2.'

As O'Grady puts it, Cork's mentality slipped a little. Waterford stayed in touch and Seamus Prendergast gave them a two-point lead with time running out. Tom Kenny pointed, but Cork's last attack died in Ken McGrath's left hand. The Waterford star was fouled coming out, and that was that.

'The biggest problem was we had a game plan and we didn't stick to it—draw the man, give it on,' says O'Sullivan. 'We didn't do that; we hit the ball long. If we'd drawn the man and moved it on we'd have done better. Dropping the game plan cost us. When Mullane was put off, we felt we could do what we liked, but we didn't.'

'We lost by a point,' says Murphy. 'But it was going for a long time beforehand.'

'The momentum of the game shifted,' says Joe Deane. 'They took all their chances, they hooked and harried and blocked. It faded away from us and we couldn't get to grips with it. In the circumstances it was one of the greatest comebacks of all time, and one of Waterford's greatest wins.'

O'Grady gave the opposition full credit: 'Fair play to Waterford; they won fair and square. We couldn't get back into it. When a fella is sent off, decisions always seem to go against you. We had chances in the last few minutes but fellas lost their composure a little bit. Kieran Murphy, who'd been injured, came on and made a great run, but when he passed to Ben it was intercepted.'

'You didn't know what was going to happen in that game,' says Ronan Curran. 'It's like, we got a goal, we're on top, hold it out. They get a goal and it's back to square one . . . You're thinking, what the hell's going on here? As a back you'd prefer to be involved in dull, boring games, maybe, but looking back on that one, it's good to have played in it.'

Brian Murphy might have been public enemy No. 1 to Waterford fans after the entanglement with Mullane, but they didn't have a face for the wanted poster. The irony was that a lynch mob wouldn't have had too far to look, either. Murphy's girlfriend was from Dunhill and he spent the following days in the heartland of the Deise. 'I went down to the Spraoi in Waterford the week afterwards. Sure there wasn't one person recognised me; there was no bother.'

It was different at home. Cork weren't criticised for defeat; they were crucified.

'We were criticised after the game about the extra man, but that was stupid,' says O'Grady. 'It's the opposition which decides who the extra man is, and they decided to leave Diarmuid O'Sullivan loose. You can't afford to go with five backs, because that creates space for the opposition attack, which is just what they want.

'There was a huge backlash in the papers and on the radio, fellas giving out about Timmy McCarthy. Someone said to me it was because it was he was tall, he had a white helmet and was always near the crowd because he was a wing forward.

'We didn't play him the following match. Maybe that was good in hindsight, because he was fired up then when he came on, but I spoke to him about it before the Tipp game. But the criticism . . . Some people's loyalty to Cork is based on a few bob on the team or whatever.'

The practicalities weren't straightforward either. The qualifier with Tipperary was fixed for Killarney, and O'Grady explains how that happened.

'We'd been out on the steps of the Anner Hotel after the Munster final and Frank [Murphy] said we were drawn against Tipp; what would we want?

'The last game of the home and away arrangement had been the 2000 Munster final, so I presumed it was Pairc Uí Chaoimh. Failing that, I proposed a toss, but we weren't going to come back to Thurles. Frank came back later and said they weren't agreeable, that they wouldn't toss. I think Tipp felt Cork wasn't a good hunting ground for them, and they suggested Limerick. I said we wouldn't go there, so I suggested Killarney.

'It went to the Munster Council, but I knew our supporters would get to Killarney. They were used to going to football games there compared to the Tipp crowd.'

The team had a crucial training session after losing the Munster final that got them back on track.

'We had a heart-to-heart team meeting the Wednesday night after the Munster final,' says Ó hAilpín. 'O'Grady said, "The other games don't matter, they were half-pace; the championship starts now." Of course, we were thinking, Christ, we trained hard for those half-pace games.'

Ever mindful of the tempo at training, Joe Deane took solace in the preparations for the Tipperary game.

'The quality of the sessions after the Munster final convinced me we had a good chance. I felt we should have beaten Waterford. We'd been better than them for three-quarters of the match and a lack of killer instinct had cost us. We wouldn't have been afraid to play Waterford the following week, for instance.'

Travelling to Killarney the week before the game was part of the preparations.

'We did a bit of ballwork and so on at the same time we'd be playing,' says O'Grady. 'The pitch was desperate, I remember, and the groundsman told us which dressing room we'd be in. There was a big bath in the other room and I asked if we could use it for recovery, but your man told us no. Ken [Hogan] had been down and had booked that one.

'Then he asked if I'd noticed the scoreboard, and when I looked he had Tipp's name on top. Now he probably thought it was a big psychological advantage to Tipp, but I just said what counted on the scoreboard was the numbers after the team names. He wasn't too impressed with that.'

O'Grady's predictions about the Tipperary turnout came true. Thousands didn't make the game and were turned back by traffic jams coming into Killarney. The game itself was held up by twenty minutes to accommodate latecomers, and when it began the coach was vindicated further.

'As we finished our puck-around, I asked Kieran Murphy to go and take a few shots from a specific part of the field, and to pack it in when he was finished,' says O'Grady. 'The first ball that came to him in the game itself, of course, was the exact same spot, so afterwards I was able to say to him what great coaching he'd gotten. He gave a *tour de force* that day, in fairness.'

Wayne Sherlock was assigned to Tipperary wizard Eoin Kelly.

'I asked Wayne to mind Kelly in Killarney,' says O'Grady. 'I told him specifically to keep Kelly outside him; no matter how many points he got he wasn't to be given a chance of a goal. It's like DJ Carey with Kilkenny—if Eoin Kelly gets a goal for Tipperary, it's huge psychologically.'

The drama built up even before the throw-in. Donal Óg Cusack was suffering with a muscle tear in his chest.

'I'd already had an injection that week and friendly as I am with Dr Con, I know there was nothing in that injection,' says Cusack. 'That morning I felt I was in trouble, and I knew O'Grady was very anti-injections, but for the Tipp game I asked Dr Con not to tell Donal because he mightn't play me.'

The medic brought Cusack into a toilet cubicle and gave him the injection, and the goalkeeper's pain subsided as he took the field.

A tense game came to life just before half-time.

'The Tipperary penalty . . .' says O'Grady. 'We put a lot of planning into defending penalties, but one section of the plan broke down. I can't remember who was supposed to be in that part of the field, but they weren't there.

'But I didn't mind so much, genuinely, because we'd stopped the penalty. The goal was a scrappy enough affair, but the important thing was Donal Óg's save from Eoin Kelly.'

Then there was the row.

'Jerry got a late belt,' recalls Ronan Curran. 'He's such a big player for us, everyone was up for the game after the meeting, so we all got involved. It was a sign that maybe we weren't going to get pushed around. We might have felt that maybe Kilkenny pushed us around a little the previous year, so we were standing up for each other.'

'When Jerry got the slap, it was miles late and he and the Tipp player were both out over the line,' says O'Grady. 'There was some argy-bargy. It was old-style Cork and Tipp. Up to then the match was a bit *lag*; the crowd weren't involved. Both teams were trying not to lose the game in the first half, but the shemozzle knocked the shackles off. We were four down at the break and it was all hands to the pump.'

Another significant development came before half-time. Diarmuid O'Sullivan was driving along the sideline with the ball when John Carroll arrived with a thunderous shoulder. O'Sullivan went down, but bounced straight back up.

'He steamrolled me that day out on the wing,' says O'Sullivan. 'If I'd stayed down on the ground, it would have been huge, so I struggled back into the square for the penalty.'

'If I'd been John Carroll I'd have done the same,' says O'Grady. 'Diarmuid was open and he went for it.'

When Cork got into the dressing room at the break, O'Sullivan collapsed.

'When I went in at half-time I just fell on the floor of the dressing room,' says the full back. 'I just had to try to get myself together for the second half.'

Aside from the drama the atmosphere was good, however.

'At half-time we were four or five down, but it was the most relaxed dressing room I was ever in,' says Brian Murphy. 'Fellas really believed we could do it. O'Grady said he was a lot happier in that dressing room than he'd been at the break in the Munster final, even though we'd been winning that game. Fellas had a better attitude in the Tipp game. We realised it was up to us and nobody else.'

Diarmuid O'Sullivan offered a response to his marker early in the second half.

'Just after the second half started, Carroll put his hand up and I said to myself, well now, Jack, and let fly, and he was taken off,' says O'Sullivan. 'In fairness to Carroll, he'll take it and give it, but he knew there'd be payback coming.'

'I thought Diarmuid was immense in the second half,' says O'Grady. 'He came out with some terrific ball to relieve the pressure.

'People have a notion of Diarmuid being rough and tough or whatever, but he's a very good hurler, very refined. We'd done a lot of work on tackling properly, and at one stage he tackled Benny

Dunne just as we'd practised, did it brilliantly and came away with the ball—and Barry Kelly penalised him.'

With the game in the balance, the Hollywood script was enacted. Timmy McCarthy came on.

'I've been criticised from time to time,' says McCarthy. 'It's annoying, but it's worse for your family and friends. It's there and you have to accept it—it's not going to disappear now. I got a fair bit after the Munster final that year, but it was more hurtful for my family and friends. I can't hear it, but you'd hear it afterwards, read it in the papers. It doesn't bother me that much, but it would affect you at times.'

Inevitably, it was McCarthy who buried the game's decisive goal. His namesake Niall added another to put the icing on the cake, but the take-home memory from the game was Timmy McCarthy's wicked shot. And his celebration. He doesn't hide the satisfaction: it was sweet.

'That was definitely two fingers up to a lot of people. I was thrilled. I enjoyed that goal. Sometimes you could hurl a lot of ball without scoring and people don't realise, while they think you had a great game if you got the ball twice and got two points.'

'It was a huge win,' says Diarmuid O'Sullivan. 'When Timmy came off after that he said to one of the selectors, "You won't drop me again."'

After the game the players refused to speak to the media. Not a management call, says O'Grady.

'It wasn't, and I got some stick about it. The players felt that the loss to Waterford was personalised. I never asked them about it, but it stemmed from the fact that the year before they were getting calls at work from different people. We'd brought in a system to regulate requests for interviews, with allotted time to set up interviews.

'In Killarney John Motherway, then the PRO, said the press was outside. I went out and took questions.

'The players decided not to speak as a group. They got no prompting from me. The way we worked was that if a player came to us and said, such-and-such is on to me to talk to him, what'll I do? And I'd say, do you want to talk to him? If not, then don't.

'It's an evolutionary thing. A fella is 18, 19 and he feels under pressure; he's 25 and he's loquacious; and then he's 30 and he's sick of the whole thing. A lot of the time the reporter prints the interview exactly as he got it, but the headline may be different. Fellas who have a bad experience when they're young may get a turn against it.

'My opinion was that if a fella was willing to give interviews, then fair enough; players were getting commercial opportunities, and I was in favour of them making the most of those opportunities.'

The players had been wounded by the post-Munster final onslaught of criticism. John Gardiner gives their view: 'You go out to win a game, and it was the first time I saw the papers go through fellas one by one. Timmy got slated, Curran got slated, and we thought it was a disgrace.

'Every decision made is made with the agreement of every single player. It's not one guy deciding and telling everyone else what to do. A player will say something, we discuss it, and if right is right it all comes out.

'The most important thing is what's best for the team. That time we felt the best thing to do—for us to win an All-Ireland—was not to talk to the press and not to get distracted. They can write what they want. We believed that at the time and that's what we did.'

'It was incredible,' says Diarmuid O'Sullivan. 'I refuse to listen to a certain Cork radio station because of that time. Some of the comments read out were incredible. And these are people who'd expect you to give them an interview then afterwards! It wasn't criticism. It was degrading. It was hurtful to fellas.

'I'm convinced there's only about ten to fifteen per cent of the people in Croke Park who are genuine Cork fans—families of players, people who go to league games and so on. The rest of them feel they're entitled to say what they want on the basis of going to one or two games.'

'I wouldn't have been conscious of the criticism,' says Joe Deane.

'I wouldn't read the papers before and after games we're involved in, because some writers you'd think, well, he has some idea of what he's talking about, but a lot of them haven't a clue. I didn't read the papers that time. We were disappointed because winning the All-Ireland was all that was acceptable to both us and the public, and that loss made it harder.'

Not all the players were party to the silent treatment. Donal Óg Cusack and Seán Óg Ó hAilpín had been sequestered away in Fitzgerald Stadium for drug testing. It didn't mean their manager had forgotten them.

'The two of us were in the room for the test with two Tipp players when O'Grady arrived in,' says Cusack. 'He took over the room. He questioned everyone as to who they were, he questioned the drug testers about their credentials, he said he wanted a Garda escort for the players back to the hotel, and there was an escort there for us when we finished.'

The criticism hadn't ended with victory over Tipperary. Donal Óg Cusack had been targeted by howling fans in Fitzgerald Stadium looking for long puck-outs. The keeper had the self-belief to ignore them; his family couldn't avoid it.

'The day in Killarney, my sister was fierce upset. My aunts couldn't get over it. My housemate's fiancée asked him to go down to tell me to puck the ball out long. O'Grady believed in that system, and if he believed in it, I was going to carry it out. But I could sense that people wanted me to drive it out long.'

'We didn't see the puck-out as just restarting the game,' says O'Grady. 'We saw it as our first attack, and obviously you'd hit the ball to where you'd have an advantage. We got desperate flak because one puck-out was intercepted, but you have to live with that. If you lose one or two, so what? It's still better than just lashing the ball up into the air for the defender to bat it forty yards back down the field.'

Timmy McCarthy is generous in evaluating the flak O'Grady refers to.

'Puck-outs are planned. We've done the short game to bring

teams forward and so on. But people aren't going to understand half the tactics. A lot of people are just casual supporters or in the corporate box, and they're needed as well. It's a game for everyone. And if they can't follow everything, that's fine too. It's a pastime, after all.'

# WHAT'S DINNY DONE TO US?

Motivation was never going to be an issue for a Cork-Tipp clash, but Cork drew Antrim in the quarter-finals. O'Grady spent a week wondering what he'd say to his players to motivate them, and the players were as worried as the manager. Joe Deane recalls warning people he met that Antrim were going to beat someone sometime, and being answered with scepticism when he suggested that it might be Cork.

Antrim had done well against Tipperary the previous year, and O'Grady feared an ambush. Then, as Deane says, Cork prayers were answered.

'On the Wednesday I got a phone call from [team logistics manager] Jim McEvoy to read the paper,' O'Grady says. 'He said that my worries about what to say to the players had been sorted out by Dinny Cahill.'

Cahill, the Antrim manager, had launched an amazing attack on Niall McCarthy and Brian Corcoran. He said Corcoran was past it and that that would be proved during the game. Criticising McCarthy, one of the most popular players on the panel, didn't go down well either.

'We were expecting to win, everything was lax and we were going through the motions in training,' says Ronan Curran. 'Then everything changed. I can't understand it. The fellas he got onto— Corcoran is a legend to us and Niall is one of the most respected lads on the team. That night at training Donal O'Grady said it to us. The session went really well and everyone was up for it.'

'Referring to them by name . . . I said to the lads that it had become personal, and it was up to them to sort it out,' says O'Grady.

To make matters worse, Antrim were booked into the Burlington Hotel the night before the game along with Cork, and a couple of their players had wandered into the Cork team room. It was innocuous enough, but it still went into the mix as Cork prepared.

The day of the game there was some uncertainty about which team was warming up at which end; Cork were in the left-hand dressing room and thus entitled to warm up at the Canal End, but Antrim went out first and took up position there.

'Jerry Wallace used to go out and lay out the cones for our warm-up,' says O'Grady. 'As I was talking, Diarmuid burst across the dressing room: "That's it, they're after kicking Jerry's cones around!" That was the final insult for them.'

O'Sullivan won the first ball: 'I went through the first tackle, popped it to Seán Óg, we went downfield and got a point, and the game was over. We knew it. They knew it.'

'I'd said to them that I wanted the game finished early, and it was,' says O'Grady. 'If you'd been looking for something, it couldn't have worked out better. I remember in 1986 with Cork we'd struggled to beat Antrim. We needed seven goals to do it, so it worked out perfectly. Corcoran got two goals and Niall was very good.'

Cork ran out easy winners, and the Antrim players weren't too grateful for their manager's outspokenness.

'Criticising two of the most popular fellas on the panel . . .' says Brian Murphy. 'Everyone was taken aback. Antrim were going well at the time, but that was the thing we needed. One of their players said to me, "What's Dinny done to us?"'

What indeed.

'Dinny came into the dressing room afterwards and said that what was reported wasn't quite what was said,' says O'Grady. 'But it solved a problem for me. I didn't think we'd be beaten, but I didn't want to be struggling with ten minutes left.'

O'Grady was genuinely worried about Wexford in the semi-final. Though their team was in decline from their 2003 form, they had done well against Cork earlier in the season.

'We played them in a challenge before the Limerick game and they ran a drag with us for a long time,' says O'Grady. 'I was worried if they got that going again we'd be under pressure. We did a lot of planning for that, so mentally the lads were prepared for it. There was nothing in it for the first twenty minutes.'

Then Tom Kenny drove straight down the middle before ramming home a superb goal from the 21. It destroyed Wexford's self-confidence and with Jerry O'Connor reeling off points from midfield, Cork won with something to spare.

'There was a goal of the year competition afterwards and Tom's came in at eight or nine,' says O'Grady. 'Michael Jacob's goal for Wexford in the Leinster final won it, and I remember thinking, there's seven or eight places between them.'

For the final, the lessons had been learned—about the schedule, about the experience, about the motivation.

'Stopping the Kilkenny three-in-a-row was huge,' says O'Sullivan. 'Let's cut the bullshit. It was huge among the players—as it was for them against us in 2006, obviously.'

'You go to Croke Park and the programme is imposed. You're told what time you're coming out,' says O'Grady. 'We'd say sometimes that 3.05 pm was too late; we needed to be out for 3.02 pm. We said that the previous year we'd been out too late, so we changed that.'

In Pairc Uí Rinn the previous week at training, the manager had asked the players to come out the same way they would in Croke Park.

'I noticed when they were coming out of the tunnel, they were hitting the ball at the goal, which was what, 80, 85 metres away out at an angle,' says O'Grady. 'I was thinking, why make your first experience in Croke Park a negative one?

'I told them to jog up towards the goal and to go as far as the 21-metre line if they had to, but to stick their first shot over the bar. At least that way their first experience would be positive.

'We'd decided that fellas were tearing out on the field without being warmed up. The morning of the All-Ireland we went for our stroll, and Seánie McGrath brought the lads in together. I told him to hop up on a wall to speak, and he explained how he wanted them to come out on the field.

'We'd learned. If the Artane Boys Band was in front of you coming out, then you went out through them, and if a few of them fell down, well, so be it.'

And the experience stood to Cork. Dr Con Murphy puts it high on his list of positive experiences: 'There are certain matches, at certain times in your life, when there's a feelgood factor in the dressing room that doesn't always occur. That was the case before the Kilkenny game, and Brian Corcoran contributed to that hugely. He was a quiet man by nature and at half-time he went around to each player, telling them he hadn't come back to lose an All-Ireland final to Kilkenny.'

Not quite everything was accounted for. O'Grady felt a cold chill as the players ran out.

'The only thing we didn't prepare for ahead of the final was penalties. We'd usually do that before a championship game, but our last session was too wet, and we'd abandoned it rather than have them standing around in the rain. I remember thinking, we never practised that . . .'

John Gardiner reinforces the lesson of experience: 'The main thing was that we'd been there before. We knew you'd have to be here at this time, there at that time. You'd be out on the field longer than you'd ever been before, the anthem and the parade, all that.

'That makes a difference. We practised it. Two nights before the final we went to Pairc Uí Rinn, ran out, had a photograph taken, marched around for the parade, stood then for thirty seconds and we got introduced to the President.

'O'Grady was the President. Of course.'

'We wanted to play Kilkenny,' says Donal Óg Cusack. 'It was better that it was them. We were focused; we'd had meetings in which every player spoke. And 2003 was valuable. You develop a pattern very quickly as to how you prepare for games, and fellas would have been more comfortable. But it was a game we had to win.'

In the game itself all the Cork plans almost came unstuck in the first minute. Martin Comerford pulled on the first ball and it flew towards the Cork goal.

'Wayne went for the ball and slipped,' says Diarmuid O'Sullivan. 'So did I, and Eddie Brennan was through. It mightn't have been much, but I think Gardiner got something on it.'

He did.

'When I turned around, all I could see were Wayne and Diarmuid on their backsides, sliding all over the ground,' says Gardiner. 'DJ Carey and Eddie Brennan were queuing up to get a goal.

'I got a hook, just a small touch, on Eddie Brennan as he took the shot. He should have passed it inside to DJ, really. The next thing was Wayne flaked me with the hurley across the backside and sent me back out to wing back.'

There were more complications. Soon afterwards Brian Murphy had to go off.

'Brian got a migraine, but he also got a desperate flake on the leg,' says O'Grady. 'The interesting thing was that John Browne was going very well in training, though he'd been going back and forth to England. I remember saying to him to hang in there during the season.

'Pat [Mulcahy] would have been disappointed because he'd

worked very hard, but I didn't think he was quite at the level. John Browne came on, caught the first ball, drove out and blew Derek Lyng out of his way. He was totally relaxed.'

Alan Browne, John's older brother, had booked holidays in Paris and eventually found a bar which was showing the match. He got a surprise when he realised that his brother was on the field. The following day Browne Jr confessed that he hadn't even brought his helmet or glove to Dublin. He hadn't thought he'd be needed.

'Browner was on the top of his form, though he wasn't on the team,' says O'Sullivan. 'He had skill, pace and a nasty streak. All you needed.

'He brought one hurley to Dublin and he played a game that was fantastic. That was Browner for you. He brought in a fierce confidence with him that day. Now I'd have been as happy with Pat Mul coming in, but Browner came in and gave a great display.'

So did Seán Óg Ó hAilpín. Afterwards O'Grady would point to Kilkenny placing Henry Shefflin on the wing back as a statement of intent.

'Why would you put Shefflin on one of our best, only to dominate him? I think it was Seán Óg's best year. I'd have given him man of the match in the 2003 games against Wexford. In the final Shefflin had been on him for a while, then Gardiner, but in 2004 I felt he was tailor-made for Seán Óg.

'The important thing was to keep to the plan and to keep our composure, whether we were ten points up or ten points down. I felt if we could do that, we'd be fine. I was very confident. I had no doubt we'd win. Of course, I never had any doubts before a game we'd play—except the 2004 game against Wexford, oddly enough.'

'I was hoping I'd be marking Henry,' says Ó hAilpín. 'It all goes back to personal performance and 2003 just came and went for me. I felt Henry got the upper hand that day and that's why I wanted to mark him. If he didn't start on me, it wouldn't have mattered that much. I was ready anyway, but he started on me.

'Now, he's a class act. I marked DJ a couple of times and I thought you wouldn't get better, but Henry's got to be better. That's the reality. I was doing okay on him from play, getting my fair share of ball, and in the second half they moved him into the full forward line. I was just happy to get a chance to make up for the previous year.

'O'Grady would have a different perspective, but as a back you've a man to mark and you limit him as much as you can.'

When Ó hAilpín needed back-up, it was there. Gardiner remembers Shefflin going all the way through in the first half, being shadowed by both Cork wing backs: 'He couldn't play the ball, and Aodhán McSuibhne gave a free out. That was the theme for the day.'

'The first half was to and fro. They went for the jugular early on, but it started to unravel for them just before half-time,' says Ó hAilpín. 'Corcoran was getting on top, Joe was getting on top, and the signs were good. It was like 1999—keep them goalless.'

In the warm-up area at the break Corcoran spoke to his team mates again: 'Remember how you felt after last year's game. Don't come in feeling the same way; I didn't come back to lose an All-Ireland; I came back to win one with ye.'

A green flag would likely prove a match-winner, and in the second half Henry Shefflin ghosted away from the Cork defence for a sight of goal. As DJ Carey hand passed the ball into him, the Cork supporters held their breath, but the full back line believed in the man behind them.

'You have to have confidence in the lads around you,' says Diarmuid O'Sullivan. 'When I played with John Browne and Fergal Ryan, we had confidence in each other, and it was the same in 2004. I knew we had a chance because I know what Donal Óg has done to make himself the best goalkeeper in Ireland. I knew he could save it, and so did the other players.'

'Shefflin does that. He backs off the play, and I remember thinking, he's free, I can't go to him,' says Cusack. 'He doubled on it well, and O'Grady had always been keen on me standing up, so I had it in mind to stand up, and I saved it.'

That was only half the job. As Cusack puts it, the real satisfaction came in what followed.

'The best kick I got out of that was the way we reacted after that,' he says. 'We'd gone through that a thousand times. Wayne knew if I had the ball, then odds on I'd try to find him. The selfish way to think for me would have been, I made the save; I'm a great fella now, but we wanted to do the right thing.

'I gave it to Wayne. Niall came short for it, and we worked it through to Joe for a free. That was the greatest kick of it.

'The second half was one of the most enjoyable halves ever. They could have scored four goals in the last ten minutes, but that was never really going to happen.'

The omen was recognised further up the field.

'I'd hit the bar earlier in the game and was thinking, here we go again,' says Joe Deane. 'But as the game went on we got ahead, and when Donal Óg made the save and we got a point, I was thinking, it's going to happen for us today.'

Mortally wounded, Kilkenny's defence started showing gaps. With minutes left, Kenny had surged onto a neat ball from Deane for a fine point. Ronan Curran took that as the *coup de grâce*.

'I think, like us in 2006, Kilkenny were tiring. It was the exact same situation with the teams reversed. They'd just beaten Waterford in their semi; they'd been beaten by Wexford . . .

'When Tom got the point it was like the Clare game the previous year—you know you're going to win, so you can enjoy the few minutes. I looked up at the scoreboard and we were six points up and I thought, we're safe here, before thinking, calm down, anything could happen here yet. But it's a great feeling. You know you're safe.'

The game ended with Cork eight points ahead. John Gardiner had the ball in his hand at the final whistle, and to his eternal regret he banished it out over Hill 16. It was his only regret.

'Winning an All-Ireland . . . it is what it is,' he says. 'You meet the people close to you, your mother and father, your brother, and you only see how happy they are for you. You're too close to it yourself, even though you're delighted. Fathers crying. All that. It's unreal.'

'It was relief,' says Ó hAilpín. 'Straight after the whistle [panellist] John Anderson came over and jumped on top of me, and it was sheer relief—that we won the game. I can't stress how bad the doldrums were in 2002, it was that bad. If someone had said then we'd make an All-Ireland final in 2003 and win it in 2004, we wouldn't have believed it.

'I never saw the players until we got back in the dressing room. There was huge enjoyment, but relief was the overriding feeling. It was sweet.'

Timmy McCarthy agrees.

'Definitely relief. We'd seen the lowest of the low and reaching the top again was brilliant. The supporters backed us all the way. They spent big money to follow us when we needed them, so there was great satisfaction. The supporters deserved that.'

'I suppose it was vindication of the lads,' says O'Grady. 'There was no triumphalism. We were the best in Ireland. Having come through the strike and lost the year before, everything fell into place. It was nice for them to prove how good they were—good enough to win it.'

The 2004 final isn't such a welcome topic for one or two players.

'No, not a good subject,' says Brian Murphy. 'These things happen. Noel Hickey was having a stormer in 2007, but he pulled a hamstring. You never know what's going to happen. I had a junior football game the following week, so I got on with it. I've never watched the game since, though.'

'There's nothing to say,' says Pat Mulcahy. 'I was out injured for the year and came back on the panel for the semi-final, but Brian was outstanding.

'The final was hard. I was delighted for the lads. I'd been there for years as a sub; I'd made the breakthrough the year before and it had been an unbelievable buzz. And now I was a sub again and they'd won. I vowed to myself that I'd win an All-Ireland medal on the pitch.'

Diarmuid O'Sullivan is characteristically straightforward about the win in 2004.

'It put fellas who questioned us back in their box. We didn't feel we owed it to anyone other than ourselves. We'd put the time and effort in and we felt we deserved it for that. It answered a lot of criticism.'

The result validated the team's approach—the support play, the puck-out strategy. Donal Óg Cusack never felt a need to justify that approach, despite the criticism. He felt it was common sense.

'Our point was always this—don't be a *mé féiner*. If a *mé féiner* was smart he'd know that by giving to the team he'd benefit more individually as well. We'd often say we get more of a kick out of being a team than anything else.

'The other thing is that the structure suited our team; if another style suited the players we had, I'd have been happy to use it. But I've seen nothing to say you shouldn't have a plan. You can improve it and refine it, but you have to have a plan.'

His mentor, Ger Cunningham, backs Cusack up: 'No matter what you're going to do, there'll be criticism. When it comes off it's great, but when it doesn't you get plenty of criticism.

'It didn't worry him in the least, and he was the guy who had to carry it out—and more importantly, he was pushing to carry out the puck-out plan. He believed in it, and it wasn't being imposed on him. It was just a natural evolution of where we were going to go with it. Donal Óg didn't have the longest puck-out, but he was fantastically accurate.

'In 2004 the shorter puck-outs went against him once or twice, early in the All-Ireland final for instance, but he never stopped believing in the strategy. He was criticised when one to Seán Óg early on went astray and Kilkenny scored, but no one picked out the couple that went to Tom Kenny which we got scores from later in the game.'

In the final, Ben O'Connor could feel the victory coming. As captain he knew the duties which began at the long whistle.

'With about five minutes to go you knew,' says O'Connor. 'You wanted the ball all the time; you knew it wouldn't go wrong. It's seldom you'd feel that in a big game, an All-Ireland.

'A lot of people try to make a big deal out of the captaincy, but you take no notice of it. People might say, he'd say that anyway, but what would I say to other fellas on the team? Tell the likes of Sully or Curran what to do? Everyone has their own way to prepare. You're only going out to take the toss. It is a big deal and it isn't a big deal at the same time.'

Ever mindful of the small details, the manager had covered the captain's speech.

'Going up on the train O'Grady asked me if I'd a speech ready,' says O'Connor. 'He told me he'd get it done for me. He and Eddie O'Donnell said they'd write it out phonetically, though I said there was no need. I was getting ready to belt out the speech, but Eddie handed the speech to me, and when I got up there the note blew away.'

It didn't matter. As O'Connor picked up the cup he could see no grass, just red. The Cork supporters were all over the field.

Returning to Cork was everything he imagined it would be, recalls Ronan Curran. John Gardiner suggests it put 2003 to bed for a lot of the players, himself most of all.

But the manager didn't stay on. He had just about fitted in a second year. A third didn't figure in his plans.

'If it was a professional area, I wouldn't have had any problem staying on,' says O'Grady. 'But I didn't have the time to devote to it, not to do it properly. I barely had the time for it the second year. Maybe I gave it too much time, but I gave it the time I felt it needed.

'Now, if some fella had said to me, "Look, you can have your salary while you do it", I'd have jumped at it. But it wasn't to be. And anyway, you could have a situation where players are amateur and the manager's professional, which could be tricky.'

One last side effect of 2004 was that hurling's smallest superpower had to accommodate its most distinguished visitor.

'The Tuesday we brought the cup back to Newtown,' says Ben O'Connor. 'The lads back home had organised it, and around 3 o'clock I got a call to find out when we'd be back, because they had detours organised around Newtown. We had a bus to come back into the village. It was mighty.

'Up on the trailer, you wouldn't know a quarter of the crowd—people from Limerick and what not. The fact that you had roads into Newtownshandrum blocked off at three o'clock in the afternoon—that was enough.'

# RUN, FORREST, RUN

John Allen didn't see becoming manager of the Cork hurlers as the realisation of his life's dream.

'Not at all, no. I remember saying to Eddie O'Donnell one time at training that whoever followed Donal would have a fair job, given his no-nonsense attitude to training, his self-belief, his determination to get it done, to say what needed to be done.

'I knew the players better than most because I'd known them as friends in the dressing room. I knew there wouldn't be an issue with us taking over. In 2003 there was pressure on them, having got what they wanted. Having come through that and seen how well Donal did, knowing he'd go after two years, and knowing Seánie O'Leary had no interest, I knew I might be asked.'

He was. It didn't take him long to make up his mind.

'It wasn't a certainty by any means, but when I was asked I felt it was a huge honour and that outweighed everything. Dealing with players, press, the board—that was all in the ha'penny place because of the honour. But it wasn't planned.

'The only plan I did have was that I would have thought I was more of a people person than Donal, that I would have more skills that way. I felt that was what I'd bring to the table and that I'd try to manage the team as democratically as possible, by consensus rather than by rule—that everyone would have a say, and then when it came to tactics and so on, we'd talk about what we'd do. It was all about consensus.'

Erudite and well travelled, Allen's inquisitive mind and relaxed manner were familiar to the players, and they responded.

'It was that smooth,' says Timmy McCarthy. 'Donal was great when he came in, but after two years you nearly had enough of that. John came in with a different approach. It was the right sequence. Donal was tough; he put in the perfect structure. John came in and maybe gave the players a little more leeway to make decisions. He brought in a slightly different approach which was just right.'

Pat Mulcahy also welcomed the new appointment, though he gives due tribute to Allen's predecessor.

'I could have listened to O'Grady for good. He was one of the top two or three trainers I ever had. John Allen's big advantage was that he'd been there for two years. He knew the basis of what we were doing, and he made one or two changes.'

'Donal and John are different people, obviously,' says Dr Con Murphy. 'At that stage the players were evolving, say someone like Donal Óg was a big help to John, but it was a seamless changeover.

'There wouldn't be that many fellas who would speak before a game, but at player meetings senior players talk. Donal Óg, Joe, Diarmuid in particular, though Ben, Jerry and Seán Óg would speak up as well. When Brian [Corcoran] spoke he had massive presence, because he wouldn't talk that often.

'In 2005 we were more confident, we had a blueprint and so on. What helped as well was that we didn't play Kilkenny. Galway were a new challenge and were different. They were the coming team and it probably suited us to have a new target.'

'John was totally different,' says Gardiner. 'It was O'Grady's way or the highway, while there was some compromise with John. Donal

Óg, Seán Óg, Diarmuid, they could all come forward with their ideas. With O'Grady there was no talking back.

'For instance, I remember one time we were outside Highbury on a trip with $O_2$ to see Arsenal, and O'Grady wanted to make sure we were all there. He had us all line up outside Highbury like children—thirty grown men—and he counted us to make sure. Fellas were going into Highbury looking at us and obviously thinking, who are they?'

'There was no need for a big change,' says Donal Óg Cusack. 'John Allen didn't have an ego. He was intelligent and he knew the players; he'd been with us in 1999, so he knew us.

'Kieran McGeeney once asked me who the best manager was I'd worked with. I said that in terms of putting structures in place, it was Donal O'Grady, but that John Allen was the man Kieran should talk to. Donal was a groundbreaker and didn't have the luxury to sit back and say things could be done better: he was breaking the ground.

'But John was able to improve the structures. John couldn't have done what Donal did, but he made the system even better, and he made better players of us.'

The endorsement of the senior players in the group also strengthened Allen's position.

'My attitude was that you could have debates and arguments internally about structures and so on,' says Cusack, 'but once you decided to go to war, that was it. If a couple of fellas were wondering about John [Allen], Seán Óg as captain made a speech in Fermoy early in 2005 saying that whatever John said went; that that was non-negotiable. Was that a threat? It was.

'The fellas against us would have said we had too much power, but we never crossed the line. John was always the boss—and he *was* the boss. He could certainly be saucy enough to be the boss.'

That he could. Diarmuid O'Sullivan confesses that friendly as he was with Allen, 'we had our rows as well'. Allen believed in the structure, in having the player representatives in place who would sort out tickets and gear. As Cusack said, he had other weapons O'Grady didn't have.

'John made speeches on the mornings of games and you'd see fellas with tears in their eyes. That's not something O'Grady would have been doing. John spoke once before a game about how our opponents' manager had belittled him at a function, and I was ready to kill the other manager after hearing it. John could get inside you like that.'

Na Piarsaigh had won the county championship the previous year, and that gave Seán Óg Ó hAilpín the Cork captaincy. But his tenure had a harrowing start.

Early that year a Midleton youngster, Robert Holohan, had gone missing. Search parties were scouring east Cork for him and team trainer Jerry Wallace, who had coached the boy with the local GAA team, came to the new skipper.

'Jerry said to me, "It'd be a strong statement if you went on TV because he would have been a big Midleton GAA fan, a big Cork fan,"' says Ó hAilpín. 'I felt uncomfortable first doing it because I felt it was kind of out of my remit. But it was a case of if I could do anything, grand.

'That's how I got involved. It wasn't because I rang up and said, look, I want to help ye. It wasn't for my own personal gain or profile. It was to help the family in any way I could. Looking back on it now, do I have any regrets doing it? None whatsoever. In my life, there's a couple of things that put things into perspective over the years and certainly that was one of them.'

When the child's body was found soon afterwards, Ó hAilpín read a prayer at the funeral Mass.

'I remember I had the gearbag in the boot to go training after the funeral. It wasn't team training, just to do a bit on my own. After the funeral, I was driving to the gym and I did a U-turn and went away home.

'That was an example where there's more important things than sport. It was a very sad day and a very sad ending.'

Thankfully, John Allen's early challenges were more team based. An internal issue gave him the chance to establish his authority.

'One thing that stood to me when I became manager was something with Pat Mulcahy,' says Allen. 'He played with his club even though we had agreed a policy with the clubs that the lads wouldn't play. I forget the specifics, but Pat was told on Thursday he wasn't to play on Friday. He played, so we dropped him. That defined my managership, if you like, that I wouldn't be dictated to.'

Mulcahy remembers the specifics well.

'There was a league game with Cork on Sunday and everyone was allowed to play on a Thursday night with their clubs, but for some reason the Newtown game was on Friday. I said to myself, look, the lads played last night . . .

'We had a disagreement. I felt starting off that year that maybe we could be going back to the old ways, that the quiet fella wouldn't be listened to unless you kicked up a fuss, that I could be pushed aside. Maybe I was paranoid, but that's how I felt and I decided to make a stand.

'Whether I was right or wrong, the end of the year justified that. But at least I felt I'd made a stand. I felt that after that they were going to have to give me a league game or two—either to hang myself or to make a name for myself. I'd rather it that way than just slip away into the background. Produce an average performance here and there and it would have been tough luck. The team would have been the same as the previous year. That's what I didn't want.

'I wasn't going to wait around for that and I decided I'd stick my neck out, whether I was right or wrong. I felt I was right; John would say otherwise, but I got the league game against Kilkenny and picked up the man of the match award, even though we lost. It worked out.'

Cork overcame an under-strength Waterford side in that year's Munster semi-final, an oddly decaffeinated game that never threatened to reach the heights of previous and subsequent games between the teams.

The Munster final, however, was one of the games of the year. It was Cork-Tipperary in Pairc Uí Chaoimh, but the drama of that Sunday had a lengthy preamble.

A row had been simmering between GAA players and RTÉ all summer due to the broadcaster's unwillingness to allow players to drink GPA-endorsed Club Energise while being interviewed after games. Alan Brogan of Dublin had withdrawn from one post-game interview as a result. Complicating matters was the fact that Irish rugby star Brian O'Driscoll habitually swigged from an energy drink he endorsed while being interviewed after games. The new manager put RTÉ on notice that it was a problem that needed to be resolved.

'That two weeks before the Munster final, I spent a lot of time on the phone with people from RTÉ and so on,' says Allen. 'I'd flagged that issue with them because I knew after the semi-final that RTÉ would be on to me to talk, and I also knew the GPA weren't happy with how GAA players were being treated in that context, with the energy drinks.

'I figured it was a chance for me to help out the players, so I flagged it because I wanted it dealt with before it became an issue. But it sputtered on and sputtered on. I had Ger Canning, Tony O'Donoghue and Marty Morrissey all on to me to talk to them, and I said I'd no problem doing so if the issue was sorted to everyone's satisfaction. I felt the players were being wronged. It's not like I wanted them holding bottles or whatever, but it seemed silly that there was one rule for rugby players and another for GAA players.'

As was customary before big games, Cork had a press night the week of the game, but their approach to the energy drink issue still hadn't been settled. They'd decided not to co-operate with RTÉ, but the precise nature of that non-co-operation was still up in the air.

'It went on and on, and the night of the press conference, Paschal Sheehy was on to me and we agreed he'd just take a statement from us,' says Allen. 'I was talking to Seán Óg all that day about what the statement would say and so on, and there were still meetings about it late in the day, but I said, right, that's fine. Then, on the night, Seán Óg told me he didn't need a statement; he knew what he wanted to say, but Jim O'Sullivan asked a question, then Paschal asked a question, and Seán Óg started to answer him until John Gardiner started kicking him under the table.'

'Yeah, I wasn't supposed to answer,' says Ó hAilpín. 'I said, look, we're not talking because of the Club Energise situation. Alan Brogan had brought it up after he'd won a man of the match. He said he'd be drinking Club Energise and they stopped him.

'You couldn't say it affected us when you saw how we played in the first half. Maybe we should have had a stand-off before every game if that was going to be the result.'

'It was maybe a distraction, but you can get used to having distractions too,' says Diarmuid O'Sullivan. 'We spoke to John and we said we needed him to back us, and he did.'

In the absence of Wayne Sherlock, Brian Murphy was becoming the man-marking specialist.

'I don't know if it's a compliment or not,' says Murphy. 'I remember before we played Tipp, [selector] Joe O'Leary said, "You're getting the short straw. You'll be on Eoin Kelly." For the next game I asked if there was any chance of the long straw.

'Every position in the full back line is man-marking, though, and your performance is dictated by the lads outside you. If they're not putting pressure on the man delivering the ball, then you might as well come ashore and let your man have a free shot. Give an inter-county corner forward five yards and he's gone.'

Murphy's team mate Joe Deane showed the proof in the game, distracting Tipp keeper Brendan Cummins for Kieran 'Fraggy' Murphy's vital goal, but the final really turned on a first-half penalty for Tipperary.

'We were four points up, I think, and hurling well when Tipp got a penalty,' says Curran. 'Eoin Kelly took it. Donal Óg made a great save, and then we did exactly what we were supposed to do.'

The ball broke from Cusack's hurley to Pat Mulcahy.

'It might only happen once in a game, something you practise, but that could be the winning of the game,' says Mulcahy. 'The second Cusack saved the ball and it came to me, not for a second did I think about lobbing it up. I was always going to give it to John [Gardiner].'

'Having practised the penalty you'd feel, this is only going to happen if we play perfectly,' says Gardiner. 'But that's what happened. I carried it upfield and gave it to Fraggy.'

Kieran Murphy—Fraggy—then pointed from distance to give Cork a five-point lead. It was the perfect example of the Cork possession game, and how productive it could be, but it wouldn't have worked if not for the painstaking preparation that went into it.

'We'd practised that for ages in training,' says Curran. 'We took six or seven penalties a night and went through what we'd do, and in the game we did just that. We got the ball up to Fraggy, and he got one of the best scores in the last four or five years. Everyone at the time thought, that's perfect, and we drove it on from there. If they'd scored a goal we were under pressure, but instead we were five up and the confidence rose.

'The penalty save and the score changed the whole thing. It just shows what can happen when a team gets a run on you, like with Tipp in 2007 against us and Limerick in 2006.'

'The call was "Forrest" if we were going to run with the ball,' says Donal Óg Cusack. 'It was "Run, Forrest, run" from *Forrest Gump*. O'Grady would have us stand around and walk through the moves. And then you see it works. Brilliant.

'See, we believed you needed a structure. If you've a lot of riches you lose structure, but we wanted to get the best out of ourselves, and we fundamentally believed in structure, and working on that structure. Fellas disagree with us, but we don't care. What I do know is that every professional sport in the world, sports which invest millions in improvement, they all have structures.'

Cork gave an exhibition for the first half of that Munster final.

'Was it as good as we ever played for thirty-five minutes?' says Cusack. 'Yeah. It was no wonder we put in such a performance. Management was excellent, all the players were into a professional way of life . . . the 2004 team holiday, we spent a lot of it training. The Munster final performance was no surprise, the camp was happy, we were All-Ireland champions and the whole thing was going well.'

In defence Diarmuid O'Sullivan was having a rare tussle with Michael Webster, the Tipperary full forward. The thousands of Cork supporters on the Blackrock End were vocal in support of their hero, raining down threats on Webster's head: "Sully's gonna get you."

'I have that game on DVD and when Cian [O'Sullivan's son] puts it on you can hear that,' says O'Sullivan. 'There'd be a smile, but you don't really hear it in the game. If you listened to everything you hear out on the field, you'd be in a bad way.

'I suppose in a way it's flattering, if you think about it. It meant you had the respect of people that they were using that name, but in other ways, if you had a bad game fellas would turn it around—he's just playing to the crowd, and so on. That's far from true. It just comes from the nickname, but that's the downside. Still, you're putting yourself in the public eye.

'He [Webster] is the kind of fella who strikes me, if he concentrated on hurling he'd be a very good player. He showed that with Loughmore-Castleiney in the club championship. But that day he was driving me off my head, running around the goal. If he thought I was going to chase him around the goal, he must have thought I came down in the last shower. It's bad enough having to run around the field itself . . . if he concentrated on hurling, he'd be far better.'

O'Sullivan wasn't the only player having his name sung by the supporters in red. Joe Deane's sparkling display in the corner led to a familiar chant.

'I didn't hear it much in the early years,' laughs Deane. 'It might have started off in 1999, when we got a bit of a run going. I don't remember one particular day when it started. The boys would slag me in training about it or chant it in a pub to annoy me, but I always thought it was a great compliment to have your name chanted. You could have a lot worse chanted about you.'

Tipp looked a beaten docket at half-time.

'We were twelve up and we were warned about it at half-time,' says Ó hAilpín. 'We were told, put yourself in their shoes; their pride is hurt. But you can't help it. We fell into the trap and towards the end they were coming at us.

'It was a great win, but if we'd carried on as we did in the first half, our sense of invincibility would have gone through the roof. As it was, our confidence got dented. Tipp had chipped away and chipped away. They got a goal, but Fraggie and Neil Ronan got points to put them away.'

'Everything was so good that it had to fall apart,' is O'Sullivan's succinct description.

'In the second half we took our foot off the pedal a bit,' says Curran. 'But there was a thing for us about playing in the Pairc that day. I'd never played a championship game there before and the atmosphere was unbelievable—people are on top of you, and the players rose to that.

'The row with RTÉ had brought the team closer. It was something we thought was right. We were all fighting for the same thing, so it probably helped us. It happened in 2004 as well when we refused to speak to the papers.

'At times people forget we're amateurs, we're going to work the following day. In 2004 we stuck together because some lads got fierce grief even though we'd only lost by a point. In Killarney that day Brendan Larkin asked me for a few words but I said, sorry, Brendan, we've taken a decision not to talk. Sure it gave ye something different to write about.'

'I never felt we were going to lose that game,' says Pat Mulcahy. 'I thought we were a lot more cohesive than they were. Because of the previous year, we were always thinking of the All-Ireland. That was just another match.'

'In ways it was like the All-Ireland final of 2003,' says Ó hAilpín. 'We were like Kilkenny, we'd been well on top and then they came back, like we did in 2003.'

Afterwards RTÉ awarded the man of the match to Paul Kelly. The Tipperary man had had a good second half, but John Gardiner was immense throughout. He wasn't too bothered.

'The Munster medal is worth more than the man of the match, though my mother might disagree,' says Gardiner. 'To be fair to Paul Kelly, he did get seven points from midfield, even if it's unusual to give the man of the match to the losing team.'

'The whole thing took up a lot of time all right in the run-up to the game,' says Allen. 'Paul Kelly got man of the match in the game, but he mightn't have got it if the dispute had been resolved.'

As Cork faced into the All-Ireland series, Ben O'Connor started to notice the wear and tear.

'To me burnout isn't physical. It's in your head, when you're just going through the motions. Once I've the head right the body is all right.

'In 2005 I had a problem with my knee—the cartilage. I had it early in the year and thought I'd get away with it. Then it got too late to get it done, so I had to go through the year with it. I got it done but then I got a problem with my hip, and I had it operated on at Christmas 2006. If I'd my time again I wouldn't have had it done, because there wasn't much of an improvement.

'Injuries are a killer. I was lucky enough up to that, getting away with it, but running year on year, you don't have a chance to recover. That's where you're caught.'

Cork would need Ben O'Connor later in 2005. As Ronan Curran notes, they'd also need a slight adjustment in attitude.

'There is a different attitude towards you when you're on top. In

2004 there was no stopping Kilkenny and in 2005 there was no stopping us. Not that much can change in a year, but you'd hear people saying we'd be unstoppable for years and so on. We knew that wasn't true.

'We had to guard against going out to defend ourselves instead of attacking. To win something you have to attack rather than defend. Things don't materialise if you have the attitude that you're waiting for something to happen rather than making it happen.'

They'd need to make things happen soon enough.

# IS FADA AN TURAS

Given the drama of the semi-final, the quarter-final against Waterford is largely forgotten.

'It was one draw we didn't want,' says Ó hAilpín. 'You meet a team a few times and eventually they'll have their day. But we beat them.'

The win, powered by Brian Corcoran's clever drop-shot goal, gave Cork a semi-final against Clare. There was a general expectation that Cork would have little trouble against an ageing team, but Clare didn't read the script.

Early on the Banner were in charge. Manager Anthony Daly came with a reputation for innovation, and he managed to unhinge the Cork defence where they felt strongest—at centre back.

'It's very noticeable at full back, you can see your centre back is getting dragged around,' says Diarmuid O'Sullivan. 'That's a huge problem. No matter how good you are in the full back line, if the lads outside can't stop the supply, then you can't hold the forwards inside. And it was clear that Clare had a plan.'

'I felt the first half was even. There were only a couple of points in it,' says Pat Mulcahy. 'Maybe at that time teams were getting to know our style a little, stopping our runners. But they got a couple of points after the break and instead of the score being 8–6, suddenly it was 14–8, 15–8.

'I remember thinking, we're not out of it, but we're going to need a goal to win it, after five minutes of the second half. We never looked like conceding one, but we looked like we needed one.'

Clare kept the energy going into the second half and were six points ahead going into the final quarter. John Allen knew he couldn't just watch: he had to make a decision.

'I was on the line saying, right, here I am, first year in the job and I'm not willing to make a big call. My thought was if I don't make a call here, we've lost anyway.

'We worked by consensus nearly all the time, and I went up to the lads and said, we'll do this. We'd already discussed potential changes. Ronan hadn't been playing that well at times that year, but we hadn't expected Brian to be beaten that day.

'There was no real issue—we were six points down—but my feeling was that even though we worked by consensus, I'd be hung out to dry the next day. I'd get the blame as the manager. So I said, this is what we'll do. We did it, and it just worked. We talked it over, but time wasn't on our side at that point. Our backs were to the wall.

'To stray off the point, fellas said to me since, "Why didn't ye do something equally radical in the 2006 final?" I'm still of the opinion that we'd won so many games that had gone down to the wire with that set of players, and it wasn't as if there was anyone who was really poor—apart from Pat Mulcahy, whom we might have brought off earlier—that we said afterwards, we left him on way too long. That didn't happen. We were just staying with them as much as we could and hoping the same thing would happen that had happened in the previous four years—that we had enough in reserve to come towards the end.'

Allen took off Brian Corcoran and Ronan Curran, two All-Stars, bulwarks of the team. He put on Wayne Sherlock and Neil Ronan and moved Gardiner to centre back, with Pat Mulcahy on his flank. Sherlock bolstered the full back line, and Ronan immediately had an impact.

'Clare were flying,' says Mulcahy. 'Lohan was flying, the backs were doing well . . . I don't think Curran was playing that badly. The tide might have been turning even before he was taken off. There's always a period of dominance in a game when you have to make it count. If you do, you're sorted, and ten minutes after half-time they probably thought they'd won it.

'Then Ben got a point out on the wing, the midfielders came into it, Seán Óg came into it, and the whole thing turned. And when the tide turns it's hard to stop. We had time, too, remember—we had fifteen, twenty minutes to reel them in. Thirteen points after sixty-eight minutes wasn't huge scoring anyway; our problem was probably up front.

'Everyone goes on about the substitutions, and Neil made a difference up front because he's lively, but I think the tide was turning our way anyway, and that the changes didn't have the impact maybe the media made out.'

'I felt halfway through the second half that we could do it if we kept focused,' says Donal Óg Cusack. 'I thought Clare should have started a fight to upset things or waste time or whatever, but I felt if we could get into our rhythm, we'd get there.'

Others weren't as optimistic.

'I thought it was curtains,' says Brian Murphy. 'Some of the lads might have thought differently, but I thought we were gone—that we needed at least one goal. At the start of the second half we were saying, we'll raise it, but with ten left I thought we were gone. I couldn't see where the goal was going to come from.'

'It reminded me of the first game against Wexford in 2003,' says Seán Óg Ó hAilpín. 'I don't think the team were playing well within themselves. That's being honest with you. Based on that, I thought that was it. If Clare had got another point or two . . . It's funny, the difference between six points down to even seven or eight, even psychologically. If they had got an extra two points, it would have been psychologically a burden too much for us.

'Clare looked hungrier, and they were getting the scores, but I'd agree with Brian. I thought we were gone. The moves were a factor, but it was back to what we knew best. The last ten minutes and you back yourselves.'

Trainer Jerry Wallace remembers the calmness of the players. As Cork started to whittle away at the Clare lead, he brought water out to the defenders. 'Gardiner, Curran, Tom, Jerry and Pat Mul were in a group, and I remember Gardiner's words distinctly: "Don't worry, Jerry. We have them."'

'It started to happen,' says Brian Murphy. 'Ben got a point out on the wing, then Tom, then Jerry . . .'

'We took over for the last few minutes,' says Gardiner. 'The ball was raining in on top of me for the last few minutes—and to be fair, if Curran had been playing he'd have caught them as well—but it was an unbelievable game.'

Clare faltered, and Cork started to reel them in. The goal chance, when it came, fell to Ben O'Connor.

'Jerry came through,' he says. 'Tom passed the ball to him; there was nobody near me because my man went to Jerry. He left it in to me and I never hit a ball as hard in my life. If I'd mishit the thing it would have been a goal, but it went over.

'We were hoping the clock wouldn't run out on us. The fitness levels told and fellas weren't giving up. At one stage Tom and Jerry had gone upfield and Jerry said, "I'm not able to go. Cover my man", but as Tom jogged out he said Jerry was out ahead of him.

'It was one of those days. Fellas would say they're not able, but they still wouldn't give in. But that was the benefit of the training. You might do a tough night's training, but that extra little bit you'd do after would stand to you. You'd curse them on the night for making you do it, but it stood to us that day.'

And it was Tom and Jerry who won it. Kenny won a ball in a thicket of players, drove forward before timing his lay-off to Jerry

O'Connor perfectly. As O'Connor turned outfield he stuck out his tongue: relief. It had been close, but the win was forged in teamwork.

'I felt that was one day when the teamwork was vital, the possession game,' says Mulcahy. 'The last point, the winning point, came as a result of a good hand pass, whereas Clare had had some bad wides. That was the difference. When they had fellas in good positions up front, they didn't lay it off to lads in better positions; our bit of cuteness stood to us.

'From my perspective it was probably the most satisfactory game. I was thinking throughout it, I'm not losing this—the lads have their All-Ireland medal from last year, I want to win mine.'

'We always had that attitude, that there was always a chance,' says Diarmuid O'Sullivan. 'That was the mentality. We'd been to the bottom of the pit, and we always fought and fought until we couldn't fight any more, and I felt we had a chance.

'But it was still a huge win. The Cork–Clare thing was still big, and it was a massive relief to win it.'

Clare were shattered at the final whistle.

'They were, and I was conscious of it,' says Cusack. 'I like [Anthony] Daly, and I'd know he'd want the best for players and that, but when you're out there you have to be selfish; you have to be ruthless. And afterwards it doesn't sink in immediately. You're so relieved, so happy yourself, that it wasn't you.'

There were other signs of the team's maturity.

'That was a fierce physical battle that day,' says Cusack. 'In previous years we'd have gone around them, but we were as physical as anyone that time. We were happy to take them on. Daly was a good coach and we'd have expected him to come up with something. A lot of teams put a tactic, a structure, in place to counteract us, but the majority of them weren't able to keep that going. The first team to keep their discipline with that was Kilkenny in 2006.'

The victory is Allen's sweetest memory from his time in charge.

'The Clare game was the best. The game wasn't won until the final whistle. The fact that we were scoring, that we were running at them, suggested we might win without getting a goal. And we did.'

The close shave stood to Cork. While Kilkenny and Galway provided a hugely entertaining shoot-out in the other semi-final, which Galway won, grinding out a nail-biter reinforced to John Allen and his men that they had plenty to do.

'We were always going to win the Clare game. That was the talk beforehand, at least,' says Diarmuid O'Sullivan. 'Afterwards we knew well we had stuff to work on, and we had a very intense two weeks after that, working on the things we needed to improve. Those two weeks were two of the toughest we had that year, but we needed it and the Clare game was a big warning to us.

'John was only interested in one thing, minding his own house— getting his own players right for the job coming up. He'd feel that if that was right, everything else would take care of itself. And that came across to the players. We knew that as the time came close, that we were ready.

'There's no way you could buy the experience some of our lads had, and that stood to us against Clare as well.'

Joe Deane takes up the theme by comparing the game with previous semi-final nightmares.

'We'd had chances against Offaly in 2000, but we didn't take them. Against Clare we had a chance; I felt we'd come at some stage. And Clare had given it absolutely everything, and they were bound to tire in the end. Once we started getting the points they started coming, one by one, and that showed the maturity compared to 2000.

'I felt better after that game than almost any other. The buzz from the Cork crowd after that was as good as winning any All-Ireland. I suppose people thought we were gone, but it was a great comeback.

'And you could see the devastation of Clare. That was noticeable. They'd put so much effort into it. We were hot favourites and they'd given it everything. It was probably that group's last chance of beating Cork and making an All-Ireland final, but the other side of that was that it was a huge win for us.'

In the dressing room after the Clare game, Ger Cunningham had nudged Ben O'Connor.

'It could have cost us, missing the goal chance,' says O'Connor. 'Ger Cunningham said to me afterwards, "You should have stuck that one." I said to him, we didn't need it today, Ger—the next day.'

The management had other concerns. Brian Corcoran was always likely to improve as he recovered from an arm injury which had restricted him against Clare, but Ronan Curran was a different case, particularly as the credit for the semi-final victory was widely ascribed to his removal from the game.

'Well, I take a different view,' says Curran. 'We were going well up to the Clare game, but they had it planned out very well. When you'd look up the field you'd see acres of space in front of the half back line, and I remember thinking, they've something planned here; we could be in a bit of bother.

'We were going okay, but then two small breaks went against us; Tony Carmody was onto them, and bang, bang, two points. Suddenly we're under pressure.

'Any centre back will tell you the start is important, because if your man gets a couple of points, you're under pressure. Maybe you shouldn't feel it, but it's only human nature to start following him, because you're hoping he won't score again. That leaves space behind you, and then you're doing everything you've been trained not to do . . . and that's what happened to me. I was dragged out of position, but those are the tactics; you've to deal with that.

'Brian Corcoran was struggling a bit as well and when we were taken off, I was disappointed but felt I deserved it. My head wasn't right. But everything started to close up then, rather than anything we did.

'I think Clare started to lose their discipline. I spoke to Davy Fitz later and he said looking up the field towards the end of the game, all he could see were bodies, where in the first half there'd been space. He just had to launch it upfield. Fair dues to John Gardiner.

He's well able to play centre back, and he was flying, but I'd love to have been out there. But my head wasn't right.

'Clare probably thought they had it won when Brian and I went off, but John, Jerry, Ben and Neil drove it on. That's what our lads can do. Ben and Jerry can take you to pieces in five minutes if they get a run on you.'

Ger Cunningham asked Curran to call to his house the following week.

'He said, "You'll be centre back for the final." Straightaway there was a load off my mind. We went through what went wrong. I accepted it, and we went on to what to expect from David Forde. But it was good to hear it, that there was that trust there. Then it was a case of getting my head right.'

John Allen was confident of his side's chances against Galway.

'We'd played them three times that year and I couldn't see us losing to them,' says Allen. 'I couldn't see Niall Healy getting three goals off Diarmuid, for instance.

'Earlier in the year we'd gone to Kuala Lumpur on the way to New Zealand and I went to a Chinese temple to pick out a fortune straw and the message was, you'll have to settle for being second best this year. And that struck a chord with me.

'Before the game there was a lot of talk about Conor Hayes being the captain of an All-Ireland winning team, a league-winning team and now possibly an All-Ireland winning manager. I was wondering if it was their destiny, but I still couldn't see us being beaten.

'We had the best of people involved behind the scenes, like Seánie McGrath and Jerry Wallace, and we were mature enough to see how we could improve the professionalism. Dealing with the off-field peripherals was a big part of that, making sure the players just had to concentrate on getting themselves right.'

One of those peripherals had been a situation involving Niall McCarthy and Kieran Murphy. They'd worn Corona beer logos on their boots ahead of the Waterford game, and from Allen's perspective it created an unnecessary problem.

'I got a call that this was about to break, so I rang the two boys,' says Allen. 'The other players were very annoyed about it, not because the two of them got paid (it was only a few bob), but that they were compromising the team by their actions. I don't doubt that they didn't see it that way, but the other players should have known and I should have known. We put in a system after that that nothing like that would happen unless I or the players' representative knew about it.

'For the few days we were worried. Seán Óg had been involved with Paddy Power's a few years earlier and it was possible that the authorities could have said, lads, ye got a warning already, so . . . and we could have been punished.

'I suppose according to the letter of the law there was a chance they'd get suspended, but you know the way the white smoke does tend to come. We learned, maybe not officially, that there wouldn't be much about it, even though the controversy dragged on a bit. It shouldn't have happened, but we spoke about it and moved on.'

Moving on meant the nuts and bolts of handling Galway.

'When you're a corner back and you see them get five goals,' says Brian Murphy, 'you're thinking, what's going to happen the next day? Some of their forwards would have been on any team of the year.

'I remember Armagh going on about how they wanted to win the second title, to be seen as more than a one-hit wonder. What was notable was that we went to Inchydoney before that game for a meeting, and there was a slight change to the game plan.'

That change—going longer with the puck-outs—would be crucial. Its implementation would also point up the co-operation between manager and players in making decisions.

'John Allen instigated the change in puck-outs,' says Cusack. 'We had a meeting in the away dressing room in Pairc Uí Chaoimh and discussed it, but we had to make sure we had All-Star sliotars.'

Cork felt the Niall McCarthy-Brian Corcoran axis in attack would benefit from a slightly quicker, slightly longer delivery. Given the emphasis on the Cork running/possession game, they also felt the element of surprise in springing a direct approach would help.

There was plenty of interest in Galway after beating Kilkenny, but the benefits of experience were obvious even before the game. The westerners had their press evening after an open session in Pearse Stadium, which left players standing around sweating as they signed autographs and answered media questions. Cork had their press evening at a city hotel *before* a training session; at an agreed time players and management left for Pairc Uí Chaoimh. At the Galway press night Ollie Canning's best hurley was stolen; there was no team representative at the Cork press night by seven o'clock.

In the run-up to the final, Ronan Curran saw some differences in how people were treating him. He saw it as motivation.

'I could see people's attitudes towards me changing, keeping away from me a little bit. People were avoiding the obvious question. They don't know if you'll be playing.

'I was fine until the night before the final, when I got a text from someone—obviously it wasn't David Forde, who I was marking, but "supposed" to be from him—which said: "I suppose I'll be marking Gardiner tomorrow." Probably some smart alec in Galway, but when I read that I thought, well, fuck them anyway . . .'

On the day, Cork enjoyed several advantages. Seán Óg Ó hAilpín won the toss, for instance.

'Traditionally if we won the toss we would have gone for the jugular straightaway and taken the wind to put some doubt in the opposition,' he says. 'In the overall scheme of things winning the toss isn't a huge thing, but it just puts you at ease a small bit. It was crucial that we got a great start because for any crowd going up, hoping, you have to give them doubt straightway.'

For Galway, Niall Healy's three goals in the semi-final earned him plenty of plaudits, and rightly so. In retrospect the absence of the formidable Noel Hickey from the Kilkenny defence that day might lower the value of the full forward's hat-trick, but going into the All-Ireland final Healy trailed a considerable reputation. Diarmuid O'Sullivan, waiting for him at the Canal End, weighed up his options.

'My way was always to put down a marker—win the first ball and do something positive with it, for instance,' says O'Sullivan. 'But when he was walking up to me I could see how pale he was under the helmet. He was rattled. I could see that.

'He was a young lad who'd had a good day a couple of weeks beforehand. He'd had plenty of space to operate in, and I knew that wouldn't be the case against us—that Brian Murphy would be covering across for me. I could see the blood had drained from his face and I remember thinking, there's an opportunity here. He'll be a good player in time, but I might not get another chance to play in an All-Ireland final.'

O'Sullivan decided to welcome the Galway man to All-Ireland final Sunday. He took Healy's outstretched hand and drove his shoulder into the forward's chest.

'It rattled him for a while. I don't think he touched the ball for the first twenty-five minutes.'

And while Healy was out of sorts, O'Sullivan made hay, particularly when a long delivery came into the Cork full back line.

'I was standing next to him,' says the full back. 'I knew I was stronger than him, so I held him off with one arm, using my leverage pushing him away. He ended up on the ground, but I was gone.'

O'Sullivan took the ball and delivered it crisply up the middle, to where Timmy McCarthy was the man flying towards goal. However, McCarthy didn't gather the ball.

'As it was dropping near Timmy, I'd say he was thinking, redemption, I'll be sticking this up a load of fellas . . .' says O'Sullivan. 'Then his face dropped when Ben came across and grabbed it. If Ben had missed that, Timmy would have choked him.'

O'Connor had been lurking near by, and the discussions before the game were about to pay off.

'Diarmuid hit the ball straight down the middle,' he says, 'which wouldn't normally be our way of playing, but we had discussed going a bit longer when the chance arose, so it wasn't unexpected.

'I'd been over in the left corner, but I'd come outfield. I saw him clearing it and I'd started making my way in that general direction. I turned fast and looked behind me, and Ollie Canning had fallen. I knew he'd stumbled, that I had a half-yard, and I took off. The ball bounced right in front of me as I came across.

'Timmy was facing the goal, and he should have taken it—I had my back to the goal—but I got it, turned and hit it. Normally when I get the ball, I'd try to put it away from the keeper, but I didn't look; I just let fly. I should probably have put it to the other side of the Galway keeper, but that's how fast it happened. Lucky enough, it just popped in.'

Even at that moment—and hitting a goal in an All-Ireland hurling final must be as heightened an experience as any Corkman can enjoy—O'Connor stayed in character. He didn't lose the run of himself.

'Just as I struck it I got a push in the back, so I ended up on the ground. I saw it go in, but while you might run around or something if you were on your feet, after falling, the initial excitement was kind of gone by the time I stood up. I was probably as well off. I might have done something stupid if I'd been on my feet.'

Donal Óg Cusack pays tribute to his club mate's part in the goal: 'Diarmuid now is focused on getting the best out of himself. He wasn't always like that and he'd say that himself. The result is the thing. You're not into the bull and you'd be calmer.

'That day Sully said to me after a couple of minutes that he was knackered. I said, sure you always feel like that, and he knew that. And a minute or two later he was saying he felt great. With experience you'd be calm enough to have a conversation like that.'

Cork kept that lead all through, and the change in style helped.

'The only real difference was in Donal Óg's puck-outs, where he went longer,' says Mulcahy. 'Jerry got a point from a Brian Murphy hand pass; Ben got a point from a hand pass from me, which was typical of our style. But the fact that Donal Óg hit the ball a bit further might have caught them on the hop a little bit.'

Galway rallied towards the end of the game, but Cork always

seemed to have the wherewithal to keep them at bay. When the westerners got a goal, it was almost an anticlimax to the man on the Cork goal-line. Diarmuid O'Sullivan was primed as backs and forwards tussled in the square: 'I was expecting a rocket; I was braced for that, and suddenly it was trickling towards me and I was falling . . . I looked like the greatest fool of all time. It trickled in as I fell; it was a huge disappointment. If it had been a rocket, I'd have said something.'

Despite the goal, Donal Óg Cusack was on top form. The safety-first approach of 1999 had given way to full expression as a keeper, as seen in the point he pulled down in the 2005 final as it was going over the bar.

'That goes back to Tommy Walsh's point in 2003,' he says. 'Every time I see him I think of it; I should have brought it down and that was a bigger regret than the goal. I said at that time, I'll never again not go for it. And I never have.'

'I felt it was the fastest game I played in,' says Pat Mulcahy. 'It was the one day I was absolutely knackered walking off the pitch afterwards. Galway certainly didn't close us down as much as Clare had, and while they had better forwards than Clare, they didn't seem able to score as much. I always felt because of that we'd win. If your forwards are scoring, you'll always feel you've a chance of winning, no matter what happens at the other end of the field.

'I felt that day we'd score. They came back at us a couple of times, but we found it easy to respond. We scored from a couple of puck-outs directly, and that doesn't happen against a strong defence.'

'I thought we had another few gears,' says Ronan Curran. 'Maybe Galway came a couple of years too early. They'd beaten Kilkenny, who were tiring a bit. I think that's when Brian Cody felt he'd have to change things, but we were that bit stronger. Any time they came at us, we had an extra gear and a lot of that was confidence from 2004.'

For the two corner backs, the final whistle meant the dream had come true.

'It didn't hit me for a while,' says Brian Murphy. 'I was drained, the crowd was running on, and I was thinking, a five-minute break here would be grand. But you get swept up in it, you meet people you know and it sinks in: I've won an All-Ireland.'

For Mulcahy it was vindication for the years since 1997.

'It was the ultimate. Eight years of slogging . . . I felt I'd contributed, that I'd put the shoulder to the wheel and been a valuable part of the team, that I could be proud of it.'

His club mate got a nudge from a selector afterwards about his goal.

'Straight after the All-Ireland final Ger [Cunningham] said it to me,' says Ben O'Connor. "You got it today."'

Ó hAilpín walked up the steps to accept the Liam McCarthy. His all-Irish passionate speech—'Is fada an turas é ó Fiji go Corcaigh, is ó Corcaigh go Pairc an Crocaigh'—was unforgettable.

'Even though I had it in my mind earlier in the season,' he says, 'I didn't want to do it until we were definitely qualified for the final. As soon as we got qualified, the week after, I called up to Jack Beausang in the North Monastery.

'I knew what I wanted to say, but I asked him to put a piece of snas in there, which he did. I just read it once or twice and put it away. It was always going to be in Irish, as simple as that. It wasn't that someone came to me and said, it would be nice if you did it.

'The fact was that I did go to Irish school for six years. The AG has been great to me. It gives guys up the Northside opportunities that they mightn't get. The hurling was good to me in the Mon as well; it really developed my hurling career. I did an interview and I thanked a lot of the teachers and the hurling coaches in the Mon, and my speech was a big thank you for the product that I am. Did I know it was going to have a snowball effect? Not at all. I just saw it as a duty. I spoke in Irish to Donal [O'Grady], to other teachers like Tony Duggan. It was natural.'

Ever the perfectionist, he saw a downside in the captain's armband.

'I was delighted to get the chance to captain Cork and as it worked out, we landed it, which was even better. Only thirty players in the history of Cork have ever done that. When you take the playing group in Cork, you are one of thirty fellas, which is only a tiny percentage.

'But the drawback with captaincy is you can easily get caught without being focused on your own game. And that's what I found. You're talking here and there, you're trying to please everyone and at the end of the day you need to get your house in order. My 2005 season was well below 2004. 2004 was probably my best season because I could do whatever I could and I could concentrate fully.

'Fast forward a year, there was stuff I would have loved to have done, but I just couldn't—the extra bit of fine-tuning. I just didn't have the time for it.'

For the manager there was a sense that life would never be quite the same.

'I suppose you don't appreciate what it means to your life—in a good way—for a while after it,' says John Allen. 'Only this year I can see the benefits to managing a team to win an All-Ireland. You're invited onto TV programmes, to write columns . . . You don't appreciate it.

'For the ten minutes after the game you don't get a chance to show how elated you are because the field is so crowded. I'd love if they went back to the system they tried a few years ago, keeping supporters off the field, even just for the twenty minutes after the final whistle.

'I didn't appreciate the significance, maybe until losing in 2006. Then you appreciate the whole thing. Having won in 2005, it wasn't as bad to lose in 2006. I suppose it depends on what you do with the opportunities that present themselves afterwards, but I'm so delighted to have managed a team to an All-Ireland. It has opened a lot of doors for me.'

The year would have a last twist.

Donal Óg Cusack was on the team holiday when a couple of telephone calls from home disquieted him. There were suggestions that a particular newspaper story was to be published about him, and after the goalkeeper flew back to Dublin for a GPA meeting, he came home to Cork. There he was told that the newspaper had decided to approach him or a member of the panel to substantiate loose rumours. Most inter-county players have to learn to live with lurid allegations made in the unregulated world of internet chatrooms, but this was different.

'We sent out a text to the panel suggesting a standard answer if lads got a call from this newspaper,' says Cusack. 'We felt it was the best way to deal with it.

'Sully got the call, had the answer and gave it; he'd be great in a situation like that. I thought that'd be the end of it.'

It wasn't. Reporters called to Cusack's home asking questions. One arrived into his place of work but was headed off by a vigilant security guard ('a man who's anti-GPA but a great guy,' says Cusack).

'I didn't care. My attitude would have been, let them write what they want,' says Cusack. 'But the people close to me said if it was any other player, I'd have been fighting for them. That's what happened. We dealt with it.'

There was enough to be dealing with. Diarmuid O'Sullivan recalls picking up a newspaper the day after the All-Ireland final, which trumpeted Cork's chances of three in a row. The pressure was already on.

# IF THEY COME TO PLAY IT HARD, THEN WE CAN PLAY IT HARDER

The three in a row might have been hanging over the team from early on—from before 2006 even began—but Pat Mulcahy was dealing with the captaincy. There was enough to be going on with.

'I didn't find it a hindrance on the playing side. There are certain other responsibilities, there's more attention on you, which goes with the territory. It was huge because of the three in a row, obviously. You try to take it game by game, but that's still in the back of your mind.

'It was great—but it was only great if we won. That was how I looked at it.'

For John Allen there were other considerations. He knew the team would be under pressure, and he didn't have to wait long to see the evidence.

'I don't think the three in a row was an issue early on. Early in the year there was an article in one of the papers castigating our players, and we had a meeting on the holiday in South Africa where I reminded the players that we were the team to be knocked, whether it was things like refs giving bad decisions—not deliberately, but because you're naturally inclined to favour the underdog. I was very aware that that was the case.

'I was aware the players had to be careful not to get drawn into issues in the press, or to be goaded into getting sent off—not to give anyone an opportunity to damage us, to maintain control.'

John Gardiner remembers the article. It suggested the Cork players hadn't mixed with those from other counties on a Railway Cup trip to Boston.

'People from other counties think we're clannish or whatever,' says Gardiner. 'Maybe we are, but everyone on the Cork panel is as sound as anyone I've met from other counties. Every fella with Cork is a normal guy, but there probably were some misconceptions.

'We'd organised going to a basketball game in Boston, and the rest of the lads had a few beers, but we'd organised the tickets. What were we going to do? I can see how lads would get upset, thinking, we're supposed to be here as a team; the Cork lads are off on their own. But we only had six tickets for the basketball game. If we'd had sixty, they'd have all been welcome to come along.'

Allen is careful not to overstate the persecution.

'I think pressure like that reinforces the team. I'm open-minded enough to see that journalists are looking for an angle, some little bit of tangible proof that their story will stand up. That story from the Railway Cup, that our players didn't associate with other lads . . . I knew that because we were at the top table, All-Ireland champions for two years; people would be looking to find fault. That didn't worry us because we knew it might happen.'

Still, the team was under the microscope. Brian Murphy, one of the quietest panellists, acknowledges the pressure.

'You'd talk to lads on the quiet about the three in a row. Everyone remembers the team of the seventies because of the three in a row, and it was a huge motivation. Kilkenny had come so close in 2004 . . . we'd had a good run, nobody was retiring, and with a bit of luck we could pull it off. But it was definitely discussed, at meetings we had and so on.'

'Were we after three in a row?' says Donal Óg Cusack. 'You better believe it. Every winter there'd been a sense of, don't mind the celebrations, we'll get into it, from me as well as others. But we trained well on the team holiday; fellas were in good shape. It was an opportunity we weren't going to get again.'

Ronan Curran agrees: 'Everyone was saying they weren't thinking about it, but they were. In a sports-mad place like Cork, particularly in hurling, everyone was asking, will ye do it? Will ye win the three in a row?'

Cork had Clare in their Munster championship opener. After their narrow defeat the previous year, Clare felt they had unfinished business with the champions, something John Allen was well aware of.

'There were stories they were doing unbelievable training and so on, but we gave a good performance that day.'

'We'd heard a lot about the semi-final the previous year,' says Donal Óg Cusack, 'that they felt they should have beaten us and so on—stuff they mightn't have actually said at all, but we put in a good performance. We beat them well.'

It set up a Munster final against Tipperary, the same team they'd demolished in the first half of the corresponding fixture in 2005, only to hold out for a close win after the Blue and Gold rallied in the second half. Once Clare were out of the way, Allen and his selectors started thinking about their next challenge.

'Eoin Kelly's scoring feats took some of the heat off us,' says Allen, 'but I wouldn't have been looking ahead at the same time. As a management team we were looking at the next game the whole time.

'For four years I didn't go to many places, and for one reason— everywhere you go people ask about next Sunday, or last Sunday, or whatever. When I was manager of the Barrs footballers fifteen years ago, I couldn't take being told what to do. At least now I'm not manager, so it doesn't matter what they say, but I wouldn't have been able to take people slagging off this player or that player.

'As manager I wouldn't have read the papers, so I wouldn't really have been noticing what people were saying. You're so wrapped up in your own team anyway you wouldn't be paying attention.'

Still, Allen took notice of the wizard of Mullinahone.

'Of course you'd pay attention. We'd have had a Dan Shanahan tactic for limiting him under the ball, the same with Eoin Kelly. We put the tightest player on the team on him, Brian Murphy, and we had Seán Óg Ó hAilpín in front of him for puck-outs and so on.

'People not involved in teams wouldn't see that. You saw it in the 2006 final, you saw it in Tipp-Limerick in 2007, you see it in third midfielder options . . . Managers use tactics. It's just that people don't recognise it.'

It's a point echoed by Brian Murphy.

'Being brutally honest, I wouldn't think many people recognise that. Without abusing anyone, a huge proportion of people at a Cork game don't even have a club, or are after a few pints when they see the game.

'I'd say every fella has two or three people he relies on for their opinions on a game. You might hold a fella scoreless, but he could set up two or three goals for other players—the other corner back might be coming across to save you, and his man gets the scores as a result. It's a catch-22. Then you'd hear of games where a back has conceded seven points, but six of those might be from frees, or they might have been made by another forward.'

Murphy did well on Kelly, aided by Ó hAilpín lying deep in front of the Tipp man, but Cork started slowly. Lar Corbett scorched through to score early on—'a great goal,' says Donal Óg Cusack—and it was game on.

'Yeah, you'd be thinking, we've to tune in here,' says John Gardiner. 'Babs Keating was down behind the goal with Donal Óg about the sliotars . . . I suppose we didn't really start playing until we conceded that goal.'

Cork settled when Joe Deane set up Brian Corcoran for a goal in response, but then came the apotheosis of the running game. Brian

Murphy gathered the ball in the left corner, gave it to Ronan Curran, who played it on to Tom Kenny. Kenny drove forward, and up ahead Ben O'Connor could tell what was coming.

'It was like soccer, one-two and one-two,' says O'Connor. 'It showed the game plan, that if fellas believed in it that it'd work, whereas if you went back ten years—not even ten—the first fella who'd see the goal would put it over the bar.'

When the ball came to O'Connor on the sideline, he checked and looked for an option.

'I threw it out to Timmy; he passed to Tom; I'd gone and Tom gave it in to me. O'Grady had always said, put it in front, put it in front; the last thing you want is to break your stride and go back for it. His other thing was, don't mind one hand—he'd eat you if you didn't pick the ball with two hands. In 2004 Waterford played Kilkenny in the All-Ireland semi-final and a Waterford sub went for a ball late on. He had a chance of a goal, but he went in with one hand and he lost it. And O'Grady pointed that out to us the next night at training.

'Anyway, Tom put it in front of me and I got it into my hand. And then you had another thing O'Grady would say—go that extra little bit. At times people would give out we didn't get goals, but that day I said, here goes.'

O'Connor hit a wicked drive that beat Brendan Cummins at the near post. He didn't place it. 'I just hit as hard as I could—the shortest route.'

'You'd get a kick out of that. You're practising it all the time, and then it comes off in a game,' says John Gardiner. 'You believe in what you're doing, obviously, but then it comes off in a game and you see that it works.'

The game ground down to a close enough finish—another alarm bell, says Diarmuid O'Sullivan.

'We didn't finish them. But that had always been a problem for us. Other teams would keep going and going, but we just seemed to do enough. Goalscoring was a problem for us. We had chances over the years to go for goals and we didn't take them.

'That's not running down our forwards. They did the job for us often enough, but going for goal wouldn't have been the automatic choice.'

Mulcahy accepted the Munster championship trophy. Already he was thinking ahead. They all were.

'Without being arrogant, the All-Ireland final was what it was all about,' he says. 'It was nice to win, but it wouldn't mean as much without the All-Ireland.

'I was concerned before the game, because we'd wiped Tipp off the field in Cork the year before, and they weren't going to lie down two years in a row. That was a big win because they hit us with everything, got an early goal, but we were still good enough to weather the storm.'

Cork weren't dominating, and some theorists put it down to tiredness. Mulcahy rebuts that firmly.

'That's all in your mind,' he says. 'I genuinely believe that. But having said that, if you lose half a percentage point upstairs, you're fucked. That's the difference between winning and losing.

'There were a couple of things. Teams were copping on to our style, and the more big games you play, the more chances people have of copping on to your weaknesses. I'd had a good year in 2005, winning an All-Star, but people can see you on video and they see how to play you.

'I wasn't getting the high ball in that I could grab and break out with, for instance. I was getting dragged around the place. Teams were looking to play my weaker side. And I felt training had gone back a little bit. Not much, but I think some of the team were hoping to just get to the end of the year and thinking we could freshen things up after that.'

Part of the freshening up included a visitor. John Allen spent a long time arranging it, but when it fell into place he provided the team with the ideal guest.

'We never had sessions behind closed doors the week of a game,' says Diarmuid O'Sullivan. 'When I got the text to be in the Pairc at a certain time, I was surprised. I heard on the news that Roy Keane was in town with the guide dogs and started wondering.

'I rang Jim McEvoy and asked if he knew anything, then I rang Donal Óg and asked if he knew. I mentioned Roy Keane and he said, "You might be right." He was later than usual coming down the Pairc that night, and when I asked what he was doing, he told me he'd gone home for a Celtic jersey.'

O'Sullivan opened his gearbag; he'd gone home for his Manchester United jersey.

The team trained, and Keane was in the dugout before the players knew it. He watched training and joined them for tea—pasta and chicken—then Keane fielded questions.

'It was incredible,' says O'Sullivan. 'At half eleven, quarter to twelve, John said to him, "Roy, I think we've taken up enough of your time," but he was prepared to stay another while. He spoke about the winning mentality, about preparation, everything. Fantastic.'

Limerick were the quarter-final opponents. They were supposedly in disarray, with one of the heroes of 1973, Richie Bennis, being parachuted in to salvage something from their season after Joe McKenna resigned as manager. As it happened, Bennis almost did a lot more.

John Allen is unequivocal about the match.

'It was the most intimidating game I was ever involved in, as player or manager . . . it was just obnoxious behaviour.'

Soon after the start Allen called Jerry O'Connor over.

'Donie Ryan came with him. He stood in between the two of us and I pushed him away, and he fell over. I was thinking, Jesus, I'm in trouble here. It was an awful game.'

Though Allen has support from Dr Con Murphy—'I think Limerick had massive physical presence on the day, to put it mildly; maybe that was a warning sign for the team'—some of the players disagree.

'I didn't think it was that bad,' says Pat Mulcahy. 'There wasn't a huge intimidating crowd. We probably took them for granted a little. You can talk about it as much as you want, that Limerick were tough and so on, but we were probably thinking about Waterford in the semi-final. Then there was a shower, they got their tails up and it became a much harder game. But physically? Not that tough.'

The man alongside him felt the same, but then again he had his own points to prove.

'I'd been criticised after the Clare and Tipp games,' Diarmuid O'Sullivan says. 'People saying I was finished—again—though I'd only given away something like two points from play.'

In the dressing room before the Limerick game, O'Sullivan got all the motivation he needed.

'In the programme for the Limerick game, I saw there were some individual battles made out, and mine was "advantage Brian Begley". It's nice when you go into the dressing room to have a flick through the programme, but when I saw that, I said to myself, I'll have to be right for this.

'Myself and Pat probably thrived on it. Even when we marked each other in club games, we'd play it hard and physical, and with Brian [Murphy] that was our attitude in the full back line: if they come to play it hard, then we can play it harder than them. That was our attitude. But that was a strange game. We were doing well, but then there was a shower—and we were gone.'

Out in the half back line, John Gardiner's experience was somewhat different.

'It was bad. It wasn't like any other game we've played. There was belting, but it wasn't the usual. The ball was at the other end of the field at one stage and a guy ran at me. I thought I was getting a shoulder, so I dropped my own shoulder, but I got a hurley in the face. I got stitches under my eye after it. The whole thing, it was like something you'd hear about from years ago.

'And I got booked after that. Now I'd say I get booked every second match, but that was one time I did nothing and got a yellow card for it. I've no complaints about those other yellows, but that one . . .'

Before the second half began a man ran out to the Cork midfielders and tried to assault Jerry O'Connor, only to be collared by Jerry Wallace. It contributed to the oppressive atmosphere, then came the shower, and Cork lost their way. There was a bad omen when a ball ricocheted off Pat Mulcahy's boot and shot over the bar. But when Cork won a penalty with ten minutes left, it looked like the chance to put the game away.

However, as the appointed penalty-taker, Diarmuid O'Sullivan, came up the field to take it, he was confronted by Limerick players who turned the journey into the stations of the cross, complete with falls.

'We'd been awarded the penalty. Diarmuid was the taker,' says Allen. 'But it took so long you were thinking is he ever going to get there?'

'It was probably the strangest thing I ever saw in a game,' says Gardiner. 'A fella coming up to take a penalty and he gets belted around the place. Now, he probably had a ball he was bringing up, but I don't know if people thought we had some secret ball we were going to fire out of a rocket-launcher or what. But it was incredible, seeing one of your players getting knocked to the ground—and nothing done about it.'

O'Sullivan did in fact have a dry ball with him.

'Jerry Wallace ran in to dry my hurley,' he says, 'and gave me the ball. But I knew I'd been seen taking it. When the Limerick player hit me, I said to myself, if I go down here I might get it out of my shorts and put it under my arm. And I did, I got it up under my arm while there were players around me.'

He eventually made it to the Limerick 21, but by then Allen made an executive decision: 'I felt he wasn't going to be in a fit state to take a penalty, so Joe knocked it over the bar.'

'I don't remember how aggressive it was or not,' says the full back. 'But John was right to tell me to give the ball to Joe, I suppose . . . it was an incredible sequence of events.'

Ben O'Connor's coolness saved the day, nailing a late free to give Cork the win. But the cracks were visible, even if Ronan Curran saw some plus points.

'Limerick are always physical, always tough. In 2004 before we played them, we did a lot of work with tackle bags because we expected that. In 2006 it was probably the most physical battle we ever had, and we were lucky we had the few years' experience, because we probably wouldn't have handled that in 2003, 2004.

'There were a few stupid, niggly things from the start. The game was stop-start, we never got a run going, and there was a big shower in the second half. They were coming in waves and we were under huge pressure. You could sense lads looking around to see if something was going to happen, but the experience stood to us.'

'I remember John Gardiner got a bad belt in the face in that game,' says Cusack. 'But apart from that, it was just a dour, tight game we didn't get a run in. At that stage the victory is more important than anything. And we won. There was a point in the second half when it looked like it was going away from us, and Limerick showed the following year that they were no bad side.

'The attitude that we were only just getting there doesn't wash with me. We were putting up an outfit that was taking on the best in the country. We beat Tipperary, Limerick, Waterford, and Kilkenny beat us by three points in our worst performance. I read afterwards that our game had been found out by the time we played Kilkenny, but we were still winning.

'That's how I look at it—not, if we could only just get over the line, or whatever.'

Huge challenges still lay ahead, says the captain.

'We had a couple of very good meetings after the Limerick game,' says Mulcahy. 'We knew we were going downhill. But we got it up for the Waterford game.'

# THE WORST TO LOSE

Waterford came to the semi-final with confidence. After beating Tipperary convincingly in their quarter-final, they had reason to be. Donal Óg Cusack could see the improvement.

'Tony Browne, for instance, has turned into a far better player than I'd have thought,' says Cusack. 'In 2006 I was sitting in the stand before the semi-final and when he came out for a look around I thought, he's ready, he's fit.

'I'd have seen them as hit or miss, but now they have lads who are in for the long haul, the long campaign rather than the odd ambush. They've sustained themselves.'

Waterford had nourished themselves on goals all year. For a team that didn't tend to score a lot of goals themselves, Cork paid close attention to opposition players who could bother Cusack. Dan Shanahan was twelve months away from his hurler-of-the-year form, but he still posed a huge threat.

'We saw him as a player who could take the ball out of the air and score goals,' says John Allen. 'That was the only day I asked Seán Óg to sacrifice his own game, and he did so very effectively. Teams have to make plans and we sat down, say on the Tuesday we picked the team, and went through the options. In the team hotel for half an hour before the game, we'd go through possible substitutions and moves so we wouldn't be facing an unknown situation.'

One possible substitution was young Cathal Naughton. In private, two weeks before the Waterford game, Allen had suggested to this writer that Pa Cronin might be an option off the bench, but Cronin's examinations had robbed him of valuable preparation time. But after that conversation the manager saw Naughton in training. He was irresistible.

'He was exceptional in two fifteen-minute games,' says Allen. 'We'd seen him at U-21 level and maybe midfield didn't suit him, but after those sessions before the Waterford game you'd have been saying, my God, who's that fella?

'He was showing, he was scoring, he was passing fellas out . . . Going into a game like that, he was just what you'd want, a player who was an unknown quantity. But he wouldn't have been up the pecking order if he hadn't shown exceptional form.'

In a tight game Ó hAilpín's discipline limited Shanahan hugely, but Waterford nudged ahead after a second-half Eoin Kelly goal. Allen and his colleagues had a call to make. Naughton arrived on the field and within seconds he'd snapped the ball up on the right sideline and pointed.

'We had discussed the move, and while I'd take credit for the 2005 semi-final moves, I wouldn't in this case,' says Allen. 'I'd told Jerry O'Connor and John Gardiner that John wasn't taking the long-range frees any more, that Jerry had the call on those. If he felt he could score them, he'd take them, and if not it was down to John.

'When Cathal came on, the free had been given. John taking the free meant the corner forwards knew he wouldn't be going for a score, so they knew the plan was that they'd break to the opposite corner before the ball was struck.'

'That was some score, the way it worked out,' says Gardiner. 'He knew what to do, but my fear was he wouldn't run. I knew what I had to do, but I was thinking, there's no way he'll make the run. Next thing he's there.'

'In fairness to Cathal,' says Allen, 'when John set up to take the free, he ran, and John gave him the ball. It took something for him to come on and do the right thing according to the plan, even though the game was in the balance.'

Ronan Curran sees a wider context for Naughton's score: 'That's the difference; there's been a big change. Cathal's a massive hurler and he saved us that day because the work had been put into him and he had the confidence to come on and do it. Neil has come in and done the same. You need everyone to work together, but that's been done now.'

Struck by a hammer blow, Waterford showed maturity. They banged over two points with five minutes left.

'They just came and came,' says Diarmuid O'Sullivan. 'That was a change in them, because they'd have wilted away in previous years. They've shown since that they'll still come, that they'd developed a winning mentality. You could see it in that game.'

With time almost up, Tony Browne gathered the ball in midfield. Ben O'Connor arrived to contest and a free was given. It was a long way from the Cork goal, but Ken McGrath stood over the ball and it was clear he'd go for it.

'That wasn't an easy free,' says Gardiner. 'In fairness, it was miles out. It took some balls to save it, but Donal Óg always mentions the 2003 final, when a ball just went over the bar, and he'd say he regrets not going for it, not pulling it down. And we'd be thinking, leave it off, leave it off.'

'Tommy Walsh,' says Cusack. 'The point in 2003.'

Ronan Curran was next to his keeper: 'I stand on the goal-line for long-range frees, and Donal Óg says, "If I call I'll take it", and I'd be thinking, I hope he calls it—a wet day, last minute . . .'

'He was saying "hold them out",' says Diarmuid O'Sullivan. 'I knew then that if he had the chance he'd play it. I knew there was something coming. He was well off the ground when he played it.'

'I remember watching the ball come in and thinking it was going wide,' says Curran, 'then thinking, shit, it's going to make it. Then he swiped.'

'I was thinking, what is Donal Óg doing? We'd take another day out,' says Brian Murphy. 'As a corner back you'd dread any ball dropping in the square, but he got a fair bat out. He'd do it in training. He had it prepared, so it wasn't a one-off.'

Cusack batted the ball out towards the wing deliberately. Even then there was plenty of work to be done, as Brian Corcoran won possession.

'Corcoran deliberately dropped the ball instead of hitting it downfield,' says O'Sullivan. 'Ken McGrath was waiting there. You had two of the most intelligent hurlers around there, and doing the right thing when it was needed.'

Cusack wouldn't have been ready in previous years to make that save. By 2006 it was a no-brainer.

'Each year the training got better and better,' says the goalkeeper. 'Ger wanted me to keep evolving as a keeper, and in 2004 he said, "You're heading into the best years of your career as a keeper", and each year we tried to make it better. We'd go after a new skill if we thought there was value in it.

'We spent time practising that, and Ger would be very tough on me. The ultimate was to stop the ball and to get it out of danger, and by the time of the Waterford game, because we'd trained for it so much, going for it was non-negotiable.'

'It was an unbelievable save,' says Curran. 'But then, out in the corner it was pure guts, swarming on the ball. It was pure guts, a great feeling to win.'

Cork were through to the All-Ireland final. The manager pays tribute to Cusack's stop and the preparatory work behind it.

'It was a fantastic save,' says John Allen. 'To deflect it out to the sideline like that . . . he's worked so hard to get where he's at. Most nights he, Ger, Martin [Coleman] and Anthony [Nash] would go off and do their training. They'd often be there when we'd be finished. You'd be pleading with them to come in . . . his touch is sublime. It's the best in the game.'

The game ended in the left corner, and Cork were through to a fourth final in a row. Had they played their best game of the year a few weeks too early?

'I felt training went well, that we were as good as what was there,' says Joe Deane. 'But unknown to ourselves we probably got a little stale. We had a great team meeting two weeks before playing Waterford in the semi-final, that we'd need to be up for it, and after that training was unreal, as good as it ever was.

'We hadn't played to our full potential that year and I felt we were coming right after scares against Limerick, and we just got there against Waterford. And remember, some people saw Waterford as being better than Kilkenny that year. Maybe we played our All-Ireland final in the semi and we were gone off the boil for the final.'

'We were scraping it,' says Gardiner. 'We weren't playing well even though we were winning games. We weren't reaching the heights we had, and though you'd hear fellas say it's a sign of a good team to win not playing well, that's not true. The Waterford game was the perfect example. We hung on and hung on, and we were delighted, but looking back . . . yeah. We were scraping home.'

The heat started to come on in earnest.

'Fellas really started to feel the pressure then,' says Diarmuid O'Sullivan. 'We tried to put it out of our minds, but it was coming and coming—that fellas could retire after it, that kind of thing.'

First they had to face Kilkenny. John Allen recognised the different challenge.

'Kilkenny weren't really into tactics, they had so many good hurlers,' he says. 'I won't say we didn't expect something. The word was out that you had to stop our two runners, but we'd come out of plenty of tight spots. I was surprised they were so tactical, but they did the same in the U-21 final replay that year. They closed down everyone.'

There was one unexpected dividend when Donal Óg Cusack got a phone call he didn't expect.

'Peter Barry rang me and said he wanted to talk about 2002, the league final and that,' says Cusack. '"I didn't mean what came out in the papers that time," he said. "Everything that ye've done since, I agree with. I respect the way ye've driven on the GPA, and if there's anything I can do, I'll do it for ye. But I want to end this bad feeling between a few of us."

'We had a great conversation, and since then I'd never say anything about them, and I spoke to a few of our lads who were involved, and our feeling was, fair play to him to have the balls to ring up and was man enough to want to sort it out. And we said we'd leave it at that.'

As for the All-Ireland final itself, Ronan Curran is frank: 'They were like frigging bees. Everywhere. All over us.'

'They were set up to put extreme pressure on our full back line; they defended from the front,' says Pat Mulcahy. 'I remember in the first ten minutes I gave away a free; I'd had possession, lost it, then gave away a free, and I saw three or four of their forwards jumping up and down, banging each other on the back. They were targeting our full back line.

'It was the same old story. We'd played so many games that they'd analysed us really well. It was the flip side of 2004, and we'd spoken about that, but we couldn't do anything about that. I felt we prepared for it well.'

Kilkenny dropped deep and invited Cork onto them, a tactic that paid dividends.

'I noticed it in the puck-outs, the fact that they had five men in the half back line,' says Diarmuid O'Sullivan. 'They had tried that before but broke after half an hour. But they stayed with it in 2006, and that made it hard for us.'

With minutes to the break Kilkenny got the vital goal. The ball dropped into the square and bounced out of O'Sullivan's hand. Aidan Fogarty made no mistake.

'Fellas said since, if only you'd caught that ball . . .' O'Sullivan says. 'Those things happen. I couldn't get my left hand to it. I was just trying to knock it out and their man did what he was probably trained to do from the age of five, stayed off for the breaking ball and buried it.'

Mulcahy recalls the mood at half-time being positive, even though the players knew they were in a battle. A few minutes after the break he was taken off. He didn't enjoy being called ashore, but frank as always, he dissects the feeling as well as he can, particularly when asked if he feels he should have been left on.

'I suppose not. I'll be straight. At the time I was gutted, depressed. I found it very hard to handle. But afterwards I felt I'd played in two other All-Ireland finals and conceded no score and one free, so of three All-Ireland finals I'd played well in two and bad in one. Sully is an outstanding full back. He was outstanding in 1999 and 2004, yet he conceded 1-4 in 2003.

'I tried to look at it rationally in hindsight. I didn't play well, but if you play in three All-Ireland finals there's always a chance that one of them isn't going to go well. The worst was being captain, which highlighted it, and with Wayne on the sideline, a quality corner back, so people were going to ask questions.

'Outside criticism like that doesn't bother me. For myself there were regrets, but I can honestly say I wouldn't have changed any-thing in the lead-up. People said the captaincy affected me; I don't think it affected me on the pitch. I just think teams knew me that little bit better and were able to expose my weaknesses a little better. But in my opinion the captaincy didn't affect me.'

Still, some videotape doesn't get much airplay in the Mulcahy house.

'I've never watched the game and don't intend to. I found that the more big games you play, the more chance there is you'll lose. I don't like it, because I fucking hate losing, but that's life and I'm stronger for it.

'If I can say I gave my all, I'm happy. My only regret would be not being mentally right going out on the pitch. And you only know that ten minutes into the game. You realise you haven't prepared for this. If I'm tuned in properly and I don't play well, then I've no problem with it. But if I'm not tuned in properly I'm furious with myself.'

Cusack, meanwhile, was optimistic even when Cork were chasing the game.

'Even in the last quarter I was telling the backs to keep it steady, that there'd be a chance. And we were in with a shout going into the last quarter. If we'd won, Cody would have been finished.

'I don't like the bull. I don't like being false with fellas. I know Eddie Brennan. He's a sound fella. I'd have no problems with any Kilkenny lads I've met out. If I were on Cody's team I'd probably love the guy, but I'm not, and that's just the way it is.'

The game petered out. Kilkenny strangled Cork, and a late goal by Ben O'Connor made it a three-point game at the finish. A false read, says Joe Deane.

'Their intensity was something we couldn't match,' he says. 'They tackled in twos and threes, and maybe if we changed our tactics as we'd done in 2005 we might have got a result, but it wasn't to be. Although we got within a goal of them, they were more than three points ahead of us.

'Nothing compensates for losing an All-Ireland final. It was our crack at three in a row, and it didn't come off. What was devastating was we didn't play well. We left nothing behind us in 2003, while in 2006 we didn't play as well as we did in the semi-final. That was the really disappointing thing.'

John Gardiner doesn't hand any bouquets to the Croke Park ground staff.

'The biggest factor that day—I thought the pitch was a disgrace. You'd play challenge games in January and the fields are better.

When was the last time you were in Croke Park and you'd see the trail left by the parade? You could turn around and see the footprints of the band and the teams in the grass. I don't know whose decision that was, but it was a bad call.

'That's not why we lost, but it was definitely a factor. Kilkenny were better on the day. They were hungry, they stuck to their tactics rigidly and we found it very hard, particularly to win puck-outs.

'An All-Ireland final is the worst to lose. Don't mind this talk about losing a semi being the worst. You're gutted. In 2003 we knew deep down we'd probably be able to get back. I believed we'd be in the final at the start of 2004. I wasn't as definite at the start of 2007. If we hadn't won in 2004 and 2005, it would have been very hard. I look at Waterford and I wonder how they keep going.

'One change was that I was a student in 2003; I was working in 2006. There's a big difference. I had more time to train in winter 2003; I got straight back into it. Now you've work—even though the lads in work are very good to me—you have other commitments. Does it make it better if you've won one? It probably does.'

'2006 was more disappointing than 2003 for me,' says Ben O'Connor. 'We'd had chances in 2003, whereas in 2006 we just didn't perform. We lost by three points but we were well off the pace. The goal was no consolation. Not at all. People think the pressure of the three in a row got to us, but it was more that it was one of those days.'

'They had a game plan for the puck-outs,' says Brian Murphy. 'We were hitting it to Jerry and Tom and the half forwards created the space, but we couldn't make the space. No matter how far you hit the ball, if your player is surrounded by two or three opposition players, then you won't succeed.

'A shorter game might have drawn them out. We could have hand passed it over them, but they had a good game plan. You have to hand it to them. The goal in the last few minutes meant we were only three points from three in a row, but on the pitch afterwards I remember thinking, we'll never get this chance again.'

The bad news didn't end there. Diarmuid O'Sullivan was collared for a drug test after the game.

'It's hard after losing an All-Ireland final. You're off the field at five o'clock, and I was still in the drug testing room at twenty to eight. It was a hard place to be. They don't let anyone in to see you; there are two or three people standing in the same room as you. Hard.'

O'Sullivan told his team mates to leave Croke Park, saying he'd see them later in the hotel. They stayed. When the full back was finally released by the drug testers, the team left the stadium the same way they'd arrived—together.

# HE'S NOT GETTING AWAY
# WITH THAT

The cold light of a September Monday helped Allen adjust.

'I'd been involved for about eight years, two as manager, and the law of diminishing returns was bound to set in. There comes a time when the players have had enough of you and you've enough of them and I'd decided two years was enough.

'I suppose in retrospect one change would be that I'd have involved the players more, particularly the subs; I'd have kept them in the picture more. But it was a dream. Apart from the last day, I'd never had to take criticism for losing a game. If you did things differently, you don't know how they'll go, but in a final you don't have a second chance.'

And there were great days along the way. After the semi-final against Waterford in 2006, the Cork panel and management headed to Heuston Station for the train home. When the Cork people already aboard saw them, they applauded as the party made their way down to their carriage.

'It was probably the most genuine, spontaneous reaction we got in the three or four years,' says Allen. 'They looked out the windows at us and every single carriage clapped us as we walked down the platform.'

Pat Mulcahy knew it was the end of inter-county action for him.

'After ten years there were other things in life. I felt I'd given it my all. There were good young fellas to come in and maybe I wasn't quite as driven. That was the lack of half of a percentage point upstairs I mentioned. That makes a huge difference.'

Mulcahy's long duel with Wayne Sherlock for a starting berth never became a problem, says the 2006 captain.

'He was a super player to be alongside; he's super-confident,' says Mulcahy. 'In 2005 he was injured and in 2006 it was hard, probably tougher for him than me, but we got on great and I never had any problems with him, or him with me.'

Perspective arrived for everyone soon enough.

Joe Deane had noticed a hardening in his testicle throughout the summer, but by early October it had swollen considerably and the player was a little worried.

'Even at that stage I wasn't that concerned,' Deane told Tony Leen of the *Irish Examiner* early in 2007. 'But within a few days the testicle was two or three times the size of the other one. It was getting sore and awkward and I rang Dr Con again.'

The team medic put him onto a urologist and the diagnosis was swift. Cancer.

'He assured me the recovery rate is very high, of the order of 96%,' said Deane. 'But I was going to lose the testicle anyway. He was straight down the middle with the information. He didn't beat about the bush either. He wasn't telling me I was going to be fine the next morning. And he raised the possibility of chemotherapy . . .

'At the back of your mind, there are moments when you are thinking how bad could this get? Could I die? Let's face it, you hear of people dying of cancer every day, and I wouldn't have been *au fait* with the differences between testicular and other types of cancer in terms of seriousness. I had read Lance Armstrong's *It's Not About*

*The Bike*, and knew there was the capacity for further problems. For a brief second it crosses your mind, but it never took a hold.'

A CT scan revealed small traces of cancer in his stomach, but broadly speaking, the prognosis was encouraging.

'The blood tests had shown there was cancer,' said Deane. 'But I don't think I ever got to a point of turning corners. I was never so far down the road that I felt, I'm in trouble here. I always felt very positive, getting the operation done, getting the treatment and getting better. Never felt a stage where I was turning any corner.

'The following Tuesday I remember getting out of bed, and I was feeling great. I wanted to start the chemotherapy immediately. My oncologist explained about the cancer in the blood, but did say on the first visit that I wouldn't necessarily have to go for treatment. But I wanted to get the process started, get it over and done with. I did the sperm banking in Dublin for three days, and everything else to make myself ready.'

If Deane had to have chemotherapy, he might be back in contention for the All-Ireland quarter-finals in August. He was setting himself a tight schedule, but then there was a chink of light. The oncologist told him the traces of cancer in the blood had dissipated. There was no need for chemotherapy.

'I said, that's great. I wasn't jumping around or heading off on the piss. Okay, it was a bonus, but as time was going on, the vibe I was getting was that the treatment was by no means certain. I'd be a positive person anyway, so I was nearly expecting it going in.'

Deane wasn't shy about urging men to get themselves checked out: 'The thing is for fellas to get checked out as regularly as possible, and if there is a situation, always be positive. Always. Males are more bravado, especially younger guys, and it's very difficult for them to speak to their father or doctor and say, I've got a problem with my testicles.'

Lowlights of the period included the tabloid reporter who called to the Deane household in Killeagh, but others behaved better. The men who spent summer Sundays coursing Deane around Thurles and Croke Park were quick to make contact. Steve McDonagh,

Damien Hayes, the entire Tipperary squad, DJ Carey, Gary Kirby, George O'Connor—they all sent letters and cards. A pleasant surprise, yet given the individuals involved, no surprise.

In the summer the unmistakable yellow helmet was again seen at corner forward, and no allowances were being made by opposing corner backs. That was just the way Deane wanted it.

John Allen's departure meant a vacancy. He himself had recommended continuity, and most observers felt that was a tacit endorsement of Ger Cunningham. After a few weeks, however, Gerald McCarthy was appointed manager. He brought a considerable reputation into the dressing room—five All-Ireland senior medals, as well as a stint coaching Waterford as recently as 2001—but it was a surprising break with the previous regime.

For his part, Cunningham concedes he didn't go bald-headed for the job.

'I haven't gone on record since that time,' says Cunningham. 'I never went on the record at the time saying I was interested in the job, but having been involved for a couple of years, if the opportunity came your way . . . was I prepared for it? Did I want it?

'I couldn't really say, because you can't really assume anything when you're involved with the Cork team. And when the call didn't come, I never really pursued it to the situation where I put everything in place to be in a position to be appointed. But when the call didn't come, irrespective of having played for twenty years and having been a selector for a couple of years, not even to get a phone call to say, thanks very much for this or that, we're going a different road . . . That would be fine. Anyone who puts his name forward, you have to expect knocks as well.

'What was disappointing was the six or eight weeks around that time, the talk and the assumption that you might take over created huge pressure. A lot of people assumed you were taking over and it was hugely stressful.

'I felt after being involved, the likes of myself, [selectors] Patsy

[Morrissey], Joe [O'Leary] and Fred [Sheedy], none of us got a phone call to say thanks. We worked hard; it was finishing and we were walking away, but the dismissiveness . . . It was as if you didn't exist. The positive side of that was it got me back involved with the Barrs.'

The negative side was that the players picked up on the dismissiveness, as Cunningham puts it. On the team holiday in Mexico, Cusack remembers some of the players showing him an interview which they'd printed from the internet.

'Gerald had said he didn't like "their" hand passing game,' says Cusack. 'My first thought was, what does he mean by "their"? We felt we had enough fellas waiting in the long grass for us after losing the All-Ireland final to Kilkenny, but then someone who was joining us in the war, if you like, was giving them ammunition.'

'Were we unhappy with the treatment of Ger and Patsy?' asks Seán Óg Ó hAilpín. 'Definitely. The argument against continuity is always, isn't it great to have a change, but I maintain Ger and Patsy would have changed things themselves a bit. They'd have taken the blueprint and tinkered with it; they would have made their changes the way John Allen did with Donal O'Grady's blueprint. But at least the structures would have remained.

'Those structures and foundations weren't carried through by the 2007 management; they said they did, but if they had been, we wouldn't have had the rumblings people heard in Cork in 2007, the teething problems.'

Rumours weren't long rattling around Cork about discord in the hurling camp, and they weren't entirely without foundation. Early in the year Cork played Waterford in Dungarvan and two of the strongest personalities involved clashed.

'Donal Óg has been coached to puck the ball out short to someone if that player is free,' says Ó hAilpín. 'Only he can call it, and he wouldn't do it every time, and there was a situation at half-time in that game that Gerald asked Donal to go long, to cut out the short puck-outs.

'When the team went out for the second half, Donal was last out and he said to Gerald, "If the same situation comes up, I'll go short again." Gerald saw that as a challenge and looked for a meeting with Donal Óg.

'That was an example of the management not knowing what they were getting into. Under O'Grady and Allen, if a player was called in like that, he'd have another player with him, because it could be intimidating for a player to face the entire management team like that. So Donal Óg said he wanted a player representative with him, and that seemed to be news to the selectors, and it took a couple of days to set up that meeting.'

'Gerald would have felt I'd said something to him in Dungarvan,' says Cusack. 'I felt I did it in my way, relaying what was in my head as honestly as I could. [Selector] Martin Bowen rang me and said Gerald wanted to meet me regarding a disciplinary issue. I said I thought it was an over-reaction, but added that Seán Óg would come in with me. He said they wanted to see me alone.'

The selectors offered to allow county board chairman Mick Dolan to accompany Cusack as a compromise. It wasn't a runner. Eventually the selectors agreed to allow Ó hAilpín to accompany Cusack, and the goalkeeper told Ó hAilpín beforehand that the meeting wouldn't have much to do with the incident in Dungarvan.

'It didn't, either,' says Cusack. 'Other issues came up and we had a debate about them—that I wasn't interacting with the management and so on.

'I'd have been seen as a positive influence over the Cloyne and Cork teams by the managers I'd worked with, yet here I was being told about discipline and they wanted to suspend me. If you looked at it negatively, from our side, this was the lads coming at the person regarded as one of the strongest on the hurlers' side. I couldn't believe it. I said to Gerald that I was saying what other fellas were thinking.'

Cusack wasn't suspended in the end, but the smoke didn't clear. Ó hAilpín is too honest to beat around the bush about the appointment.

'Personally I felt Gerald was the wrong man, that he was the wrong appointment from day one. Ger Cunningham was the man who should have got it. I think the reality hit home for Gerald and the selectors when it got to ground-level stuff. It was said they knew what they were going into, but they didn't.

'We had problems. They were kept quiet, but 2007 I see as a very sad year, particularly when you see the likes of Wayne Sherlock walking away. For me it was the season one of our best colleagues ever walked away. Wayne rarely complained; he got on with the job—more action than talk—and it must have been bad when he walked away. And it was.'

There were other issues. Training had changed, and as Ó hAilpín puts it, the players weren't comfortable with the new approach: 'Corner backs did overhead pulling, the goalkeepers were mixed in with outside players for training . . . we had moved on to training that was specific to your position. We thought that day was gone, so of course we were suspicious.'

Management knew the players weren't happy, and the players knew the management weren't happy. A meeting was held in Pairc Uí Rinn in April, and the air was cleared.

'We had a frank meeting,' says Cusack. 'We reiterated our points. We said maybe ye don't trust us and we don't trust ye, but it was a good meeting, and everyone drove on after it.'

'In fairness, management put a few things to the players that they weren't happy with, that we weren't pulling our socks up,' says Ó hAilpín. 'We accepted that. We made our points, and they took those things on board, and after that, things started to change around. What put a good twist on the whole year was the suspensions thing.

'Our suspicions would have been that Gerald and the selectors had been planted by the board to put manners on the hurlers, that we were too big for our boots. When we said that to Gerald, he took it as an insult and he gave his reasons as to why that wasn't the case. We took that on board, because he pointed out that he'd had more run-ins with the county board than anyone else. To be honest, we were probably small kids when he had those run-ins.'

On the surface Cork were doing well. They beat Offaly, Clare and Wexford, though they struggled to beat Down away, and qualified for the semi-final against Waterford.

'On the face of it, that suggested we were doing well,' says Ó hAilpín. 'But we knew we weren't ready.'

Waterford edged them out in the league semi-final—an ominous sign for the year ahead.

Clare were the opponents in the Munster quarter-final. It was a cold day, with the low attendance giving the occasion a national league feel, but nobody remembers that now. What everyone remembers is the prologue: Semplegate.

There were plenty of conspiracy theories in circulation afterwards about what sparked the melee between Cork and Clare players, but the truth is a little more prosaic than the more *outré* suggestions. It was all because of a speech.

'Those speeches before games—they only go in one ear and out the other,' says Ó hAilpín. 'Gerald would have given a last few instructions; you'd take those on board, but you're ready to get out, a few deep breaths and you're waiting to get your first touch.'

'Niall McCarthy never spoke in the dressing room before, and if he'd said nothing in 2007 we'd have been out on the field,' says Cusack. 'Niall stopped us and gave us a speech. That's the truth.

'I remember going down the tunnel and seeing their door opening and Frank Lohan coming out. I was thinking, this is dodgy enough, because you wouldn't have seen that before.'

'I remember Niall speaking, but I didn't realise the significance of that until later,' says Ó hAilpín. 'It was business as usual. Donal Óg was behind the Hero [Kieran Murphy], top of the queue, and I was halfway down. I saw the Clare jerseys coming out and thought it was unusual, but it didn't throw me off. The last thing I expected was a war in the tunnel.'

'I got a touch from behind and your instinctive reaction is to hit,' says Cusack. 'That's what happened.'

'As I turned out to the pitch I saw Donal Óg get belted twice by two different players from behind,' says Ó hAilpín. 'I thought, what's going on here? One of the lads who hit him legged it away to the right and I thought, he's not getting away with that. That's why I was on camera heading that way, after him.

'I didn't want to get physical, but both of us ended up tussling on the ground. I didn't hit him and he didn't hit me, but unfortunately I was caught on camera. When I was accused of "contributing to a melee", I argued that I wasn't involved in the melee.

'To be honest, when I looked at the video, what I did was nowhere near as malicious as what a few lads did, lads who got away scot-free. I went after a culprit who got away scot-free himself.'

The dust-up didn't last longer than thirty seconds, but even as the ball was thrown in, Cusack knew the repercussions would be serious.

'At the start of the game I was trying to put it out of my head, but I knew there'd be trouble. I'd gotten flaked—when we went through the video footage afterwards, the lads had a good laugh about it because I got a lot more belts than I gave.'

Cork won comfortably enough, and the goalkeeper tried to defuse the situation after the game, saying it was a storm in a teacup.

'We deserved a sanction,' says Cusack. 'You can't be doing that. But we felt what followed wasn't fair, and that the lads were coming for us.'

The post-game analysis focused on the fight—not surprisingly, given the bloodless game which followed it. Ó hAilpín knew there was trouble ahead when his phone trilled at midnight the following Tuesday: 'Gerald rang me at midnight and said I was one of the lads in trouble.'

The controversy meandered on and on. Eight players were named as contributing to a melee and faced punishment, though several more seemed to have participated. Having lost, Clare were awaiting the qualifiers, but Cork had an urgent date with Waterford looming.

The GAA didn't seem in a hurry to reach a resolution, and Cork's preparations suffered as a result.

'The lads who weren't involved in hearings and so on, it was like the elephant in the room,' says Ó hAilpín. 'We weren't talking about it; the other lads didn't know if they should mention it; the selectors didn't know who they'd have to select, all of us or none of us. The fellas who'd replace us didn't know for definite but had to prepare as if they were playing. Gerald Mac and Jerry Wallace were going to all the hearings with us—and also had to prepare the team at the same time. Of course it disrupted preparations.'

Cork had a fair ace in county secretary Frank Murphy.

'It might sound strange now,' says Cusack, 'but I knew Frank would fight tooth and nail for us; there was no question about that.'

But even though John Gardiner was cleared, the other three, Ó hAilpín, Cusack and Diarmuid O'Sullivan, had to endure more uncertainty.

'We'd decided to limit the effect it would have on the team,' says Cusack. 'Usually I'd be the last to speak at the last session before a game, so we called the lads in at training that week and said while we were fighting the suspensions we wouldn't line out against Waterford.'

'And it went to the last minute,' says Ó hAilpín. 'We were at the Portlaoise meeting on the Friday, and then we went on the Saturday to the DRA. So we came back from Portlaoise at midnight and then we got up the following morning to head back to Portlaoise for the DRA meeting. This was the day before the Waterford game. Even if we'd been cleared there and then, we wouldn't have been right to play. We were in no shape to line out. We hadn't been sleeping; we hadn't been training properly. We couldn't have played.'

'It ended in a very fair hearing,' says Cusack. 'And we were out. Seán Óg's suspension . . that was a joke. He never raised his hands above his shoulders.'

Cusack's replacement would be Anthony Nash, whose preparations weren't ideal.

'The worst thing I've seen was Martin Coleman being told he

wouldn't be playing,' says Cusack. 'I was fierce upset over that. But I was also worried for Anthony—not that he wouldn't take it on; he'd be well capable—but because it wasn't the right way to put a fella in.'

The trio's absence contributed to the atmosphere in Thurles. Both teams came out to a rousing reception, but when O'Sullivan, Ó hAilpín and Cusack emerged from the tunnel after that, Gerald McCarthy made a point of shaking hands with each of them. The Cork support hailed them.

'People were good to us,' says Ó hAilpín. 'When we came out before the Waterford game, the reception meant a lot.'

'I'll never forget the reception the Cork supporters gave us that day in Thurles,' says Cusack. 'The only thing I'd compare it to was the day we came back after the Waterford semi-final in 2006. We were passing Cork supporters queuing for the train and when I put up my fist they gave us a huge reaction, one I'll never forget.

'But while it was a disaster not going out with them, I genuinely feel so much part of that team that if they won and I wasn't playing, it would be as good for me. At this stage it's about having pride in our team. That means as much to me as the enjoyment of playing.'

The game was one of the season's highlights: even without the three key players, and shipping five goals, Cork hung onto Waterford's coattails and refused to let them get away. With time almost up and Cork three points down, substitute Shane Murphy's last-gasp effort almost secured an unlikely draw, but his shot rattled the crossbar.

'His shot dipped,' says Ó hAilpín. 'We half-jumped off the bench because we thought it was going in. If that had gone in, it would have been some win against all the odds. It would have been a great win against Croke Park, if you like.'

The hours of preparing a case and fighting together had one unexpected dividend: it bonded players and management.

'During that whole controversy I think Gerald became a players' man, and I thought 2008 would be better as a result,' says Ó hAilpín. 'Did I think he was the wrong man for the job? Yes. Did I dislike him? No. Was he off the mark with preparations in 2007? Yes. But I think 2007 was a learning experience for him as well, and we bonded, even though it was a bad way to have to do it.

'When we shook hands with him out on the sideline, it was a sign of unity and defiance.'

The three suspended players issued a statement subsequently to the *Irish Examiner* expressing their dissatisfaction with the disciplinary process—a process that changed significantly in the aftermath of the Semple Stadium controversy. Then it was time to move on.

Cork's journey through the qualifiers went to plan with defeats of Offaly and Dublin, and they had Tipperary for their last game. The prize for beating Tipperary was a date with Wexford in the All-Ireland quarter-final, and on a dull evening in Thurles the word wasn't long getting out that Eoin Kelly wouldn't be playing. The Cork supporters relaxed. They weren't alone.

'It wasn't "one of those nights",' says Ó hAilpín. 'What filtered through to the players was what the supporters felt—that we'd win. There was talk all wasn't well in Tipp. Dublin had tested them and Offaly nearly beat them, and we'd beaten Offaly well. And I know that it doesn't work like that—if you beat one team and they've beaten another, you'll beat that other team—but we were sitting ducks in Thurles.'

Cork started well, but Tipperary stayed in touch. And as the game wore on and Tipp kept ahead, Cork fell into what Ó hAilpín calls the classic trap.

'Everyone expected the next fella to do it instead of taking the responsibility themselves. You go into a game you're expected to win and you can't turn it on. They deserved it. There seemed to be more Tipp support there at the end of the game. By then all of Tipperary was out on the field.'

Tipperary held out for a narrow but deserved win, and there was no shortage of opposing supporters to rub salt in.

'I always liked Tipp people, but they were nearly vindictive that night as we were coming in,' says Cusack. 'I was arguing with a linesman about coming outside the square, but a supporter from Tipp made a comment in the tunnel to the dressing rooms. He got involved when he shouldn't have. I remember thinking, this is all we need, another tunnel incident.'

Cusack turned away from the buffoon and headed for the dressing room. Cork had two weeks to prepare for the All-Ireland quarter-final, which meant rearranging county championship fixtures. The players discussed matters on the team bus before leaving Thurles, asking the management team for a few minutes' privacy to do so; that decision would reverberate around the county in time, but at that stage of the year Waterford was the next date on the calendar.

'It was the best game we played all year,' says Ó hAilpín. 'But the Waterford goals killed us. They've a great knack of getting goals, and they disrupt opposing defences by rotating players. Is that a deliberate plan? I don't know.

'Dan Shanahan was obviously the star, but Stephen Molumphy was a key man. He dropped deep and played a lot of ball, and played it to the right men.'

Despite Waterford's goals, Cork had the better of the game, and with time running out the Rebels were four points up. Given the game's dramatic conclusion, there was no shortage of experts to say they should have held out, a suggestion Ó hAilpín takes issue with.

'It's easy to say we should have closed the game out at that stage. But how do you close a game out in hurling? I remember a couple of lads were rushing to take sidelines for us, and I was at them to slow down, but that's about all.'

With two minutes left, Paul Flynn cracked in a shot that Donal Óg Cusack dived acrobatically to save. The ball looped up into the air and Molumphy held his nerve, waiting underneath to bat it home and cut the deficit to a point.

Waterford repelled Cork's last attack, and a long delivery by Brian Phelan found Eoin McGrath lonely as a lifebuoy in the Cork half. Everyone expected the equalising point, but McGrath had other ideas.

'The second he ducked his shoulder I thought, Jesus Christ, he's going to go for a goal here,' says Cusack. 'I'd have imagined he'd tap it over. I saved his shot, but I thought Shanahan would flick it.'

Cusack deflected the ball out and across the square; it passed Shanahan, and Flynn connected.

'It hit Sully and was rolling in when I got my leg to it,' says Cusack. 'As I was going across, I dragged it around.'

Referee Brian Gavin blew for a free, penalising Cusack for lying on the ball. The keeper didn't take the decision well; nor did his manager. Both played the consistency card.

'When I look at it now, being honest, it was fifty-fifty,' says Cusack, 'though in the heat of battle you don't think like that. If people feel we're paranoid, look at the decision that same referee made for the Ken McGrath free in the 2006 semi-final.

'The ball got stuck under my leg. It was never really underneath me, but by the time I got it around I knew Flynn was coming, so it was too dodgy to open up. But I could have been given a free out as well.

'I'd look back with disappointment, because it was a fifty-fifty decision. And we were four points up and didn't close out the game. I was never as mad after a game. We could have beaten Waterford, but we didn't.'

'What annoyed people was that the referee had given bash balls for the same thing earlier in the game,' says Ó hAilpín. 'With ten minutes to go he probably would have thrown it in, but given that stage of the game . . .'

Eoin Kelly pointed the free to take the draw. Replay.

That week the Cork defenders met to discuss how to handle the Waterford backs. They felt that Dan Shanahan would pull Ronan Curran out of centre back if he was followed, so they'd play their positions.

'We felt we should have the confidence to beat our man one-to-one,' says Ó hAilpín. 'But for all our talk it meant nothing. In fairness, 2007 was the Dan the Man Show. He was outstanding. Give him a half-chance near goal, he'll bury it.'

Shanahan scored the goals as Waterford booked their spot in the All-Ireland semi-final. Cork's season wouldn't see August.

'We felt we'd turned the tide against them the first day,' says Ó hAilpín. 'We probably felt the replay was more of an advantage to us, even though we'd lost the lead. We lost the replay on 31 July; we weren't even playing into August, and for the last few years we'd been spoiled, playing All-Ireland semi-finals and building up to the final.'

Cork were out of the championship. The Semplegate fiasco had made it an unforgettable year, but 2007 didn't end for Cork in July. Before Christmas they'd be the focus of attention in the GAA world, and beyond, once again.

# | WITHDRAWING SERVICES

On 11 November 2007, in the doldrums of the GAA season, this writer was given a statement issued on behalf of the Cork senior hurling and football panels for publication in the *Irish Examiner*. It outlined the players' dissatisfaction with a recent decision by the Cork County Board to deprive managers of the right to choose their own selectors and detailed their willingness to withdraw from inter-county action if that decision wasn't reversed.

It was 2002 all over again.

'There was a sense of, do we have to do this all over again?' says Cusack. 'Absolutely. It was a place we shouldn't have been. We knew where we were heading, because I was talking with Joe [Deane] one night and I said, I don't believe we're doing this again.

'But he explained it best of all. He said, "We don't need it, we don't want it, but is it important we do it right? It is." We genuinely saw it as a duty, as something we had to do. And if we didn't, there was a danger of thinking, if we don't fight this, why did we fight in 2002? That would have been disrespectful of the lads who fought with us then.

'But we tried to strike a balance. We were sending a message, but we were also aware it was November. There was time to sort it.'

The Cork footballers had asked Cusack for advice, as they'd be the first team affected by the county board decision, but suggestions that the hurlers were driving the strike through them receive a swift retort from the goalkeeper.

'Bull,' Cusack says. 'If anyone thinks people would tell Graham Canty what to do, then they don't know him. The hurlers would have asked me what the footballers were like, and I said the fellas I was dealing with gave me no reason not to respect them. We'd proved we could stick together in the strike in 2002, but when I was meeting the footballers first, was I trying to figure them out? Yes, I was.

'We said it as honestly as we could to them that in 2002 the footballers had been a hindrance to us with the exception of one or two like Ronan McCarthy and Conrad Murphy, who were very good. I know the footballers got pissed off with me over a few things I said, but I was trying to be honest with them, and everyone was the better for it.'

The way Cusack puts it, going on strike wasn't much of a decision. There had been suggestions that the teams withdraw from action in the dressing room before the first national league games of the season, but that was rejected in favour of a more gradual approach.

'We had a meeting in Cloyne,' says Cusack. 'We had another issue going on in the group that time and we would have spent an hour on that and ten minutes on the strike issue.

'Subsequently, there was massive debate, but not on the main issue. Every fella believed in the one thing, and any debate was on the nuts and bolts of handling the thing. The board tried to suggest we weren't representing the views of the panels at one stage in the negotiations, and we pointed out that if that were the case, they wouldn't be sitting across the table from us in the first place. We were smart enough to come with what the group wanted.

'That's the reality. We couldn't do something others wouldn't back us in, because we would have tripped up. Fellas would break, and they'd be dead right to.'

'We had two options,' says Ó hAilpín. 'One was that we didn't need all that and could walk away, but the other option was to realise, if we did that, then what was 2002 all about? What were the last few years about? We felt we'd have more sleepless nights down the road if we didn't act, because we had the chance to act. So we did.'

For long stretches of the three-month strike there was little to report, but early on Cusack felt the board showed its hand when its Central Council delegate, Bob Honohan, spoke to a local radio station and suggested that if clubs wanted Cork players to present medals, they were directed to an agent, adding that there were personal vendettas at play.

Honohan wasn't presenting the official views of the board, but the players felt it indicated the administration's thinking.

'Our insight into the bad side of the board—the bitterness and the small-mindedness, staying in the cave because we don't know what's outside—came from Bob Honohan,' says Cusack.

'Everyone who knows us knows our attitude. If our best player can earn as much as he can, we say best of luck to him. We understand a rising tide lifts all boats, and we try to spread those things around anyway. That's how we've done our business.

'In that interview he had a go off us and spoke about money, vendettas, 2002, all of that. We were thankful for that. He proved our fears to us.

'I might come across as single-minded, but sometimes you'd say to yourself, am I too close to this, do I need to have another look at it? But that interview—any time I'd have been thinking about this thing, I reminded myself of that interview.'

The players' statement had been issued ahead of the next scheduled county board meeting to avoid personalising opposition to any likely football manager who'd be appointed, but most observers were wrongfooted by the appointment of Teddy Holland on 20 November, an appointment overwhelmingly backed by board delegates.

Though Holland had steered the Cork minor footballers to the All-Ireland title in 2000, he was a relatively obscure choice. Still, his appointment meant that Cork had a football manager, and the players' urgency in issuing their initial statement looked a wasted exercise. A couple of meetings between the new boss and his players went nowhere, and milestones were passed one by one. Challenge games weren't played. Panels weren't selected. Soon it was Christmas, and flipping to a new year on the calendar upped the ante.

'Our thing was that once it turned Christmas the pressure would come on the GAA, with games and so on,' says Cusack. 'Keeping our side together was our big worry.'

The players had been through the mill, of course. They still had Diarmaid Falvey in their corner, and his dedication was a major asset; the fact that he was always available to the panel—to both panels—strengthened their resolve. The players rolled out spokespersons on a regular basis, but unlike in 2002, the board had an able media operator in PRO Bob Ryan. The Inniscarra club man stayed in touch with the press, and in the absence of action by the GAA hierarchy locally and nationally, he often seemed to be the only one dissenting with the players' points.

In December the GAA had decided not to get involved, but with the new year the pressure increased. A championship without Cork would carry an asterisk for the winners and put doubt in potential sponsors' minds; the GAA market was likely to take a nasty knock at a time the economy as a whole was becoming nervous. With this in the background the Cork footballers were on their team holiday in South America—complete with members of the board—but no progress was made there either. A dramatic gesture was needed.

The arrival of Kieran Mulvey changed the landscape considerably. The chief executive of the Labour Relations Commission was asked by GAA President Nickey Brennan to get involved, and he chaired talks towards the end of January.

By that time Cork GAA was a complete nightmare. Solicitors' letters were flying. The main actors' phone mailboxes filled every day. People were avoiding each other on the street. Friendships were torn asunder. Families split down the middle. Rumours were rife, and every day there was a round of outlandish suggestions—that Holland had resigned; that the players were going back if Holland stepped down for a fortnight; that John Allen would take over as interim manager. One of the more excitable local free sheets considered a front-page splash on Holland's resignation, fuelled by revelations from one of his co-workers in a city car park; it had to be pointed out to them that their source worked in a different car park to the football manager.

On 23 January Holland broke his media silence, telling this writer he wouldn't be resigning. By that point he and the others involved in the dispute didn't have their own lives any more. The strike had taken over completely.

'You'd be going to places and people would say it to you,' says Cusack. 'A chap in Intel said it to me once, that the rights and wrongs of the strike were all that was discussed at the lunch table. The fella I work next to was driven mad by my phone, it was going off so much if I left it after me at the workstation.'

'The three months were torture,' says Ó hAilpín. 'If I saw another hotel room . . . It was going to bed at 1 am after meetings, up for work, phone calls all day about the strike, texting back and forth. I couldn't concentrate properly in work, and the people I work with didn't want to raise it.

'People on the street were asking about when we were going to go back, and to be honest, I was thinking, forget about this year, and I wanted to say that to people, but I didn't want to give them that kind of bad news; it means so much to them. I was telling people, look, we'll see how it goes, but that was further from the reality than they realised.

'If it didn't work out, it meant people were prepared to walk away for the year. For the younger lads they'd manage it; they'd get back. For the older lads, picking it up at 31 or 32? I don't think so. And we mightn't have gone back anyway; you have to have a bit of backbone about you.'

'I'd get over all that,' says Cusack. 'My worry was how it'd affect the team, particularly the younger players. But those younger guys— we believe in them, that they're good men. Kevin Hartnett is a good man, someone we'd respect. Would he do something if he says it? Yes. Would he speak up if he disagreed with us? Absolutely. There needs to be respect and standards. Those are good values for any team.'

The parties met Mulvey in an engineering office in Mahon in the city and Cusack set out the players' stall: 'The first thing I said to Kieran Mulvey was, we're representatives of the players; we're not politicians; we won't act like politicians here; we'll relay exactly what the panels feel.'

Those talks broke down, and the footballers' first NFL game, against Meath, went west. When RTÉ's *Prime Time* broadcast a lengthy segment on the strike, however, the players regained the initiative.

'We were told that Bob Ryan would be on *Prime Time*,' says Cusack. 'So I said we needed someone to go on, and nobody else wanted to do it. The lads had wanted me to do more, but I felt people would be saying, there's Cusack again, and had rowed back.

'There was a good reaction to it, though.'

Cusack performed well on the television slot, and unfavourable comparisons were made between his articulate description of the players' position and the silence of the county board.

Going into February others began to comment on the dispute. Taoiseach Bertie Ahern called on both sides to resolve the matter, while in an elegant reversal of roles, Roy Keane described the situation as 'Cork's Saipan', likening it to his departure from the Ireland camp before the 2002 World Cup finals.

Another round of talks with Mulvey and new GAA Director-General Páraic Duffy came to an end without resolution. Events took a decisive twist with an opinion poll published in the *Irish Examiner* on 9 February. It showed overwhelming support for the players.

'That was huge,' says Ó hAilpín. 'That showed what we felt all along, that the people were on our side. It was a breakthrough.'

Binding arbitration had always been the last throw of the dice, and Mulvey offered that to the board as an option. They accepted his proposal on 12 February.

'Kieran rang me the night of the county board meeting,' says Cusack. 'He said they'd agreed to enter arbitration and I said I needed to go back to our lads. We felt we couldn't enter into it unless we knew the parameters. On the Thursday I knew it was a huge day. We got more details and we met again, and then we felt it would be a PR disaster for us if we didn't enter into it. I rang Graham [Canty], and Anthony Lynch was with him, and we met in Cloyne with Joe Deane.'

There was a feeling at that point in Cork that the players were in charge, and that arbitration was a toss of the coin which they had only a fifty-fifty chance of winning. A local radio station was referring to it as the 'arbitrary process', and the thinking among some observers was that that malapropism wasn't far off the mark.

'We made a judgment call on where we were,' says Cusack. 'I would have felt under as much pressure as I ever felt in my life heading into arbitration that evening, and waiting for the decision that Friday.'

Board and player representatives met with Kieran Mulvey in the Rochestown Park Hotel that Thursday evening. The meeting lasted forty-five minutes, and *Examiner* photographs of the participants emerging afterwards showed the strain on their faces clearly—and little wonder. As late as that morning Cusack had had anonymous phone calls warning him of a 'trap'.

It was St Valentine's Day.

Cusack went to work the following morning and on his way home at lunchtime he received a text message from Kieran Mulvey: the decision had been e-mailed out.

'I rang Joe; he was in Ballinacurra and he said he'd meet me at my house,' says Cusack. 'As it happened, Ger Cunningham had called to my house with balls for the ball alley, so he was there too.'

The three sat in front of Cusack's computer. The slight delay caused by remote access squeezed out the tension even more, but the three eventually were able to scroll down through the document.

'The pressure was desperate,' says Cusack. 'I met Joe not long after he was diagnosed with cancer and he was under a lot more pressure the morning of the arbitration decision. But once we read it, it was over.'

Mulvey had recommended that Teddy Holland and his selectors stand down, but left the mechanics of that process to the county board. There were significant developments, such as two player representatives on the committee to select inter-county managers, but that was the fine print. The strike was over.

'The only sin we committed was winning,' says Ó hAilpín. 'The board never talked about the previous four years, when we were winning; they didn't see the last four years as successful themselves, which is an indication.

'They should have been as proud of that as anyone else, but deep down inside they didn't feel that because they weren't as involved as they wanted to be. The thing is that we didn't care who got the credit as long as Cork was successful. We want them to be part of it, but they saw 2002 as losing ground to the players. That's not how we saw it.

'To be honest, there's no way in a county like Cork players should have to call a strike, if right was right. We thought 2002 was over and done with, that if there were problems that at least they'd be new problems, but the lessons weren't learned in 2002. It was the same stuff creeping up again.

'Did we boast about the Mulvey decision? No. We just got back training.'

Cusack says it was more stressful than 2002: 'You have to be a certain person when you're doing it, and you're characterised as a certain person, and so are all the players.

'We went straight from the GPA grants negotiation into that, and that had been stressful enough; but if it had to be done, it had to be done. If you saw some of the diaries of some of my days . . . leaving meetings, locking up the bar, bed, up at 7 am and ringing fellas, then work.

'But I had great trust in the lads. Some of them I trust absolutely, and they took a lot of the load.'

Cusack sums it up—the strike, the bond, the wins and the heartbreak. The journey. The team.

'I respect them. All of them. I respect John Gardiner so much that I would do anything for him to succeed as captain, more so than I would for myself. Seán Óg Ó hAilpín is the most honest man I know. When I was having hassle in 2005, I spoke to Seán Óg about it, and Sully came to me and said, "Something's wrong. I can tell from the way you were speaking to Seán Óg." He didn't know what I'd said, but he could tell there was something wrong. There's great loyalty there.

'Have we seen guys having a go at us in papers and so on? Yeah, we've seen it, but the way we've always looked at it was that if we believed in something, then we had no problem in fighting for it, even if it meant being drawn into public debate.

'If we had to put ourselves up there to be shot at, then I think that was a price we were willing to pay, even if that meant criticism from other players. Then our attitude was, fuck them. We always took on fights for other panels and backed the GPA even when it would have been easier for us to look after ourselves, as we had sorted an excellent set-up for ourselves at that stage.

'Is that a Cork way of doing things? Maybe. John Allen asked us to put "Corcaíoch" on our shorts, and we did, and were proud to do so after he told us the meaning of it to him. That's the way we are, and if that's the way we are then we'll stand up for the way we are.

'We believe that Cork should mean more than representation. If we give it this time and get this associated with it in the public eye and spend this much time together, then it has to mean more than that. In thirty years' time, when we're only meeting each other once or twice a year or at funerals or whatever, we should be able to say, I did my best with him. I respect him. We did our business and we did it our way.

'We believe in that.'

# INDEX